RECLAIMING RELIGION

FROM

THE CHURCH

BY FRANK CANATELLA

Printed in Victoria, Canada

National Library of Canada Cataloguing in Publication

Canatella, Frank, 1926-
     Reclaiming religion from the church / Frank Canatella.

Includes index.
ISBN 1-55395-430-0

     I. Title.

BJ47.C35 2003   241   C2003-900102-4

TRAFFORD

This book was published *on-demand* in cooperation with Trafford Publishing.
On-demand publishing is a unique process and service of making a book available for retail sale to the public taking advantage of on-demand manufacturing and Internet marketing.
On-demand publishing includes promotions, retail sales, manufacturing, order fulfilment, accounting and collecting royalties on behalf of the author.

Suite 6E, 2333 Government St., Victoria, B.C. V8T 4P4, CANADA
Phone   250-383-6864   Toll-free   1-888-232-4444 (Canada & US)
Fax   250-383-6804   E-mail   sales@trafford.com
Web site   www.trafford.com   TRAFFORD PUBLISHING IS A DIVISION OF TRAFFORD HOLDINGS LTD.
Trafford Catalogue #02-1145   www.trafford.com/robots/02-1145.html

10   9   8   7   6   5

RECLAIMING RELIGION
FROM
THE CHURCH

TABLE OF CONTENTS

RECLAIMING RELIGION
FROM
THE CHURCH

Our task should be understood as an attempt to break out of a closed system of thought and not to adopt one........Robert F. Murphy

PROLOGUE....As a young man I felt called to the religious life while simultaneously feeling reluctant to become a priest or a brother. I couldn't at the time imagine a religious life that was neither. I finally did spend nearly a year in a Trappist monastery as a brother but I had to leave. With the idealism of youth I had chosen the Trappist after being told that it made the greatest demands on its members which I interpreted as the greatest challenge. I didn't find it so. The excuse I used for leaving at the time was that I needed a more hands-on approach to doing good. The truth was it just didn't feel right; I didn't feel engaged.

Writing this book has helped me to understand why. While trying to resolve other questions about the Catholic church and religion I indirectly discovered the connection between the later questions that arose concerning religion and my early confusion. I can now understand why atheists might think that God is dehumanizing if in fact the church speaks for God. If I linked God and the institutional church I might be an atheist myself. Many of the people I grew up with while not becoming atheists have become irreligious, putting God aside with the church.

Gradually a clearer set of ideas began to emerge from the tacit jumble of feelings and thoughts about God and religion with which I spent childhood and adolescence. I discovered during this process unaccountable differences between what and how my mother had taught me and church teaching. Without a word about right and wrong my mother conveyed a moral sense that left me free to choose, to make mistakes and to learn. Acquiring a morality in this way ultimately enabled me to make decisions based on conviction rather than on just relying on authority, or worse, acting out of fear. The code I came to live by grew out of experience. I listened to what my teachers and others said concerning the way I should behave but what I learned at home was the only standard against which to measure what anyone told me because I trusted my mother without reservation. My mother's grant of freedom sometimes made what others said seem strange. Not until I became an adult could I fully appreciate the gift I had been given. A person who is forced to do right deserves no credit, anymore than a person who is forced to commit a wrong should be held accountable. And fear is only second to love as a motive force. In plain language, if we are not free to be bad, neither are we free to be good. The freedom to choose is a function of correct knowledge which is not what the church tried to give me. Even when I was taught that a certain behavior was wrong I now see that the reasons for it being wrong could not be convincing to a thinking adult. The church of that time depended on fear and guilt to keep the faithful in line instead encouraging us to meet the challenges of life.

That method of teaching (indoctrination actually) failed to have its full effect on me because of the way my mother taught me. My mother was a faithful Catholic, one the hierarchy liked to call the simple faithful. So I lived in tension. She never went beyond the eighth grade in school so she did not have a lot questions for the church. She was a South Louisiana peasant. She presented morality to me by way of example rather than as a set of rules, and never, never did she ever make me or my siblings feel guilty. Reflecting on my behavior I would become aware that I had done something I shouldn't have, but it was always an intellectual awareness, not a feeling and I came to it on my own.

Acting according to the pattern established by my mother I always imputed the best of intentions to others. I understood that my teachers were simply passing on what they had been given, apparently untroubled by my kind of questions. Years later when a visiting priest who came to speak at a faculty meeting said that the Catholic Magisterium considered docility one of the chief virtue. I reacted strongly. For reasons not clear at the time I quoted from Revelation. We should be "either hot or cold." I may not have had the right quotation but I meant to express the belief that I had been called to be passionately engaged with life, including religion, perhaps especially religion. From that perspective docility made no sense. It seems that until I began to write this book that I had only been able to back into some kind of clarity about religion.

I came to realize that religion is about groping for the sacred and the sacred is about connecting with people. We may think of ourselves as immersed in God and God as immanent in us, but in one sense we do not have access to God except as God dwells in the people around us. This means that even unbelievers engage in religious activities when they try to connect with other humans. No one need be an outsider, one of the better reasons to reclaim religion from the church. As presently constituted the church is a tribe requiring that there be insiders and outsiders, a lethal dichotomy in an increasingly crowded world.

This book began one day during the morally unsettled sixties. My good friend, Behrman Thibodaux said, "Tell me something. Are the Ten Commandments still valid?" What a strange question I thought. I responded with, "I don't know. I suppose so." If one of my heathen friends had asked that question I might have let it pass. Behrman however was one of the world's innocents. Like the Starship Enterprise he seemed to have a shield around him that deflected evil. So instead of forgetting his question I began to seriously reflect on the Commandments for the first time. Like everyone else I had taken them for granted; they were just there. From my later reflections I realized that the just-thereness of people, things and ideas taken for granted conceals worlds of new perspectives which may be why my first discovery surprised and pleased me; I had learned something significant about religion.

The Commandments were not for the Jews the code of personal, transcendental morality the church presented to me, the keeping of which would gain me heaven. The Jews were an extended family. They considered themselves the People of God and the Commandments prescribed how the community as a whole could maintain a relationship with God and among themselves so that they would survive and prosper *as a community*. They had no concept of eternal salvation for communities much less individuals. As a Catholic I had an identity in common with millions of people but no sense of community with them. I would attend Mass to fulfill my personal, Sunday obligation to avoid committing a mortal sin. Hundreds of others in church were there for the same reason but with no necessary connection between us except proximity and our formal identity as Catholics. We were a bunch of individuals trying to get to heaven or stay out of hell. As I studied and reflected I learned that fulfilling the sabbath commandment cannot be done by a single act and that worship should be communal. In the chapter on the Commandments I'll explain further the meaning of this and other commandments.

Up to the time of Behrman's question the Commandments were for me rules. If I obeyed them I would have a positive relationship with God and I would save my soul. My behavior pleased or displeased God; its effect on humans was secondary. I understood at the time that we all produced effects in a transcendental realm from which we got no feedback. The institutional church offers a kind of virtual feedback; we can presumably learn our status with God by talking to a priest who lets us know where we stand. That my relationship with other Catholics is secondary to the project of saving my soul is reinforced by how the church administers the sacrament of penance. If I hurt someone and sincerely confess it to a priest I am given absolution and a penance, usually some prayers to say. It would be good if I made an effort to become reconciled with the person I had hurt but under the terms of the sacrament that is not necessary. The priest has reconciled me with God and that's all that matters.

According to scripture the church has it exactly backward (Mat. 5:21-24). I should be encouraged to become reconciled to the person I've hurt. Priests could serve as reconciliation counselors and in difficult cases perhaps arrange a meeting with the offended party, but if I do the reconciling on my own I don't need a priest. I have taught that God is immanent in all of us and developing a relationship with God depends entirely on how I relate to other humans in whom God is also immanent. I do not have access to a transcendental God, only to people. If God is immanent as the church itself teaches we gain access to God through people. We all have relationships with other humans with varying degrees of intimacy. Once we accept the reality of God's immanence, an entirely new way opens up for us to relate to everyone particularly in our intimate relationships. But I'm getting ahead of my story.

I had known from religion classes that the Commandments originally came on two tablets. That knowledge didn't become meaningful until I began the study prompted by Behrman's question. The first tablet spelled out the relationship between God and the Jews while the second dealt with proper relationships between and among Jews. After being asked which was the greatest commandment Jesus simplified the whole set by summarizing the two tablets into what he called the two greatest commandments: love God and love your neighbor. Furthermore Jesus demonstrated during his time on earth that these two commandments merge into one. We love God by loving our neighbor which further suggests the reality of God's immanence. St. Paul confirms the new reality with, "If you love your neighbor you have fulfilled the law." Jesus reinforces the new commandment of love by quoting Hosea: "I desire compassion not sacrifice" (Mat. 9:13). Compassion is for people; sacrifice is for a god or gods. God doesn't need anything we have; we need each other.

Pope John Paul II and others contend that Jesus, in his Sermon on the Mount, made the Commandments, more restrictive, harder to keep. The logic goes like this: Whereas before people were forbidden to murder, now they can't even get angry. That logic is flawed. Behavior is directed, always moving toward some goal, whether conscious or not; anger is a step toward murder. It is easier to avoid taking that step (becoming angry) than stopping when I'm on the verge of pulling a trigger. Similarly with lust. It is easier to stop fantasizing about having sex with someone because those thoughts could lead to adultery than to climb out of bed with that person because I'm about to commit adultery. Jesus changed the dynamics of moral thinking in regard to sin and the Commandments even though we have not yet fully understood how he made it easier to avoid sin by attending to God, immanent in our brothers and sisters. I now believe that I understand what he meant by: "My yoke is sweet; my burden light" (Mat. 11:30). My morality determines how I will act with, for and toward others. Clearly then my morality has direction, either the difficult one Jesus warned against or the easy one of prior reflection on the consequences of the direction I am taking.

When Prof. Richard B. Hays analyzed the moral vision of the New Testament he seems to have taken the same position as John Paul II. He writes,

> In most of the six antitheses [of the Sermon on the Mount], the teaching of Jesus constitutes an *intensification*--rather than an abrogation of the Law. The Law prohibits murder, but Jesus prohibits anger; the Law prohibits adultery, but Jesus forbids even lust (1996:324). [My emphasis]

I'm not familiar with Greek or Latin scriptures but in none of several English versions of the New Testament that I know does Jesus speak of prohibiting anger or lust. He announces that a person has already gone too far in the wrong direction by being angry or by lusting after someone. Knowing this, enables a person to catch an incipient movement before it becomes too difficult to stop. A story from one of my high school religion classes will illustrate how direction is a factor in moral thinking. We had a discussion on boy-girl relationships. A lot of questions were asked but the sum of them came down to: How far can I go before offending God? The answer, of course, is no distance at all. Not because God would be offended; we can't hurt God. Nor should we just stop moving in that direction. Rather, we should not, as Jesus taught, move in that direction at all because we risk offending a person. That was not what the religion teacher said, nor was it what my classmates wanted to hear. There was a line in the sand; you crossed it and you were dead. My classmates all knew where the line was--just about where the girls skin began. To illustrate, if a boy accidentally touched a girl's breast and experienced pleasure in the touch, he had sinned mortally. That is he would go to hell if he died without confessing. There are no degrees of crossing a line. The magisterium tells it this way: The *least* amount of sexual pleasure outside of marriage is mortally sinful. They still teach this.

The teacher said nothing about an alternative direction and not a word about the joys of a proper intimacy, which is possible with anyone, of any age or gender, at any time without limit. That was sixty years ago and the church had no theology of intimacy. It still doesn't. The young religion teacher couldn't talk about alternative ways of being intimate. It had not been on the agenda of his formation, although I'm certain he must have heard the concept of God as immanent. Paul, for example said we are temples of the Holy Spirit. Apparently no one had made the connection for my teacher between that concept and boy-girl relationships. Otherwise he might have said, "Do you know that to touch a girl is to touch someone sacred? That God is immanent in the person you touch? Anyone who approaches another person with the idea of becoming intimate must do so with humility." Offending God might seem abstract to a fourteen-year-old boy. However, the issue could have been made concrete by rephrasing the boys question. "How far can I go before offending the girl?" No one had taught the good brother how to deal with young, male hormones. The alternative implied in the way the church teaches is: stay outside the line and endure the frustration or take a cold shower. No wonder men of old went to the desert. In his initial enthusiasm Paul talked about freedom from the Law with some of his first converts but they misunderstood. He had to pull back somewhat when things got out of hand. They apparently understood Paul to mean that being free meant there were no rules. This behavior is typical of people who do not grow up free. A young woman I know was educated in a convent boarding school, K through 12. She had straight A's the whole time in addition to becoming an accomplished pianist. After one semester on her own at the state university she was on academic probation. We are not born free. We sense a need to be free but we must learn to be free by being inducted in it from an early age or we will experience difficulty becoming free later.

The possibility of freedom for Pelagius may explain his conflict with Augustine. Augustine could not imagine the kind of freedom Pelagius talked about. If a person is standing before a line that can't be crossed, fighting a strong impulse to cross it, that person will have an entirely different perspective from someone who is simply moving away from the line in the opposite direction. Augustine and Pelagius both erred by projecting their own position onto everyone else, thus delaying an evolution in moral thinking for centuries. Augustine would have agreed that with grace one could do what Pelagius said was possible. Is there ever a time when grace is not available?

My mother had never forced me to be good. Mostly without words, and certainly without moralizing she made it clear that choices had empirical consequences and that I should consider them before I acted. Also, if I were the one who made the choices there was no doubt about who bore the responsibility and to whom the consequences belonged, good, bad or indifferent. From my mother's behavior I inferred that the consequences with which I must be particularly concerned were those that affected others. I never had a curfew; no one censored my reading; if the liquor in the house was off-limits no one told me, and so on. I had noticed small differences between me and my friends. I would hear them ask for permission to go to the local lake whereas I would simply say, "Ma, I'm going to the lake." She simply trusted me to choose well or to learn when I erred. I learned about the empirical consequences of behavior early. If I didn't study, I risked failure; if I didn't brush my teeth, I got cavities; if I didn't move fast enough in the morning, I went to school hungry, and so on. The freedom I had been given meant never having to prove that I am a free person. More importantly, any mistake I make results from my own choice and so presents me with an unambiguous lesson. My reference for what and how to choose developed within me. When the reference for what I should do is in someone else's head I will always experience difficulty with moral decisions because no one could teach what I should do in every possible circumstance. Also life cannot be lived according to formulas learned once and then used for the rest of one's life, which is why operating from principles may be better than a set of rules. I adopted the order of my mother's priorities. They were clearly people and ideas. Things came in a distant third.

While the institutional church is not intentionally arbitrary in the sense of making up rules just to test the faithful there was so much I didn't understand and the reasons given for doing or not doing something were less than compelling, hence seemed arbitrary. That "God says so," or "We say so," might convince a medieval or a South

Louisiana peasant who believed that the Magisterium spoke for God and controlled the gates of heaven but heaven was part of the problem. It is too distant in time and space to effectively motivate many people, including me. I am now firmly convinced that my task on earth is not the pursuit of eternal life as the church teaches. It strikes me as too me-centered. Besides, orthodox teaching has it that I cannot earn or merit heaven; whatever reality it may have is a gift. I managed to get the kind of profound and long-lasting satisfaction humans apparently were made for through my relationship with my mother and other humans.

Getting what we actually need such as food and water gives us satisfaction as do our pseudo-needs (wants) such as beer or candy, but there are certain needs not consciously recognized by us until the moment they are satisfied. Even then we may not be able to name or describe them. Or we may be able to give them names but the reality that is the need so transcends not only the meaning of the name but even whatever penumbra of connotations adhere to it. I'm thinking of intimacy, particularly an unalloyed kind such as one might find existing between a mother and child. An unexpected hug from a close friend will remind me by the satisfaction it gives that this is something I need, and if the satisfaction is proportionate to the need, as I believe it is, it would not be hard to make a case for expressions of intimacy being a greater need than food. Such satisfactions are truly empirical even if only the person getting it knows, although it may be evident to others from various indices such as facial expressions. Anyone who has ever seen a mother and a baby affectionately squeezing each other will know what I mean. I bring up the matter of satisfaction to make a point about moral behavior. Staking a homeless person to a meal because the person is a member of the human family can provide satisfaction. The depth of satisfaction depends on how free the gift is. If we expect gratitude we are not giving; we are attempting to trade. We may derive satisfaction from trading just as with any "want." However, we should have no difficulty seeing that if giving provides our satisfaction we will get it every time; whereas satisfaction that is dependent upon some measure of return can vary from much to not at all.

An apparent intimacy based on the expectation of what one will receive is commerce and contradicts any possibility of intimacy. Moreover, to engage in such trading means that the profound satisfaction possible (the real need we have) in an intimate relationship will not be experienced. The need will on some level be missed as evidenced by unnamed and unnameable dissatisfactions, but *the need* as such can never be known under these circumstances because satisfaction comes from movement in an opposite direction. If the satisfaction I refer to is not available early in life or one fails to understand how it relates to a fundamental need, one goes through life with a handicap from which one may never recover. In the words of James P. Carse

> what is needed is that others relate to me in ways that call from me resources and responses that I need to be human, but did not otherwise experience as needs at all (1985:59).

I will further explain this need when I deal with Primary Relationships in chapter 9.

The way for me to live rightly and derive the satisfaction I need means acting with, for and toward all humans just as I did with my mother, i.e., intimately insofar as it is possible. Obviously others won't make it as easy for me as my mother but as previously noted, behavior has empirical consequences even if only internal and the consequences of right acting toward other humans are inherently and deeply satisfying. Right acting does not mean avoiding a certain behavior for fear of going to hell or gaining heaven. There is no satisfaction standing before a line wishing I could cross. And if I have learned that the satisfaction of crossing it is limited and temporary, crossing the line may lose its attraction. This is what I mean by learning from empirical consequences. However, this is no sure way to learn because we may not get the satisfaction we expect from an experience and still look forward to the next one to provide it if we don't think there is an alternative source of satisfaction. The church does not feel that it can take the chance of letting us learn this way. It has such a horror of offending God it must prevent us from sinning whatever the cost. Children acquire a morality based on conviction if they learn by making mistakes and are gently corrected with reasons why something is a mistake, e.g., how it may affect members of the family negatively including the transgressor. Right acting means connecting with others through care and concern. Ask the people in community at a Worker's House, the Bruderhof or any other community of persons committed to each other and to the service of others about the source of a continuously satisfying life.

From 1935 when I made my first communion at age nine until 1969 when I started to follow up on Behrman's question, I was a faithful and, most of the time, an even fervent Catholic. By 1969 I had six children and a seventh on the way. Behrman's question ultimately changed my faith and redirected my spiritual journey to a path that I have followed till now. Knowing what I know and feeling as I do if the Church were just an institution I would leave.

When Charles Davis left he said he could not be a follower of Jesus in the church, meaning the institution, he failed to note that the bishops at Vatican II described the Church as the People of God claiming the title the Jews had. Leaving the church differs from leaving the Church. Many important ideas that came out of the Council, none compares in importance to this clarification of what constitutes a Church. If church officials had understood how radical a statement they had made it might not have passed. Think about it, the reality of the Church exists apart from the institution. Certainly there is some overlap, perhaps a great deal of overlap, but the two are not identical.

Who are these People of God? Jesus left little doubt about that--those who do God's will; those who care for the poor, the sick, the outcasts; the peacemakers, and so on. *Anyone* who is primarily concerned with the life and well-being of the whole human family fits that description regardless of faith or lack of it. Ironically Vatican II was an Ecumenical Council and that one statement put an end to the ecumenical effort as it had been originally conceived. What could a person's sect or denomination mean when even an atheist committed to service and justice for all of humanity is by definition one of God's People?

This understanding of the Church casts a new light on our task. We no longer need to convert people to one denomination or another. We are called to spread Jesus' message of love and service. In our time we don't even have to talk about love and service. With the possibility of nuclear destruction and contamination of the biosphere threatening the survival of life on earth we can preach a pragmatic self-interest. If humanity doesn't survive neither will the individual members, but seeing that humanity survives involves the very human task of bringing justice to the world. Those working to bring justice to all are God's People even if they disdain the title. There are many for whom a grand cosmic scheme based on eternal salvation might not appeal outside of the institutional churches but survival has a strong appeal to everyone. With its power and influence the institutional church could play a major role in humanity's survival. But the Vatican sees its task as mainly the salvation of souls, leaving it to divine providence to dispose of the world however it wants because everything is guaranteed to be made right in the next life.

The Vatican tries to keep everyone's eyes focussed on minutiae instead of pointing to the larger picture painted by Jesus in the Sermon on the Mount. In his recent encyclical *Veritas Splendor* Pope John Paul II keeps hammering away at the need to *keep* the Commandments ignoring the fact that he prescribes minimal behavior. Thirty-two times he repeats that refrain--keep, observe, obey. He contradicts St. Paul when he tells us that even with the most "rigorous observance" we cannot "fulfill the Commandments." John Paul II explicitly states that we save ourselves by obeying the Command- ments. To prove this he cites the story of the young Jew who asked Jesus how he could gain eternal life. Because Jesus replied, "Keep the Commandments," John Paul anachronistically applies the church's present view of one-at-a-time, individual salvation to Jesus' response. Jesus spoke to a Jew, for whom keeping the Command- ments meant, "Stay connected with your people." Or, "Don't break community bonds." The Commandments could not have been a formula for personal salvation to the young Jew. They should not be for us. Salvation is a corporate affair or it is nothing. No one will go to heaven alone by *keeping* the Commandments. I'll have much more to say about this way of thinking about all the Commandments, which is the "good news,"in a later chapter when I attempt to further clarify the difference between keeping the commandments and fulfilling them. Jesus invited the young man to engage in moral refinement, to go for the ideal, as he did for everyone in his Sermon on the Mount. John Paul II by contrast extends a call to minimum behavior.

I never once talked with my mother about the Sermon on the Mount nor did I hear her speak with anyone else on that topic but she seemed to understand what Jesus meant by fulfilling the Command- ments. She took a positive approach to every aspect of life and she promoted the life and well-being of every person she knew.

The Catholic magisterium teaches that we sin by breaking a rule thereby severing our bond with God. Sin has to do with human bonds, either breaking them, failing to maintain them, or perhaps even failing to make one when offered an opportunity. For as noted earlier, if we love our neighbor we have fulfilled the Law. Offending God is just a manner of speaking. When we sin we harm one or more persons or the larger community. Our standards of what is harmful have changed over time but the principle remains the same. We cannot do anything to God, who according to the church is immuta- ble, but we can harm one or more persons, possibly a whole commu- nity. This concept of sin flows from the new commandment of love, i.e., we love God by loving our neighbor, so by the same reasoning we offend God by harming or neglecting our neighbor. Defining sin in this way can bring to light behavior we possibly have not thought of as sinful. It can also clarify for us the non-sinfulness or degree of sinfulness of matters the church has ruled on absolutely. Any act that affects one or more persons has a moral quality to it, either negative or positive. A negative effect is precisely sin. The sinfulness is proportionate to the harm done. The church teaches, commit a mortal sin and you are dead. Can there be degrees of mortal sin? Can we learn from mistakes if every mortal sin has the same value?

In our highly interrelated world not having an effect on others is virtually impossible in just our everyday activity. Driving a car, for example, produces greenhouse gases affecting global climate. Our contribution may be small; still it's a contribution and it is negative. Is our contribution larger than it need be? There is much below the horizon that we won't take note of if our eyes are on the Commandments. It's almost as though Jesus addressed the future rather than his own age. The Commandments do not say, "You shall not be unjust," but that is the sin bringing the world to the verge of destruction. The present scale of injustice is built into the economic structure of the world. It is so massive that it is no one person's responsibility but in a very real sense we are all responsible.

The Catholic magisterium teaches that the natural law and the Commandments are the same and that Law is written on our hearts, that the Law is universal and immutable (*Veritas Splendor* p. 137). They also teach that through the use of reason humans can arrive not only at a knowledge of God's existence but also the good they should do and the evil they should avoid. St. Thomas Aquinas following Aristotle asserts that we are rational animals. His assertion is itself evidence that we are in fact rationalizing animals. In our reasoning the conclusion we come to is determined by the assumption with which we begin. St. Thomas worked backward from a chain of reasoning that proved the existence of God. In our time, even Catholic theologians accept that we cannot prove the existence nor non-existence of God. Thomas Aquinas states explicitly that the first principle of the natural law is "do good and avoid evil." Thomas skipped a step and the church hasn't picked up on it yet. Had Thomas been a serf instead of being ensconced in a religious community he might have recognized that the first principle of the natural law is *survive* and because we are necessarily social we must survive *together*. Thomas' first principle presupposes survival as though it were not an issue. This dual principle takes on a greater urgency in a crowded world where more than half the people in the world don't have enough to eat. All proscribed and prescribed behavior, i.e., the good we must do and the evil we must avoid can be derived from this two-part principle including the necessity of fighting against injustice. "Do good and avoid evil," as a first principle enables the church to define good and evil as something distinct from survival, one of the reasons they can add to the natural law the ban on artificial birth control which can work against survival. We cannot ignore the fact that how we act with, for and toward one another affects our survival chances, in other words our morality.

To understand the relationship between survival and the natural law we need only look at it from the perspective of the early Hebrews, a small tribe surrounded by hostile neighbors. The relationship should become increasingly clear to us at this time because survival of the whole human family is threatened. Survival requires a corporate effort and if I correctly understand the lessons Jesus taught, and that may be the case for survival in the next world whatever that means. If as noted above we can derive from the law of surviving-together all that we ought to do and not do we should have no problem seeing the connection between Jesus' law of love and acting together for the sake of earthside survival. It is cut out of the same cloth.

Meantime back on earth the magisterium is promoting conformity to what it considers certain important aspects of natural law, mostly having to do with sex. A history of the church's attitude toward sex is revealing. From the beginning until now sex has been considered tainted. St. Ambrose said, "Married people should be ashamed of themselves." The church at one time taught that the pleasure in a conjugal act was unavoidably sinful. Theologian Thomas Bokenkotter tells us in *Essential Catholicism* that "Gregory the Great taught that [even in marriage] a person could no more have intercourse without sin than fall into a fire without getting burned" (p. 328). More recently John Paul II declared that a man should not lust after his wife and he recently canonized a married couple who through most of their marriage gave up sex. Clearly the church's anti-sex attitude survives, a distant reminder of stoicism's legacy. The stoic ideal was for a man to be in complete control of his passions and sex provided the most problems in gaining and maintaining such control.

It is in the matter of contraceptive practices that the church's natural law teaching affects the most people and the effect is mostly negative. Two relatively common cases will illustrate. First, a woman's doctor informs her that with another pregnancy she risks dying. The church's approved method of birth control, periodic continence, commonly known as the rhythm method has failed twice for the couple who now have six children. In order not to commit mortal sin by using an artificial method or by surgical intervention, either vasectomy or tubal ligation, the couple must remain celibate for the rest of their lives or take their chances. In the second case a man with hemophilia has acquired AIDS from a blood transfusion. That couple must also remain celibate for life because the use of condoms is prohibited as unnatural, hence mortally sinful. By what line of reasoning is celibacy natural?

If as the magisterium insists that natural is good and unnatural (e.g., contraception) is bad then sex and pleasure, being natural, are not inherently bad. One or more persons must be harmed for there to be sin. Harm can occur in sex through coercion, fraud, lying, abuse, or putting a person at risk of death, as in the two cases cited above, and so forth. The sin in coercive sex is not that it is sex but that it is coercive, and certainly not that it is pleasurable. Understanding the harm to persons in adultery is relatively easy, but not in fornication per se. The church equates the two along with masturbation which is not even sex. Also the proscription against homosexual behavior is an ancient, cultural artifact that derived from its negative affect on a tribe's survival. It further reflects the distaste some males feel for possible male-male sexual contact. It suffers by the same analysis as other magisterially defined sins. We have to wonder who is harmed in a loving, committed, homosexual relationship?

As noted above, reasons given by the church for why an act is sinful are not very convincing, especially to young people who ask, "What's wrong with premarital sex?" There are good reasons but the church either doesn't know them or doesn't feel that they are any more convincing than, "God says so," or "We say so as agents of God," or if you die with your pants down you will go to hell. The best way I know to keep young people from early sexual involvement, given that there may be no necessary, overt, empirical consequences, is for them to have a deep trusting relationship with one or both parents with whom they can have conversations over a period of time on the meaning of sex, the nature of true intimacy and especially the sacredness of persons. The fear of hell won't cut it. If a youngster has experienced the profound satisfaction that comes from an intimate relationship with a parent, it will be easier for the parent to explain that sex is not by itself intimacy and why a sexual relationship makes more sense as part of a total intimacy. There can be serious consequences from early sexual involvement that are not easily explained because there are no necessary empirical consequence for anyone as a basis for reasoning to its being a violation of the natural law. This is the most likely explanation for why it was not considered a sin for the early Hebrews to have sex with slaves, concubines or even prostitutes when no religious ritual was involved. This means that all the church's has going for it in its condemnation of unmarried sex is its credibility which became seriously compromised by the *Humanae Vitae* fiasco. Its failure to recognize degrees of sexual sins is also not helpful in that regard. If a boy can go to hell for the pleasure of touching a girl's breast he might as go to hell for having sex with her.

Church policy shouldn't encourage that kind of thinking. I'll have more to say about that later. The old list of bad empirical consequences--pregnancy, disease, disgrace--seem to be avoidable possibilities that no longer deter young or old. However, methods for preventing pregnancy and disease are not fail-proof and anyone considering sex outside of marriage would have trouble justifying the risk. The possibility of harm cannot be taken lightly. It is a move in a direction that Jesus warned against. A parent who lacks the lifelong loving trust to discuss these matters with a youngster can only ask forgiveness for failing to connect and say with David, "Let me say, now I have begun." That act of humility might bridge the gap, although I know some people who regard apologizing to youngsters as wrong on the grounds that it diminishes authority. The authority has already been compromised in such cases. An apology may restore it.

In summary, the Sermon on the Mount is about community, minimally a community of two, which should begin at home and begin early. The Jews were a community but with a tribal boundary. Jesus wanted to eliminate all boundaries between people hence his cavalier treatment of dietary and purity codes which are tribal markers and not essential for community. He reclaimed religion from the institution of his time by stating that sabbath regulations were subordinate to people connections. Violations of the Commandments can destroy community but we cannot just avoid destructive behavior; we must think of community as an ongoing creative process. If we are moving toward the creation and maintenance of community the Commandments recede into the background. Perhaps that's what St. Augustine meant by, "Love and do what you will." Everything in the New Testament is better understood in the context of community. For example, when Jesus says, "Judge not and you shall not be judged," he was saying that the person who judges is either disconnecting from the person judged or is putting an obstacle in the way of connecting instead of responding with compassion to someone who perhaps has fallen. Compassion bonds; judging disconnects.

What I am teaching should not be confused with certain advocates of a new morality who say in effect that certain sins are not so bad. Jesus pointed the way for us to become God's People by distancing ourselves from all sin. By default we must take the lead in doing what is necessary for humanity's survival since the church is on another path. Religion not linked to humanity's earthside survival must be reclaimed from the church. Perhaps as a first step we can actualize potential community bonds among those we see in church. But seeing each other in church on Sunday is not enough. The best approach may be small faith communities who meet regularly to discuss what contribution they can make toward local problems and to peace and justice on earth. These small faith communities can find ways to connect with similar groups, perhaps through representatives. By learning from each other and cooperating on some issues their efforts can become synergised. Later I will have much to say about how committed couples can provide one foundation, perhaps the most important one, for a global community. If the church leaders see what the People can do on their own, they may follow.

We each exist in some kind of mental box. People in other boxes have something to teach us. I am suggesting that we should move continually to other boxes that better serve human purposes. "Truth" is communal (Piaget 1954:407; Efran 1987:38). We cannot connect through private truth anymore than we can through private language. We simultaneously affirm our truth and connect with other humans if we are disposed to change and to being corrected through shared experience. Human purposes are *our* purposes, here understood to be those that promote community without sacrificing individuals. By pursuing an intelligent morality based on Jesus' commandment of love we direct our lives toward an open future, reason enough to study the suggestions made here.

These essays are not offered as *the* truth. Consequently, unqualified assertions are never intended to mean that this is the way it is, rather, this is a way of looking at the subject under discussion, i.e., views from my narrow window on the world. While examining the social psychology of survival and the possibility of progressive moral evolution on a social and individual level I will unavoidably speculate on how we might continually learn to create a more humanistic world, one in which we recognize that we are necessarily social, and that this necessity extends beyond our family, tribe, city, or nation to all humans. These speculations are rational extensions of ideas many of us already accept. The proposals here are primarily intended to provoke thought so that we can begin the conversation necessary to bring our human family together in a true community.

CHAPTER I
NAMING THE PROBLEM

Human life is more precious than any ideology, any doctrine.....
Thich Nhat Hanh

The concept of wisdom generally has positive connotations. Among other qualities it is the capacity to make decisions that lead one to fulfilling one's goals, usually long term goal's within a communal context. However, the wisdom of a capitalist entrepreneur can diverge widely from say an elementary school teacher. One of our goals here is to learn how to make decision that promote the survival and well-being of the whole human family. As active members of that family we promote our own survival and well-being. Capitalist entrepreneurs, even when trying to be a faithful member of the human family or one of God's people, are sometimes put in the position of having to make decisions that conflict with that goal because they are beholden to stockholders. So the wisdom of corporation managers tends to be inconsistent with concern for the whole human family.

Two points to remember from the prologue: 1) We are necessarily concerned with survival and we are necessarily social. If we make survival decisions that stop at tribal boundaries, we have opted for the survival and well-being of some as against others. I intend to show in this essay that this limited wisdom turns out to not be wisdom at all. 2) Any behavior that affects at least one other person has a moral quality to it, and when the effect is negative, the chances of surviving for non-tribal members has in some way been diminished, behavior that ultimately puts everyone at risk. There was a time in the past when such diminishment might be widely accepted as the will of God, an attitude specifically promoted by the institutional church if we are to believe Pope Pius X who claimed that God created the social order and that it was "blasphemous to tamper" with it. There were kings and popes (winners) and slaves and women (losers) and every social position in between because God wanted it that way which may be why the priest quoted in the Prologue told us that church considered docility one of the chief virtues. Or as Paul suggests, "Slave obey your masters."

There are probably still people who will accept victimization as the will of God. But the global media reveals people everywhere resisting that idea. Oppression in other words sets the stage for conflict with people willing to blaspheme by tampering with the God's social order. The drive in humans to survive in this life has for a long time come to trump a desire to survive in eternity. Even people of faith rightly ask: why are the two incompatible?

If wisdom is acting in one's best interest, the institutional church does not act wisely. Like the capitalist it acts to survive but in doing so it sets in motion counter currents of resistance. Father Ephraim, the novice master for the brothers at a Trappist monastery once said that if a monastery is fulfilling its mission (acting wisely) it will prosper. This is the case for any religious organization. It was how the Jews understood their covenant. It is no less the case with the Catholic church. Vatican officials will assent to that idea; they will not however feel that it is one they need concern themselves with because of their claim that Jesus guaranteed the church against failure. The officials, in other words, see themselves as running on automatic. But the guarantee applies to the Church as the People of God founded by Jesus, not the institutional church founded by men. The Jews also had a guarantee that their covenant with God was forever. Has their covenant ended? They have to some extent failed on an institutional level but not insofar as any of them remain a People of God as is the case for Catholics or any other group. The basic qualification for being one of God's People is simply the recognition of one's self as a member of the human family and acting accordingly as noted in the Prologue.

Pope John Paul II is unquestionably a holy man. Yet he and the church he leads are unknowingly complicit in the world's besetting sin--idolatry--false or misleading ideas of God that affect or determine human behavior. I merely point out that the church is a human institution. A few years ago Cardinal Ratzinger was quoted as saying that the greatest threat to the [institutional] church is relativism (Thavis, NCR 18 Oct.1997). However, contemporary forms of idolatry constitute a much greater threat, and not just to the institutional church but to all of humanity. The threat is real because those who make decisions with the greatest impact on humanity's survival chances pay tribute to tribal gods. Whether those making decisions for us lead religions, nations, or multi-national corporations, whether their gods are explicit or implicit, their decisions affect everyone for good or ill and their gods are false in many respects. Idolatry exist more broadly than burning incense before a stone artifact. The idolatry that is problematic for us begins in the realm of concepts. The wholly otherness of God guarantees that no matter what *anyone* thinks or says of God, or does in God's name will be idolatrous to some degree. "For my thoughts are not your thoughts, neither or your ways my ways" says the Lord" (Isaiah 55:8). Burning incense before a idol may be one of the least pernicious among idolatrous acts. When done in ignorance that kind of idolatry harms no one. We are idolaters if our concept of God is comprised of characteristics improperly attributed to God and that attribution results in an understanding of God that leads to behaviors negatively effecting one or more persons, in which case the sin of idolatry is compounded. The magisterium itself inducts the faithful into various forms of idolatry.

I have already noted Pius X's attribution to God of an unchanging social order. It doesn't take a rocket scientist to see how such a doctrine would give aid and comfort to various elites such as the heads of multi-national corporations, global media conglomerates, and the church hierarchy itself. The concepts Catholics accept as truth largely determine how they will act with, for and toward other humans, in other words their morality, one of the areas in which the Vatican claims that it cannot teach error. This claim, since it is based on the guarantee against failure is as questionable as the claim that Jesus founded an institution. If the Vatican doesn't get it right most of the faithful won't either, especially those they are fond of calling, the "simple faithful," who as the Rev. Rondet says, "are the majority. Has the Vatican retracted this claim regarding the social order? Not exactly. It has made its peace with the idea of democracy without admitting that a monarchy is not the best form of civil government. They can make deals with kings, emperors and dictators but parliaments and Congresses complicate diplomacy.

The church now condemns overt slavery and makes statements about the equality of women without acting on them. However, it must still regard the status quo as an expression of God's will. How else are we to interpret John Paul's assertion that, "liberation theology is irrelevant." The intent of liberation theology is to free people from oppression and some of the subtle forms of slavery under which the losers now suffer. The Vatican has not said to liberation theologians, "We know what you are trying to do; here's a better way." Rather, officials have silenced those theologians. I have to conclude that the people who are in charge of the oppressed (the winners) enjoy divine favor and the Vatican still condemns tampering. In support of this kind of thinking is the ancient teaching that everything will be made right in the next world.

In prior centuries the lives of Jews, Muslims, heretics, witches and scientists (all losers) were sacrificed to this god who made some people better than others. There is a simple test for whether one's belief is idolatrous. If one's concept of God requires or allows discriminating against, excluding or abusing someone, or a belief is based on the idea that some person or class of persons are inherently superior to others, or that there are some persons in this world toward whom we have no obligations, then one pays homage to a false god.

St. Thomas calls us rational animals. Rationality is one of our greatest asset according to Thomas. He writes, "If it be in agreement with reason, the act will be good specifically, but if it be in discord with reason, it will be evil specifically" (*The Pocket Aquinas* p. 204). Unfortunately every chain of reasoning begins with a presupposition that cannot be proved and where one ends with reason depends on this unproven idea with which one began. Every idea of how we should live must pass the test of experience in community. We are therefore more appropriately described as learning animals rather than rational animals. The reasoning of one age must yield to the wisdom the community has garnered in the meantime. Charles Davis writes, "Truth is not reached by the individual in isolation." We attain "truth only in relationship with others" (1967:51). The process works in science in a similar way except that in people relationships we are dealing with a greater complexity and the attribution of causes tend to be oversimplified in traditional explanations as when the church identifies the source of human problems as Original Sin. No one person has a complete idea of what humans are about. An insight experienced by one person when shared with others is subject to correction, which points up the value of living in a community, particularly a diverse one.

A homogeneous culture limits the possibilities for correction. When we seem to have lost our way we must trust communal experience as a way of discovering how things really are, including religious truths. Talking together will help in overcoming some of our idolatrous habits, a large, inescapable part of our human condition.

We must learn our way out of our idolatry in a never-ending process, the magisterium as well as ordinary lay folk.

Ever since the first person conceived of the first god people hoped that appropriate behavior would elicit a sign of approbation, either a net gain in what one valued or the prevention of a net loss. Nothing has changed. Despite the occasional dispersion of the Jews for not acting as a community, despite the lesson of Job, despite Jesus saying how hard it would be for a rich man to enter heaven, the prevailing belief among the people in Christian cultures has it that God will bless us here and now in some tangible form, e.g., money, power, or fame. When misfortune strikes (the other side of that coin) people will ask, "What did I do to deserve this?" Good fortune provides its own answer. When Jesus made the pronouncement regarding riches, we learn that the disciples were not merely surprised, they "were astounded." "Who then can be saved?" they asked. Their response indicates that they thought the rich were already saved since they enjoyed divine favor. That riches could be a problem for a divine-human relationship tells it all.

In the minds of vast numbers of idolatrous citizens winning and losing of whatever sort, and often by any means, is considered *prima facie* evidence of God's favor or disfavor. Consider the prevailing attitude in the United States, toward people on welfare, non-military foreign aid and state lotteries. The tables at Las Vegas, Atlantic City and Biloxi draw hundreds of thousands seeking the favor of the gods. That kind of idolatry is based on the view of god as cosmic magician who rewards people for being good and punishes them for being bad, without their having to wait till they die. To have is to be.

Part of being human means being less dependent upon our senses for survival and more on our wits and on each other. Our knowledge of what being human means has reached a point at which social (read moral) evolution could progress in a conscious manner. We have a number of progressive ideas available to us, but we cannot bring them to bear on our problems because they contradict our dominant myth in its secular and religious versions, the myth that says the world is appropriately divided into winners and losers. This myth rests on the implicit idea of personal salvation, a scheme whereby a few are saved and many are lost. In its secular version, a few get rich and many are impoverished. A person would have to be stupid to be concerned with progressive social evolution for a global community while living according to such a myth.

Progressive evolution does not mean creating superior biological specimens through eugenics, nor by creating a middle-class lifestyle for everyone through the spread of technology. Instead, progressive evolution means creating a global community serving the best interest of everyone. We need a system within which at least everyone's basic needs could be met. Not everyone wants to be rich or even middle class, but our present system militates against poverty with dignity in highly industrialized countries and increasingly, everywhere else. Because mobility is possible in the Western economies, one's status is both "the penalty and proof of personal failure" when one does not rise (David Potter 1965:105). The technologies that could enable us to provide for greater numbers of people are used to make war, to make profits, and a host of divisive and self-destructive uses instead of providing for the survival of everyone. This is not intelligent behavior even for the winners. As Bonhoeffer noted, "The world *is* in fact so ordered that a basic respect for ultimate laws and human life is also the best means of self-preservation". It is behavior that will ultimately generate violent reactions as it has in the past--Cuba, El Salvador, Nicaragua and so on.

The problem of conceptual idolatry is not new. When disaster befell Job, his friends automatically assumed that he had sinned. Then we have the disciples asking Jesus if a man were born blind as a result of his parent's sin or his own; Jesus said, "Neither." Walter Lippmann writes, that "by the time of Hosea and Isaiah the religion of the Jews had become a system of rules for transacting business with Jehovah". Such behavior stemmed from a distortion of the terms of God's original covenant with the Jews which provided that if they acted as a community (family actually) they would prosper as a *People*. This truth still holds. Survival and prosperity are simply a natural consequence of people acting together toward that end, however under the New Dispensation the community must include everyone in the world, a perspective that makes more sense in a world made smaller by planes and instantaneous global communication.

We have no transcendental epistemology. We can hardly say anything about God that is not idolatrous, as in "God wants. . ." "God knows. . ." "God likes. . ." and so on. The churches claims that we have revelation from God, but the obvious evolution of consciousness revealed in the Bible (see Chapter 3) is evidence that revelation is an accumulation of wisdom produced by human thought and experience, a result of the fact that we are learning animals. The idea of revelation coming from God can be explained to those for whom it is important by saying God created humans to learn. We cannot explain in any other way the contradiction of the all loving God of the New Testament and God's apparent order for Joshua to kill every man, woman and child in a conquered city (Num. 31:15-16). The Jews knew from experience that women captured in war became sex objects and could lead men into idolatry. Blaming Eve for the first sin may have been an expression of that belief. It was a failure of imagination not an order from God that led to genocide as a way to eliminate a permanent temptation. The escape from idolatry is a long, tortuous journey for all of us. A learning magisterium needs large doses of relativism, prophets and faithful dissenters.

Roman Catholicism, perhaps the most successful organization in the history of the world still operates and may continue to operate for a long time. It is maintained in existence by the People of God, including many of the lower hierarchy, not by the Vatican bureaucracy which would serve the People better if it recovered its beginnings as Jesus people. Its success as an institution has depended thus far on a system of mind control over masses of people who equated faith in the church with faith in God. This basis for success is threatened by education. Even the large masses of the world's uneducated have access to information that can lead to questions that threatened their allegiance. Those in charge of the church have placed the warrant for their control in a realm beyond this one where presumably God resides. They have made themselves mediators between people and God in part by teaching us that we are obliged to act according to our consciences while simultaneously asserting that our consciences must be formed by what they teach. Another factor in making the system work is the belief by many of the faithful that there is a life after this one of either unimaginable bliss or unimaginable suffering to which the church holds the key. Several events have undermined this system of control. Chief among them are the declaration by the bishops at Vatican II that our consciences are free, and the definition of the Church as the People of God. Additionally, the People now recognize, as I have, the many contradictions between their experience and what the church teaches.

Pope Paul VI's encyclical, *Humanae Vitae*, said in so many words that persons who practiced artificial birth control could go to hell. That registered like the meteor impact that made the dinosaurs extinct. The Catholic magisterium immediately lost credibility with large numbers of the faithful, including many of the clergy. Unlike other times when the faithful loss faith in the pope and the church, such as at the Reformation and the Enlightenment, many Catholics remained in the church hoping to reform it because they understood *the Church* to be theirs not the hierarchy's.

Practicing artificial birth control is supposed to be a serious violation of the natural law, a mortal sin as the magisterium calls it. Pope Paul like St. Thomas overlooked the first natural law: survive. Many people who are neither philosophers nor theologians recognize on some level that not practicing birth control threatens their survival, a more immediate consequence than hell. The magisterium countered with what they saw as two ways out of this dilemma: Use the rhythm method of periodic continence, sarcastically known as Vatican roulette for its many failures. The second option was abstinence, i.e., remain celibate. With a choice between natural birth control that couldn't be counted on and an unnatural celibacy (estimates vary), but up to ninety per cent chose artificial birth control. There are systems known as NFP (*Crisis*, Dec. 2001), natural family planning, that are more efficient than "rhythm" but they tend to be technical and tedious and make love-making less spontaneous, hence unnatural. Paul's encyclical has aroused a skepticism that people extended to other church matters. Unsanitized church histories reveal flawed behavior by church officials during two millennia, the burning of witches and heretics, the crusades, and so on. Fortunately, the definition of Church as the People of God means that the institutional church is not identical with the People of God, as noted in the Prologue.

The time is past when the Roman Catholic church can live with these and other contradictions. The term paradox or mystery cannot be made to cover both the concept of a God of the New Testament who unconditionally loves everyone, and the God of Jewish scripture who ordered the mass slaying of men, women and children. The church does not seem to have a stake in eliminating the concept of a wrathful God which it has used to terrify and consequently control the faithful through its self-appointed role as mediator between God and persons on the brink of perdition. Catholic officials may be forgiven many things because they are trapped in their beliefs by early conditioning as most of us are in some way. But I can see no excuse for their difficulty in saying, "We were wrong," to their own faithful. Recently John Paul II has issued qualified apologies to the Jews and the leaders of the Orthodox church. I have yet to hear of an apology to his own faithful.

In a pamphlet I was given as a youth called "An Examination of Conscience," clearly identified as official by an *imprimatur* and *nihil obstat*, I was informed that I must confess the use of "bad" language. Since no one ever explained that such language was a matter of taste and not a damnable offense I was left with the impression that if I died without confessing that I had said "shit" or, heaven forbid, "fuck" I would burn forever. Perhaps this error has been corrected. If it has, it happened quietly without apology. My mother told me years ago that a priest informed her that if she denied her husband sex that she committed a mortal sin. I checked with a priest recently and this is apparently no longer taught, another teaching that disappeared quietly without apology or the admission of error. The magisterium's operative theory I've learned is that it is better to let the simple faithful believe that some behavior is a sin even when it is not than to give a complicated explanation that might only confuse them (Henri Rondet 1961:77).

When confronted with its less than immaculate past the church apologizes not for institutional failures, not for the leadership, but for all its imperfect members who cooperated with evil in such enterprises as the burning of witches and heretics, and the holocaust. In *We Remember: Reflections on the Shoah* John Paul II absolved "the church as such" from complicity in those crimes. No one, including the Pope, has yet indicated where or how this "church as such" exists. Perhaps it is some occult or mystical entity because it is not the institution; it is not the hierarchy or the Vatican bureaucracy and it is definitely not the ordinary membership. One possibility is that it is those who qualify as the People of God, the real Church, although I'm certain this is not what the Pope meant.

Historically speaking before there was an institution there were Jesus People (Crossan 1998:230-38). Men who were early leaders among the People simply followed whatever happened to be the traditional mode of transmitting ideas across generations. They created an institution patterned after the ones they knew. We needn't look far to find descriptions of who Jesus People are. Some of the more explicit statements attributed to Jesus are: Those who pick up their cross and follow; those who do the will of his Father; those who feed the hungry; those who love their enemies, and for the leadership, those who are the servants of all; those who don't lord it over others like secular rulers, and so on. Whether a People could continue through time without an institution is an open question; it wasn't tried. Current experiments among the faithful such as small faith communities seem to be successfully recreating the Jesus People.

Regarding the church's intransigence the Rev. Rondet writes, "It has sometimes been unfortunate...but in the end it has always done good. Moreover, Rome, with remarkable wisdom, knows that an assertion which may itself be good runs the risk of leading minds astray at a particular moment. Careful not to discourage the learned, it is also careful to preserve the faith of the simple, who are the great majority." Even the simple faithful, such as children, have a right not to be misled into believing they are at risk of damnation for using socially unacceptable words. The magisterium now recognizes the fact of biological evolution yet it remains reluctant to admit the evolution of morality for which there is considerably more evidence. The institutional church has wed itself to an immutable God, and as the bride" of Christ, (Louis May 1991:182), the church has assumed a mantle of immutability and infallibility.

The church could get by with verbal obfuscations at a time when most of the faithful were uneducated, all events were local and all media was voice and print, and before Paul VI wrote his fateful encyclical. Now however the whole world is bound together by instantaneous electronic media and the church increasingly faces an educated constituency not under its control. If the Vatican silences an Indian theologian this morning it might make the five-o-clock news in London and New York. The recent silencing of Tissa Balasuryia aroused a storm of protest around the world. Eventually the ban on his writing and teaching was lifted, although the reason for the lifting is not clear. The Vatican can only exercise control over books by its own clergy and publishing houses run by religious communities such as the Paulists and Maryknolls. *Papal Sins*, a recently published book by historian Gary Wills describes the church's structures of deceit. Not only is the Vatican unable to suppress this book or silence its author, they have no defense against what the book asserts because it is a matter of history.

As noted, the evil of idolatry is in its harmful effects on people. The church does not teach the idolatrous superstition that God rewards good people here and now. They also have not countered it very energetically. One effect of this belief is for people to manipulate events and people to bring about the favor of the gods. People who stand in the way, or lay claim to the resources that belong to the favored ones are by that very fact evil and any suffering they endure because of being crushed economically is seen as a sign of God's well-deserved judgment. This kind of thinking is pervasive in our culture that calls itself Christian. But if any teaching of Jesus is clear and unambiguous it is that we should be especially concerned with the care for the poor, the sick, prostitutes and social outcasts of all kinds. But he couldn't have really meant that, Right? say the idolatrous Christians even though such care and concern fulfills the two great commandments.

To teach and promote such thinking is viewed as merely a subsidiary part of the church's mission statement. Its primary task is to lead people to the New Jerusalem. With an institutional church it seems that

> All attempts to promote fraternity, however well-intentioned, stop with official authority. `You are all brethren' (Mat. 23:8) loses its validity the moment human behavior is institutionalized. Role authority creates relations of domination,

> and these cannot do without sanctions. . . Our definition of
> institution thus shows that institutions are instruments of
> power which are normative for behaviour among human
> beings. . . In the case of the Church, it can be shown from
> the Bible that a community without domination would be
> truer to Jesus' idea than an hierarchical institution (Hassen-
> huttl 1974:17).

Unfortunately for religion, humans will have institutions in which
hierarchies seem as inevitable as the tendency toward ossification.
The leaders Jesus chose wanted him to use the power of God to over-
throw the existing political institutions and put them in control, an
idea he strongly rejected. He could be considered apolitical--"Render
to Caesar. . .," etc., but his teaching would ultimately have had political consequences by undermining the standard political and economic
orders. Instead, the leadership went on to create an institution that
became itself the standard political order.

Karl Popper's description of Plato's ideal state which "is based on
the most rigid class distinctions," matches almost point for point the
Vatican bureaucracy. "It is a caste state. The problem of avoiding
class war is solved . . . by giving the ruling class a superiority which
cannot be challenged" (1966:46) based on the claim of being divinely
instituted. Plato's and the Vatican's plan for the ruling class requires
the strict exclusion of women, a policy that for the church is supported by priestly celibacy. In Plato's system women provided sex and
heirs, but the Vatican doesn't need heirs. It has a wider pool of
candidates to select from. Theoretically any male can become a
priest, a bishop, archbishop, cardinal and finally a pope. At each
stage, however, the screening process becomes more refined.

Institutions can be useful and may even be necessary to carry a
body of teaching forward to coming generations. But Jesus made it
clear that those to whom he entrusted with the leadership of his
People had to have certain qualities that diverged radically from traditional forms of leadership. He ruled out domination and anyone who
would be greatest in his kingdom must be the servant of all (Mat.
23:11). If the church cannot be reformed we need an alternative
method for transmitting the Good News from one generation to the
next, perhaps through networks of small communities as was the case
before the Church became the church But as is usually the case with
humans the old patterns are hard to break. New ways of acting got
infected by old ways. The patriarchal family structure became the
pattern for the house church where the People gathered, then became
the design for larger gatherings in buildings known as churches.

Perhaps only small faith communities based on Jesus' teaching can exist "without domination." Small groups discussing among themselves how best to show care and concern for the life and well-being of everyone has to produce better results for the survival of humanity than authoritative pronouncements from a bureaucracy so out of touch with the daily lives of the People that it could condemn them to hell for practicing birth control. Small groups could network to share ideas and experiences without a large central authority to maintain orthodoxy through sanctions of one kind or another because what has to matter in the lives of the People is that they promote the life and well-being of everyone. Such groups would be bound together by the ideals Jesus taught as the way to treat all members of the human family, especially the most vulnerable, rather than a community tied together by an abstract belief system.

I doubt that even a reformed Catholic leadership can lead us to the promised land of peace and justice on a global scale, something we must have for humanity's survival. Such an outcome would require an enlightened institution, an oxymoron. Peace and justice on a global scale can, I believe, only emerge from the People, that is, from the bottom up through pairs engaged in moral refinement and networks of pairs in small faith communities assisted by the fact that change is now a structural component in our world. Despite its unevenness there is also a history of moral progress to give us hope--the end of slavery, a start on th acceptance of female equality, the end of periodic war except among ethnic factions in various parts of the world, and the relatively peaceable dissolution of the Soviet empire.

The bishops' ecumenical efforts at Vatican II were primarily directed toward the possibility of interdenominational union to resolve the centuries-old scandal for which the Roman Catholic leadership was chiefly responsible. The bishop's perspective was too narrow. Sectarian tribal barriers at the institutional level are virtually impossible to eliminate because lowering such barriers involves the possible loss of institutional identity. At this time we need a wider ecumenism, joining with women and men of every creed and no creed to create the means of surviving in and beyond the new millennium. The "means" are not soup kitchens and food pantries although they help. We need a new way to think of how we shall act with, for and toward others, a new morality directed toward justice for all. A morality that has as its primary purpose the attainment of eternal life is bankrupt.

There are elements within that morality which belong in the new morality but agreement on those elements must arise out of the conversations we must undertake. Thus one might give money to the Salvation Army or a Catholic Workers's House because they feed the poor and downtrodden as a matter of charity and feel that one's duty has been done. Such efforts are incidental to what should be the main thrust of one's life, viz., justice on a global scale. The magnitude of the idolatry proceeding from the myth of winners and losers calls for the People working to change the structures of injustice to begin with themselves by making a commitment to simplicity, i.e., reducing the amount of the world's resources they use.

Getting people to change denominations to achieve unity is not a particularly worthwhile project. People should keep the faith they feel at home with, including secular humanism. Each faith has its own charism. Doctrinal differences generally have little or no bearing on the behavior required of God's People. The members of any religion must find their own ways of connecting with the rest of humanity. When the Christian religion began to splinter nearly four centuries ago

> What the Church needed, Erasmus argued, was a theology reduced to a minimum. Christianity must be based on peace and unanimity, "but these can scarcely stand unless we define as little as possible. . . a formula of faith . . . must be brief, `just the philosophy of Christ', which was concerned chiefly with the moral virtues" (Johnson 1976:275).

The advice Erasmus gave is still valid. If from the accretions of two millennia we isolate the basic message of Jesus, i.e., the recognition of all of humanity as a single family and the behavior that entails, the Good News might be acceptable, at least in theory, to every human of good will from fundamentalist Christian to anti-theist. This was essentially the position of Arius, condemned as a heretic. Arius thought of Jesus as a model of what humans should be. He could not have been faulted for that. If all denominations were eliminated and everyone believed and acted on Arius' belief the world's problems would vanish. If one person believes that Jesus is God and another believes he was just a great teacher, what could it matter if they both manifest a concern for the life and well-being of everyone.

If a threat to survival of the human species were immediate and clearly recognized the way we recognize an approaching storm front, virtually everyone would be concerned. But we can imagine the difficulty of achieving such recognition on that scale if people cannot quit smoking when they are personally touched by the death from tobacco of friends and relatives. The difficulty of becoming conscious of our problem, long and short range, provides an opening, hence a possible justification for institutional leadership. They are ideally situated to spread the word that we are on a path to annihilation. There can be little doubt that the survival of humanity is doubly threatened--immediately by weapons of mass destruction and intertribal feuding and long-term by destruction of the biosphere. The leadership, however, sees as its primary responsibility the salvation of souls and the fate of the world is somehow a matter for Divine Providence.

According to the theological theory known as Divine Providence, God's plan for the world and the people in it trumps human behavior when that behavior diverges from the plan, meaning that God will bring good out of evil. While the Catholic magisterium is not explicit there is a suggestion that God is active in the world, periodically intervening in human affairs to get things back on track. This is one reason people have asked: "Why did God allow the holocaust?" Such intervention while apparently supported by some stories in scripture is countered by the weight of empirical evidence pointing to our being on our own. The prayer that asks, "What can I do to stop wars?" is guaranteed to get an answer of some kind because presumably one reflects on the problem. Not so the prayer that asks God to stop wars. The partial truth in deism seems to be that the world and everything in it is crafted so well that God need not intervene. Life apparently has self-healing properties.

There are several lessons in the New Testament that point to the world as being a naturalistic place rather than one of magic and direct intervention by God. Jesus said that God causes the "sun to rise on the evil and the good, and sends rain on the righteous and the unrighteous" (Mat. 5:45), and when asked if a man's blindness was caused by his own sin or that of his parents, he replied, "Neither." I'm suggesting that for theists, the universe and the people in it can be viewed as designed by God so that good will come out of the evil that humans do as they learn from their mistakes and correct them rather than through the manipulation of events by God. Cognitive evolution seems to always produce learners and creative individuals who will take us around the next curve.

To illustrate: After centuries of war Europeans finally learned from experience that whatever goals they might have were more likely to be achieved through cooperative effort so they abolished the culture of war among themselves and formed the European Union, an entirely secular effort. The church did not find war wrong until the political leaders did. In fact in the late 19th century Pius IX looked to sympathetic civil rulers to save the papal states from Italian nationalists by means of war. In Jewish scripture the People were told that they would prosper when they acted as a family, i.e., together. Periodically they were captured and enslaved when they lost sight of themselves as a People, events that can be explained naturalistically. Praying together to end war is a good way to unite us as a People but we ourselves must act to end war. Gregory Bateson, a famous atheist, saw the primary function of religion as uniting people.

The point is that judging from what we know of history, including the Bible, if God has a plan for the world it is likely to be achieved through the evolution of human consciousness toward the recognition of ourselves as a People. This evolutionary process has been in effect from the beginning. One might say that at some point a certain kind of reflective consciousness is what distinguished humans from the proto-humans from whom they emerged. The church argues that humans can do nothing without divine initiative. Their teaching only serves to confuse. Are they suggesting that God gives and withholds grace, that God is a puppetmaster, instead of the unconditional lover immanent in all of life? As noted before, if we are not free to be bad, we are not free to be good. I am not claiming that humans are born free. Rather, their orientation toward learning can lead to acquiring the skill to be free. They are in other words free to be free. Freedom is a possibility that most humans have yet to realize to any significant degree. I see us still at an early stage of cognitive evolution in that respect. Consider the attraction that money has because of the choices it enables. That, plus the idolatrous belief that God rewards here and now makes the pursuit of money seem the way to go.

I am convinced that the radical critic of Judaism we know as Jesus started a movement to awaken humans to their evolutionary potential. He proposed a special kind of community that would eventually provide the basis for the spread of his ideas throughout the whole of humanity. However, he left for us the task of further learning required to meet new circumstances. But the process of consciousness raising inherent in his teaching was virtually stillborn, reduced as it was to a formula for eternal salvation even though the church teaches that we cannot save ourselves. The basis for community is a set of intimate relationships. The Catholic magisterium does not now nor has it ever had a theology of intimacy. The only intimacy with which it has been concerned is sex, toward which it has had an almost totally negative attitude for the better part of two millennia. Until relatively recent times it even viewed sex in marriage as sinful. I'll have more to say about this later in the chapters on commandments and in the final two chapters that deal specifically with intimacy.

If a global community is what we need for humanity to survive it is hard to conceive of how it can begin other than with pair-bonding. If two people cannot find a way to connect, what hope is their for larger groups? Pairs can then proceed to establish networks of pairs which finally breech tribal boundaries where the connection will be of necessity pragmatic rather than intimate, as in negotiating non-aggression pacts and disarmament treaties. Patriarchy and domination at any level are formulas for failure in our task of fashioning a global community. It is at this point that the greatest failure of Roman Catholicism may be clearly seen. The church has effectively turned people away from each other to focus attention on trying to relate to God, a mission impossible. We are told not to worry because the church can mediate relationships through the sacraments, especially confession. As long as the faithful were mostly uneducated and conditioned early to see the church as an all-knowing parent who had the means of surviving in the afterlife, the system worked, or at least it held together.

Those who created the institutional church put new wine in old wineskins. Religion is a call to an earthbound task. Dom Aelred Graham asks, Isn't religion "fundamentally a means of enlightenment, so that we can become adjusted to life as it actually is. . . and live in the world today?" (1971:233). The chief concern of Jesus was that people should live this life in communities of caring. The quest for eternal life is a distraction from that task. The problem of thinking about life for the sake of eternal salvation became further complicated by the Roman and Greek anthropology and epistemology used for explaining it which is why asceticism became so important in the early church. We have not yet escaped the consequences of an epistemology that said we can know things as they are, clearly expressing their essences in words, and an anthropology that starts with a hierarchy of being established by God, with God at the top, followed by religious and civil rulers, down through slaves and women to non-human animals; and finally a theology that teaches us to focus our attention on saving an "immortal soul" which "can seek no confirmation in human experience" (O'Connor 1968:25).

We saw in the prologue that the first natural law, the one we must all live with all the time, is *survive*, and because we are necessarily social we must survive *together*. From this two-part natural law all "oughts" can be derived because behavior has empirical consequences and it should not be difficult for us to discern through communal discussions those behaviors that will maintain harmony among the people we live with and those that won't.

St. Thomas taught that the primary natural law is do good and avoid evil. The good we must do is promote the life and well-being of every person, including our enemies, and the evil we must avoid is inflicting harm on one or more persons. We must especially not in any way diminish the lives of anyone for our own sake which would introduce anarchy into the process. We already have that. People who develop a consciousness of being oppressed, who feel that their hunger and misery is caused by the well-fed people of the world, could become a third threat to humanity's survival after nuclear weapons and destruction of the biosphere. Much of the crime and terrorism in the world are survival responses of those who feel they are outsiders.

Thomas skipped a step in his reflection on natural law. If he had been a serf instead of being supported in the relative comfort of a religious community he might have realized that the greatest evil anyone faced is death, an everyday, all-day concern for serfs. Of course, Thomas' reasoning started with the presupposition that the good of eternal survival outweighed all other considerations and perhaps that's what a person should be thinking of while dying a painful death from cold and starvation.

While the fate of the world may be too abstract for most people to deal with, The difficulty could be minimized if those who recognized the problem for what it is started the conversation we must have with one or few persons with whom they are closest and worked outward, creating networks of caring until everyone in the whole world comes under that umbrella of concern. We want those near and dear to us to survive and prosper as well as ourselves, but because of the kind of world we now live in a global, family consciousness is called for. Any attempt to discriminate results in a world of us against them. We already have that.

In the beginning the church saw its task as making as many Christians as possible as quickly as possible, nevermind that many of these conversions were nominal at best, as when a ruler or tribal chieftain became a Christian and all of his people followed suit on orders from the ruler. We cannot blame early church leaders for the way they acted. They could only work with what they had and at their level of cognitive development. What they can be faulted for is the failure to learn from the experience of two millennia since then, particularly during the past two centuries when they have had to back away from some untenable positions, e.g., Genesis as history, but not entirely (see Pius XII's *Humani Generis*). There is also their failure to model themselves on Jesus who came to serve rather than dominate. After Constantine, church leadership got into a mode of treating people in the manner of civil rulers, a style that has continued beyond their loss of a country to rule.

I plan to show that a morality keyed to survival is the only morality that makes sense in a world where the message of Jesus as interpreted by the church is not going to convert everyone. It is rather a message that plays into the hands of anti-survival forces by making people fatalistic and accepting doomsday scenarios as an expression of Divine Providence. I intend to show how the history of human, cognitive (that is, moral) evolution is revealed in the Bible. The magisterium's interpretations of the Bible requires them to explain away contradictions, false science and bad psychology. As Prof. Jerome Bruner teaches, we are learning animals, and as in the natural sciences the best and most interesting place to begin learning is where we find contradictions and anomalies so the People and the magisterium have a lot to work with. We are fortunate to have scripture to show us where the People have been on their journey and how far they have come, the mistakes people made and the lessons they learned. The magisterium claims that the Bible is not entirely the Word of God that some of the writers merely recorded their own experiences. In politics this is called "spin." Witness the behavior of Pius XII when finally conceding the possibility of evolution. To save the doctrine of Original Sin he said, though not in these exact words, that at some point God infused souls into a male and female who then committed the sin we read about in Genesis. The Pope overlooked the fact that here were two beings, now human, who existed among other creatures who are genetically compatible with the proto-humans from whom they emerged and the problems that entails. We could hypothesize that God scrambled the DNA of the other proto-humans, or changed the DNA of Adam and Eve, but these magical, theological contortions result in more complexity when trying to resolve the problems arising from Pius XII's attempt to save the doctrine.

The way of interpreting scripture that I suggest in chapter 4 allows believers to accept that this Book is indeed the Word of God, every bit of it. For non-believers the lessons are just as valuable because they are human lessons, arrived at through an entirely humanistic process. Only in our own time has it become possible to see scripture in this new way. When someone says, "The Bible is not history," the statement is only partially true. Although it is not history as a record of events, it most certainly is a history of human thought and like all histories it has important lessons for those who understand it. It took Bible scholarship and natural science to carry us beyond literalism. Once we look at the Bible with our new eyes a wondrous story of humanity's emergence from darkness unfolds. With regard to parables and other Bible stories Gregory Bateson, writes, "Most of the really important stories [didn't happen]--they are true in the present, not in the past. . . "

The Ten Commandments provide one of the best lessons in moral evolution found in the Bible. When we look at what the commandments meant to the Jews, what they came to mean for the church, and finally their meaning today we witness another grand unfolding of God's lessons for us coming through human effort. The church continues to insist that the commandments don't change despite all the evidence to the contrary, another instance of institutional intransigence. In a later chapter I will expose some of the problems of a transcendental morality, the kind the church teaches. At the same time I will clarify what sin means. It is not breaking a rule as the church seems to teach. If one's life is guided by the Law of Love, one's concern transcends rules. In any aesthetic enterprise, rules may be useful early on, but ordinarily a person who has been painting pictures for years needn't wonder how to render flesh tones or drapery. Similarly, in the artistic enterprise of creating a life. The rules remain as guides for the unenlightened.

There are different kinds of relativism; the Cardinal Ratzinger did not distinguish. There is a philosophical relativism according to which nothing is true. That is hardly a problem for most of humanity and so that cannot be what threatens the church. Then there is the knowledge which becomes refined over time so that we come to understand truth in an expanded or more complex way that better serves human purposes, for example, the story of Genesis. Once science established Eden as fiction we could examine the story for the real lessons it contains. All except the most fundamentalist of Christians accept that we are not reading ordinary history in Genesis. Many people will be surprised to learn that the story actually contains helpful humanistic insights but not as the story is generally interpreted. We also find history in Genesis, not with regard to events. It is a record of human thought at the time of the writing, how, for example, they attributed certain characteristics to God and believed that God expected of them behaviors, many of which we later learn were based on the culture they lived in rather than directives from God, notably the idea of sacrifice. We also learn that women were a problem for men and as is often the case with humans, the victim was blamed.

In the final two chapters I deal with the bottoms-up approach to humanity's survival by showing how committed couples of whatever gender can provide the basis for the creation of a global community by pursuing the goal of moral refinement between themselves then in a gradually expanding network of pairs in small faith communities until finally all humanity is involved. This may sound extremely fanciful, but those with experience in small faith communities know how powerful and how empowering such relationships can be. Moral refinement does not mean the pursuit of personal perfection. It is, rather, a process whereby two persons engage in an interpersonal dialectic by laying themselves out as completely and as frankly as possible. The time to think of moral refinement is early in a relationship when emotions are running high and each party to a relationship would be willing to consider the problems that can be generated by their cultural differences. The best attitude in a love relationship is to minimize expectations. I'm thinking of a relationship in which whatever one gives is received graciously as gift rather than the all-too-common attitude: "If she/he loved me she/he would. . ."

Earlier I posed the question: Who are the People of God? The fullness of the answer will unfold as we examine the many twists and turns of human thought in relation to the institutional religion. This much can be said. The People have only recently reached a level of cognitive development enabling them to take up the process of consciously expanding that development. The church might, for the benefit of its faithful and ultimately all of humanity, heed the wisdom of the atheist, Julian Huxley, who advised us that "the destiny of humans is to discover their role in the evolutionary process in order to fulfill it more adequately" (1957:209). Prof. Huxley wrote this in the context of "religion without revelation," but by *revelation* he probably meant supernatural information. Prof. Huxley might find acceptable a naturalistic definition of revelation, such as I offer in this study. We have to admit the possibility that some of the knowledge we call revelation was directly inspired by God. There is no way to tell. There is no way to distinguish it from human learning. It is our nature to learn. Christians can say that from their perspective that God created us to learn but the results are indistinguishable from the atheistic theory that we simply evolved that way, i.e., capable of learning. Distinguishing divine revelation from ordinary human learning would be difficult unless it came to us with bells and whistles.

Everyone recognizes a condition we call ignorance; it is simply not knowing. However, few us are aware of another kind of ignorance--faulty knowing, e.g., believing that the earth is flat or that the universe revolves around the earth. Such an ignorance is the polar opposite of learning to learn. It is knowledge that results in being unable to learn, temporarily or permanently. For that reason I call this condition Ignorance II, the opposite of Bateson's Learning II which is learning to learn. Much of the knowledge I had before various learning experiences I now understood as this kind of ignorance. A trivial example of such ignorance would be my wanting to go to a place that I think is west of where I am, whereas it is actually east. Eventually my ignorance will be resolved because in traveling west I will not arrive where I want to go.

Certain kinds of Ignorance II are not so trivial nor so easily resolved. Those of us who grew up in the South before the mid-1950s will remember the "Colored-only" schools, swimming pools, restaurants, drinking fountains, restrooms, and so on. All of these separate facilities seemed perfectly natural to me and my friends. We grew up in ignorance of the hurt and humiliation inflicted on a people. Some Southerners (and Northerners) apparently are incapable of resolving such ignorance. Instead of learning to learn such persons are crippled in their ability to learn, at least with respect to racism. This is an extreme form of closure, contradicting the possibility of intelligence as a survival trait. The concept is important because, "to modify our idiom is to modify the frame of reference within which we shall henceforth interpret our experience; it is to modify ourselves" (Polanyi 1962:105). The main problem from the perspective of this study is the inability to grasp that the basis of our thinking is not reality; it is our preconception of reality. What Liam Hudson writes regarding why "psychologists of different schools disagree so profoundly," is the case with anyone who studies humans, not excepting theologians; "we must first disinter the metaphorical presuppositions on which each takes his [sic] stance" (1975:23).

Until relatively recent times morality always seemed to be associated with religion. Now we know that people of every belief and no belief are concerned with how people act with, for or toward others, i.e., morality. We can legitimately refer simply to, "the People," leaving it to those with religious convictions to add, "of God." Whichever expression one uses the fact remains that the main purpose for morality has always been intra-group survival by maintaining harmony. Theoretically a person could survive alone after being given a start in life by parents or surrogates, but the difficulty of such a project does not make it an attractive option. Surviving as a member of a tribe is the way of most people, from the beginning right up till our own time, except that now some tribes are large nations.

When a tribe of whatever size feels that their survival is threatened by another tribe the first response tends to be a preparation for conflict. Preparation for conflict by one calls forth the same response from the other. From that point de-escalation becomes increasingly difficult. One of my arguments in this book is that the tribal way of surviving is ultimately unsustainable for a number of reasons, among which are the size and scope of today's economic activity, our instantaneous media connection, the finiteness of our resources, the toxic byproducts of industrialization, and most importantly the danger to everyone from intertribal war. Something on the order of the European Union has to occur on a global scale to keep humans from destroying themselves. Religion could be helpful by promoting connections that transcend national boundaries, but two of the largest and most influential religions, Islam and Catholicism, believe that nothing is so important as eternal survival. This means that like the EU's transcendence of tribal boundaries, a global community will likely result from a secular effort or not at all.

An idea can be best understood when the persons sharing the idea also share the same context of meaning. To that end we must know the presuppositions that provide the foundation for the way people think and know. Otherwise they may seem to disagree when they actually do not. Prior to the 19th century philosophers, theologians and other scholars could build systems of thought based on what they considered self-evident propositions. The discovery that all thinking is historically conditioned means that if we wish to understand philosophers, theologians, scholars of another age including Biblical writers we can only do so if we can look at the world from their perspective (Collingwood 1956). A classic example of such historical conditioning is the belief by most Christian until recently that Genesis was history. The church Fathers, notably Augustine, made logical deductions they thought relevant to Christianity based on the idea that Adam and Eve were real persons who committed real sins. We have more and better knowledge in our time to work with, but we also have the problem of a more diverse population in trying to converse on a subject as complex as morality. A conversation that takes humanity's survival as a point of departure should be less problematic because 1) everyone wants to survive and 2) behavior, as my mother taught, has empirical consequences from which we should be able to decide if those are the consequences we want and their value for survival.

We cannot avoid the conclusion that if survival is what really matters in life then we must talk our way out of certain aspects of current tribal morality, i.e., our rules for behavior determining our various relationships at every level. This essay promotes the search for an intelligent morality, one according to which everyone's life and well-being is valued making it inseparable from the requirements of creating a global community. The well-being of persons, should include opportunities for developing their minds and abilities, but that has to be a long range goal given our starting point. We must first see that everyone gets basic necessities. Equality cannot be an issue. The task of surviving requires organization, and if organization then leadership, making inequality inevitable. Although if leaders saw themselves as servants of the People equality would be a non-issue.

Perhaps that is the only kind of leadership that can succeed. An attempt at leveling society ordinarily requires the suppression of creativity resulting in a negative impact on everyone from top to bottom as we learned from the late, great Soviet Empire.

Whatever the difficulties involved in achieving a morality humanity can survive with it is not a subject we can avoid thinking about and talking about almost continuously. Our own best chance of surviving begins with promoting the life and well-being of everyone and trying to persuade others to do the same. Apathy is a big problem in getting this project started, especially since very few people are even convinced we have the problem I am describing. The responsibility thus falls to those of us who are convinced. The prognosis for a quick solution is not good when one considers the number of European wars fought before the EU was created. Still, we must do what we can on whatever scale we can. Those of us who are aware of what is a stake can make a commitment to simple living and encourage others to do the same. We need to constantly reflect on how much of the world's resources we use and the effect such use has on others. This further requires that we exchange ideas and learn from one another.

The morality we need must be generic and secular since it must be acceptable to enough people to make it work. Behavior has consequences. We should be able to empirically verify their effects on our survival chances. The morality upon which we finally agree will be simply the rules, or the principle from we derive such rules for acting with, for or toward other humans that will enable us to survive, individually and collectively. Although we may not be conscious of it each of us has a morality whether we are saint or sociopath, because everyone has rules or a principle for deriving rules for acting with, for or toward other humans, although not necessarily conscious, or even consistent. In fact they tend to be a mixed bag. We adopt rules unconsciously or even make them up as we go along. We may not agree with another person's morality; we may not like another person's morality but we have to agree that each person has a morality as defined here, i.e., the basis for how others are treated. We must each ask ourselves if the morality we live by is a proper morality, one we can all live with.

In the context of traditional, religious morality this fact is difficult to discern and understand because what does not conform to a particular religious morality is considered immoral. This dichotomy makes adherents of religious morality inherently judgmental, especially adherents of Catholic and Islamic morality. These moralities are defined in absolute and extrinsic terms. St. Thomas Aquinas says that "moral standards are external to and independent of human nature," meaning they are revealed by God. This presents a certain difficulty in reconciling Thomas contention with Pius XII and the natural law written on our hearts (*Humani Generis*; Cor. 2:15). Since God does not change, and according to Thomas, neither does human nature which is the same for everyone, the law cannot change.

Thomas uses the expression *synderesis* which means "a disposition by virtue of which men [sic] are enabled to grasp the most general principles of morality." This disposition is innate; it cannot "be weakened or lost" by bad habits or vice. "It is moreover infallible" (O'Connor p. 42). This disposition, as in the case of will or intelligence in Thomas' view is apparently located in the soul, which would account for its apparent incorruptibility. The problem with Thomas' analysis, as noted before, is not recognizing the most basic natural law, viz., survive, and since we are necessarily social we must survive "together." Thomas teaches as he does because his and the church's priority is surviving in the next life.

When Pope Leo XIII made Thomism the church's official philosophy and theology he could not have anticipated the problems that would arise on account of Thomas' now discredited epistemology and anthropology. We know for example that thinking is not the immaterial exercise Thomas thought it to be; a physical brain is required for thinking and a great deal of behavior is determined by behavioral and thinking habits acquired long before we are able to do critical thinking. Thomas' and the church's position depends on a freedom that humans do not inherently possess. Also, we know that all humans are not equally rational. "This contrasts with St. Thomas' notion of rationality which is an `all or nothing' concept not susceptible of variation in degree and which one applies to every human being" (O'Connor p.73). Morality has changed dramatically since Thomas taught that morality does not change. For instance, we now think of slavery as wrong which it was not for church until the 19th century, and racism now also considered wrong, continued in the church till past mid-20th century. What is not clear with regard to the church and racism was whether they believed it was wrong and failed to act on that belief to keep from offending white congregations or whether they actually thought it was right. These aspects of morality have clearly evolved.

The issue of whether we have souls, i.e., whether there is a part of us that can exist disembodied which Thomas took for granted is not something on which even theologians will agree. John Cogley writes, "The distinction between `body' and `soul' exists in logic, not in reality, for in reality man [sic] exists as a psychosomatic unit" (1968:84). Aristotle thought in terms of a unified existence while for

Plato we were made up of two parts. Thomas and the church are at best ambiguous, seeming to vacillate between Plato and Aristotle. *The Catechism*, first says that "spirit and matter, in man, are not two natures united, but rather their union forms a single nature." But "The Church teaches that every spiritual soul is created immediately by God. . . it does not perish when it separates from the body at death, and it will be reunited with the body at the final Resurrection" (1997:93). This is pure speculation. No one knows what happens at death and beyond. Will, intellect and emotion were regarded by Thomas as immaterial faculties so there had to be a place for them to reside, hence "soul." The ambiguity of the concept allows the magisterium to make "soul" fit with other doctrines of the church. Paul Ramsey writes,

> Where the New Testament asks, `What shall it profit a man if he gain the whole world and lose his own soul?' the word *psyche* is a translation of *nepesh* rather than one of the Greek meanings of *psyche*. The verse should read, `What will it profit a man if he gain the whole world and lose his own life?' (1962:61-62; see also Roger Johnson 1987:100, 221).

The translation offered by Ramsey can refer to a this-worldly phenomenon without denying church teaching, but the church finds *soul* more useful for maintaining consistency with its official, Thomistic theology and philosophy. If there is a resurrection after death, the logic based on the existence of a separable "soul" is not necessary. Nor is there a necessity for a temporal delay between death and resurrection if time does not continue beyond death. The point I am trying to make is that so far from being able to contribute to the conversation we must have to survive, the Catholic morality currently taught by the church presents obstacles to reaching a consensus by claiming that morality comes from God hence is immutable. Individualism, for example, is anathema to the Catholic leadership. Early in the 20th century Pope Pius X condemned movements that promoted "the freedom of the individual to think and act independently of clerical supervision and control" (McSweeney 1980:85). Note Pius X's claim that God created the social order of winners and losers. Pius XII in mid-20th century condemned the idea of free conscience because it would allow Catholics to choose another religion.

The importance of individualism is that the morality we need has to be freely discussed to arrive at a consensus. One cannot come to this conversation equipped only with dogma. This does not affect divergent moralities that anyone may choose as a personal code for whatever reason, so people in religion can maintain the morality they already have. They may not, however, make anyone else follow their code. When people lived in villages and small towns morality was inevitably parochial and was forced on everyone. Sanctions are easily applied in such situations to keep anyone from straying beyond a limited range of behaviors. Large cities offer liberation from such pressures.

Progressive moral evolution has come through a stochastic process. Input from the experience of millions of people over long periods of time have resulted in such changes as the end of slavery, the acceptance of democratic government and international law, often in the face of opposition from church officials whose idolatrous presuppositions make it difficult to change. These presuppositions and many found in conventional wisdom need to be challenged. First, however, they must be identified as presuppositions and not self-evident truths. We can find reasons for our presuppositions but never proof.

Our unique historical conditioning, our genetic makeup, the environment created by our family of origin and all the different factors that go into the makeup of our personality means that making all of one's presuppositions explicit is not possible. However I will attempt to be upfront with several of my more important ones in order to share my context of meaning and to make clear that I am presenting my perspective on reality and not reality itself. The foundation for my ideas on morality depend heavily on certain presuppositions that are not shared by everyone. However, readers should be able to say that if we grant his presuppositions then his arguments make sense. Presuppositions, provide the basis for constructing what for us is real. Most people are not even aware that their mental world is built on presuppositions and so they cannot imagine their way out of the conflicts they get into with someone who lives within a variant reality. We may say of a presupposition that it is merely a reasonable place to begin thinking, like an axiom in geometry. I agree with theologian Gregory Baum and others, that "all knowledge is based on a set of indemonstrable presuppositions" (1971:21). Some readers while not finding my presuppositions radical may find the ideas that can be deduced from them radical. My presuppositions can be discerned as the basis for important lines of reasoning; e.g., the Church is the People of God.

I address these thoughts primarily to the secular humanists among us who think this is the only life about which we can be concerned or those in religion who take their cues from "immanental theology [taking] the incarnation as its central focus and ruling paradigm. . . [T]ranscendental theology focuses on the cross and resurrection.

Immanental theology sees the divine life residing in Jesus. . ." (Avis 1989:53) just as it does in us. He was truly one of us. The basic problem with a transcendental focus is that we can only talk *to* a transcendental God; there is no identifiable response. Whatever happens is presumably God's response. With our attention on God as immanent in our brothers and sisters their voices become God's voice. If we listen carefully we can hear words of love, hurt, despair and so on, calling on us to respond with love or compassion, but in a very particular way, i.e., according to the particular need of the person with whom we are communicating as we learn from Daniel Maguire (1979:305). The transcendental (vertical) and the immanental (horizontal) views of God are in some respects complementary rather than contradictory, but while we have to respect the beliefs of those who feel they can relate to God as transcendental I see this view as problematic for our efforts to create a global community because of its association with an extrinsic and absolute morality. There is also the issue of people who do not believe in God or who question God's existence, who nevertheless must be included in our quest for an intelligent morality. The survival of humanity demands it. Traditional religious language is an obstacle to discussing morality with the unchurched. Church leaders are promoting a vertical theology at a time when it is becoming less and less viable as a means of unifying humanity. Our problems are here, not "out there." God does not need us; we need each other.

Although the explanation is somewhat oversimplified, we can think of the current tension between so-called liberals and conservatives as the result of these apparently divergent views of God. Therefore, if we wish to live as Jesus said we should, i.e., as a family, we cannot avoid adopting a pluralistic disposition. The most important difference between the perspectives on God as immanent and God as transcendental is that the divine attributes and divine revelation within the transcendental perspective are immutable, whereas regarding God as immanent leaves us open to learning variant aspects of divinity when we engage each other with reverence and respect. Simply put, we learn from communal experience.

Since the Roman magisterium operates primarily with the transcendental perspective in which God and the rules are immutable, it must adjust to one crisis after another. In our time these crises occur more frequently than in earlier centuries, because the People are more diverse hence their experiences are more varied, leading to more questioning of static concepts. Institutional church leaders feel that their main job is to lead people to the sacraments (Carney 1985:289) and to mediate between us and a transcendental God rather than in

promoting God as immanent. But if God is immanent as the magisterium itself teaches, do we need mediators? We already have a built-in
relationship with God. Perhaps we just need teachers who can show
us how to develop a consciousness of the God within and how to
relate to God immanent in our sisters and brothers. Furthermore
there is little practical difference between viewing God as immanent
and merely holding life as sacred as many atheist and agnostics do, an
important consideration since everyone must be included in the conversation regarding our survival.

When we think of the frontiers of knowledge we are more likely to
think of the natural sciences such as physics and biology than we are
to think of morality. This is surely one consequence of the glacial
pace at which morality has progressively evolved and negative reputation religion has given to the concept. Yet history testifies to the fact
that morality does indeed progress. We have only to think of the
abolition of feudal society and slavery, the trend toward popular
involvement in government, and mass education. The Ten Commandments do not mean the same today as they once did. Also in the
20th century women and persons of color have acquired the vote and
other civil rights, at least legally, clear evidence of moral progress. It
is also evident that over the long haul when the larger community
works out moral standards for itself the results are better for everyone
than when they are dictated from the top by an oligarchy, civil or
religious.

The moral frontiers are not hard to find: the ethics of intimacy;
reproductive and sexual ethics; end of life and general medical ethics;
the ethics of violence; environmental ethics; and the ethics of economic justice. These are some of the areas where the old morality does
not work or may be nonexistent. The danger in holding to an absolute
morality as does the Catholic magisterium and fundamentalist sects is
that when the rules contradict experience for someone that person may
be tempted to reject the whole system. Given this fact, those who are
responsible for moral leadership should be supportive and give guidance to the direction in which the People's energy and experience take
them instead of flatly resisting change. We can all use help in discerning the nature of a proper morality, especially a proper interpersonal morality. Instead we are being told by religious leaders, notably Roman Catholic leaders, that the moral code was given to them by
an immutable God, hence it is absolute and unchanging, a position so
obviously contradicted by history, even Bible history, that one wonders how anyone can hold it. The sorry state of the world demonstrates like nothing else can that we have a moral frontier. It is our
responsibility to become conscious of it and start discussing it.

Religious leaders will claim that we can do nothing without God, but my understanding of orthodoxy is that the availability of God's grace is not an issue. Gregory Baum tells us "the summons of grace and the gift to enter into new life are available to the whole of [humanity]" (1971:22). Many atheists and agnostics recognize themselves as members of the human family and act appropriately without a consciousness of God's grace. The availability of God's grace might be a problem for some theologians and the hierarchy but not the People. Still, given that there is some wisdom in what the churches have been teaching (Lippmann 1957:303), theologians and social scientists can find the kernel of wisdom in the old morality and explain it in contemporary language. Reasons for the prohibitions against murder, theft and adultery seem to be self-evident, i.e., they are intuitive. Sex, for example, is generally such a highly charged matter for humans that we have little difficulty understanding the original proscription against having sex with another person's mate and the consequences for community. Although as we shall see in chapter 6, reasons for these proscriptions have changed making for a significantly different kind of morality. We should remember that the Pharisees brought the woman taken in adultery not the man. The failure to note such changes has contributed to the church's loss of credibility as a moral authority.

Intra-tribal conflict over adultery in a small tribe would put everyone at risk, and although we can, in our own time, imagine a person who does not feel threatened or insecure if a mate has sex with someone else, generally speaking such behavior is more likely than not to generate insecurity and be a source of conflict. Such conflict tends to have a negative effect on the whole community because when people are hurt or feel insecure in such matters they are likely to express themselves in ways that are destructive of everyone's peace and harmony. The revelation that these acts offended God would at one time have given support and emphasis to any prohibition, especially among an illiterate populace who believed in magic. Other prescriptions and proscriptions are not so self-evident. For teachers of morality to be effective in our contemporary culture, they must understand where the harm lies in certain behaviors so that they can convince the People of how they can act in their own best interest and the best interest of everyone. This is not how it is being done. People could believe that God forbade adultery, killing and stealing because they could see for themselves the destructive effect such behavior had. In our own time most people cannot understand how contraception has a destructive effect on the community. Its excessive use might have threatened humanity's survival when the earth was sparsely populated, but that is not a problem in our time. The opposite seems to be the case. Both ideas, the prohibition of adultery and the rightness of using contraception are revelations for humanity. For a rule to be effective the People must be convinced that it is in their best interest, which is not possible unless the persons who teach it are credible or can be persuasive. The foundation for persuading people that a rule is in their best interest is the knowledge that personal survival is a subset of global family survival.

For some critics of conventional Christianity *radical* might mean a return to the roots of the movement, presumably to restore it to what Jesus initially intended, e.g. Luther's Reformation. Another meaning of the word refers to attempts at introducing any social changes, including changes to Christianity that are so out of the ordinary that they might seriously disturb the many persons who are satisfied with custom. This kind of change in Roman Catholicism might include women priests and optional celibacy for priests. The two changes cited, however, are not the changes I am advocating, although I would vote for them given the opportunity. The radical changes I am proposing are much more fundamental than that. Priestly vocations for women and optional celibacy would directly affect the calling of relatively few people. I am proposing changes in the way we think about God and what we call sins against God, but mostly about our relationships with other humans, particularly persons with whom we wish to be intimate. Some people feel comfortable with the idea of relating to a transcendent God in which case what I have to say could still be of interest by providing enlightenment for such people concerning those of us for whom an immanent God makes more sense. Developing a consciousness of God as immanent will radically alter our perception of the world and the people in it. In every encounter with another person we will be simultaneously shaping our relationship with God and the person, and ultimately with all the people in the world. Or we can, as with some atheists and agnostics, e.g., Gregory Bateson simply develop a consciousness of life as sacred.

Working to establish the Reign of God, which I understand to mean breaking down personal and tribal barriers so that we see ourselves as a single human family and the behavior that entails, has been and will continue to be a difficult task. Any kind of progressive evolution is the result of a stochastic process based on an indefinite number of trials. The evolution in consciousness Jesus and Huxley called for is no exception. What this means for people in or out of religion is that life is learning process. We can never know all we need to know from the Bible, church tradition or secular experience. What we learn from experience changes the context in which we live forcing us to learn more to adapt to the new context. This is the case for religious leaders as well as ordinary folk. Experience can reveal to us what works in establishing and maintaining community. At this stage in the development of human consciousness returning to the roots of Christianity must be complemented by an updating of much that humans take for granted. Those roots plus the radical changes in thinking that need to be made are two sides of the same coin because while Jesus gave us the basis for a program he left it for us to implement.

The critique of Catholicism in particular and Christianity in general that I am offering might not appear so radical if the evolution of Christianity had not taken the path of personal salvation as the chief goal of life and if the leadership had maintained the role of being servants of the People. I will attempt to show in this study that a morality focussed on "saving our souls", whatever that means is radically different from a morality that is directed toward creating a global community, which from my perspective is "the good news" announced by Jesus when he said, "The Kingdom of heaven has arrived" (Mat. 4:17).

Millions of people today live better than kings and aristocrats did just in the last century, but the lot of many have not improved and some have worsened. I submit that a flawed religious morality is one of the reasons for this. Teaching people that their primary task is connecting with a transcendental God contradicts the gospel which demonstrates in no uncertain terms, through the words and behavior of Jesus that it is God as immanent in our brothers and sisters with whom we must connect. "How can you love God whom you cannot see when you do not love humans whom you can see (1John 4:20-21). If Jesus brought God to earth humans have put God back. There was no malicious intent in this. It is part of the larger pattern of human evolution in consciousness. Finding God in the sky was a preliminary stage in that development. A sky God is such a powerful image that we should not be surprised that it might take a God in human form to replace that image. Humans are inherently conservative and when they create institutional structures to pass on their heritage that conservatism becomes written in stone.

Given our massive ignorance, we should also not be surprised that if humans bet all their tokens on eternal life that they feel the need for some kind of assurance that the game is going their way. All through the Bible, from Genesis on, we find evidence that humans have a strong tendency to associate good fortune with approval of the gods or God. This seems to have always been the most persistent form of idolatry, an idea we find most clearly expressed in Job and in Jesus' lesson on the problem of wealth (Mat. 19:23-26).

For those of us who find truth in the Bible, being a Christian is more important than belonging to a particular denomination. However, treating people the way Jesus is said to have done has to be more important than being a Christian, whether or not we regard the Bible as truth. If two persons are working side-by-side at some kind of humanitarian service such as operating a shelter or soup kitchen for the homeless, or teaching the children of migrant farmers to read, what could it matter that one of them believes that Jesus is God and the other is an atheist? Is one damned and the other saved? Is the work of one more meritorious than the other? Some people will answer yes to both questions because Christian morality has become a formula for salvation, but if the purpose of morality is to bring us together or to keep us from disconnecting, then the morality of such an atheist is on target. Reasonable people, in and out of religion, will think so since both are acting according to the ideals advocated by Jesus. According to my understanding of orthodoxy the one with the faith in God has the greater responsibility for setting an example but is not better as a person.

At one time the magisterium, the teaching arm of the Roman Catholic church taught that a supernatural faith is necessary for salvation (*Catholic Encyclopedia*, Vol. 12, p. 444b). Perhaps they still do. In which case the atheist cited above may be wasting his time. Pope Boniface VIII, in his Bull, *Unam Sanctum* wrote, "Hence we declare, state and define that it is altogether necessary for salvation for every human creature to be subject to the Roman Pontiff (McSweeney p.14). Humanity's needs must not be confused with the needs of institutions which are created by humans to serve humanity's needs. The emphasis on code morality promulgated by the church for saving our souls tends to obscure, when it does not actually denigrate, the most basic natural law, as noted above, viz., "survive," but in this life and "together." The Roman Catholic magisterium has for a long time had a theory, sometimes implicit, at other times explicit, that the miseries of this life will be compensated for in the next, effectively encouraging many to be passive in the face of oppression.

In the last half of the 19th century Christianity had to deal with the problem of biological evolution that contradicted Genesis as history. During the last half of the 20th century until now it is having to deal with the realization that human consciousness also evolves. However we may have evolved biologically the evidence for the progressive evolution of consciousness is overwhelming, and as in the case of biological evolution there are apparently evolutionary dead ends. Fortunately for humans, consciousness is not bound by the limits of biological evolution. Humans can become aware of a cognitive, evolutionary dead end and make the creative effort required to change directions. In the larger scheme of things someone always seems to come along to keep the cognitive, evolutionary process going--Copernicus, Galileo, Kepler, Newton, and Darwin. And in social relationships--Moses, Jesus, Luther, the Enlightenment philosophers, and more recently, John XXIII. We now know enough of history to never ask: Why does God allow this, or that; the world is ours to make of it what we will.

CHAPTER II
THE SOCIAL PSYCHOLOGY OF SURVIVAL

The world *is* in fact so ordered that a basic respect for ultimate laws and human life is also the best means of self-preservation. Bonhoeffer

Social psychology is a specialty within sociology, sometimes called micro-sociology or small group sociology. In social psychology we want to know the rules by which people act with, for and toward each other, or the principles from which they derive such rules, whether conscious or unconscious. In the very broadest sense this is morality. People generally associate morality with religion but there is no necessary connection between religion and morality. There had to have been a morality before there ever was a religion. Even animals have rules by which they act with, for or toward others of their kind for survival of their species. There may be considerably less concern for survival of individuals among non-human animals, but their rules have to be considered at least as analogous to human morality. Disagreements among humans as to the nature of a proper morality, i.e., one we can all live with, seem to be directly attributable to the belief among fundamentalists of various religions that morality has been given to us by God. Oddly enough all the people who claim God as the author of morality do not have the same morality. A God-given morality generally means, for such believers, that humans cannot change the rules even when in human terms it makes sense. From a humanistic perspective we may think of the rules as coming from God if we consider that we have been created in such a way that we would be bound to invent them or figure them out. Such an explanation is plausible given the current diversity of rules. It also suggests that we have a way to go to finish the job.

Besides not usually being subject to change, religious rules were first promulgated millennia ago and they furnish little or no guidance for confronting some problems that could not have been envisioned, in fact did not exist, when the rules went into effect, e.g., air and water pollution. This inherent lack of flexibility does little to help us deal with rapidly changing circumstance brought on by technical innovations that have lead to the globalization of communication and our economy. We have a global economy operating with the guidance of several parochial moralities. Parochial moralities contradict human experience in a number of ways, especially, though not exclusively, for people without a religious faith. A prime example would be that one could lose one's soul for practicing contraception. An unfortunate consequence of this is that secular persons look to the norms of the culture for moral guidance rather than religion and these norms are clearly tribal and materialistic. If we think it through most of us will accept that our species ultimately cannot survive with tribal norms. However, the consequences (the destruction of our world) seem so remote that such thoughts can be put aside while we pursue what we know for sure is good--money, power, fame, or simply the good life. One of the more serious inadequacies in moralities promulgated by religious institutions in the past is the lack of interpersonal morality for people who wish to have a partnership of equals, a subject that is one of the chief concerns of this book.

Confronted with the inadequacies of religious as well as cultural norms we need some criteria to help us decide what kind of rules or principles for deriving rules that we can all live with. Our most fundamental interest is first of all to survive. That gives us a clue to where we must begin our search for an intelligent morality.

The cultural norms of the United States prescribes that there shall be winners and losers. In this context the winners not only survive they often enhance their mode of survival at the expense of losers. Such a culture generates a number of problems by making individuals and groups adversaries. We need not examine the obvious risks of this on a global scale. For everyone sold on this mythology, the importance of winning produces insecurity on every level because winning is relative. We only have to think of a black judge who is a winner among the underclasses in relation to the larger society. Besides some socially recognized status, being a winner can be demonstrated by possessions, but possessions can be lost and so must be protected as well as bolstered by further acquisitions, and social status requires constant maintenance whether it derives from things or is socially ascribed because of one's career or lineage.

Religious morality has the advantage over cultural norms in that the ideal if not the reality is the kinship of all. This ideal of kinship has been contradicted during the past two millennia by religious wars initiated by institutional leaders, by colonial conquests and the enslavement of indigenous people. In addition, we have had two world wars, various genocidal frenzies, notably the Holocaust, and numberless other human tragedies for which religious institutions must accept some of the responsibility. Still the ideal of global family needs to be retained and we may find in religious morality some of what we need to develop the proper morality required for the species is to survive.

The idea of God, and the institutions that have developed as agents of God, sanctioning the rules of morality is thought to promote their maintenance through 1) the common allegiance required; 2) the possibility of being rewarded for correct behavior; and 3) fear of punishment here and hereafter for not following the rules. Perhaps such motives worked at one time, perhaps not. Nevertheless, that we do not need divine/church sanctions for morality is obvious from the fact that people generally value some kind of morality, that is, rules for acting with, for or toward other humans, but not everyone is a theist, and there are religions whose adherents have no concept of God in the Judaeo-Christian-Islamic sense. The problem, then, is to arrive at some consensus as to proper morality for all of us.

We may legitimately question the value of divine/institutional sanctions in the moral life of anyone, especially during this century of horrors. We have had such sanctions for nearly 4000 years of religious history yet the current plight of the world amply demonstrates that such sanctions have not enhanced the survival of individuals or the species in the larger sense, though undoubtedly some individuals and small groups have benefited. That the sanctions have not worked on the level of the larger society is frequently attributed to humanity's "fallen" nature. The attribution of our problem to "fallen" nature is worse than useless. It can induce apathy or passivity; the latter is preferred by the Catholic church; they call it docility. Whatever the reason for our continued moral failure it appears that unless we develop a proper morality many people will suffer and die needlessly, as indeed they now do. We have only to think of people dying of starvation at a time when food supplies are adequate but our distribution system is not. Perhaps the nebulous nature of the religious idea of reward and punishment for behavior, viz., heaven and hell, is one reason for humanity's moral failures. We will continue to have futile arguments as long as we claim to know how what we do here generates effects in a realm about which we can have no direct knowledge.

St. Augustine argued that without the idea of divine retribution or reward there would be no reason for anyone to refrain from every possible kind of evil behavior. Dostoevsky also thought this way (Ramsey 1962:11-14). The only rule then would be, "Don't get caught," in order to avoid human sanctions. The idea of divine/church sanctions grossly underestimates human intelligence and creativity. It also fails to take into account the large number of atheists and agnostics who wrestle with moral problems (e.g., see Bateson 1987, Huxley 1957, Lippmann 1964, Russell 1961, Kurtz 1988, E.O, Wilson 1999). In addition, people in other, presumably more religious ages, murdered, raped, stole, lied and had sex outside of marriage, behaviors judged as immoral or unethical by religions in our own time. In short, contemporary human beings did not invent sin.

The idea of divine retribution or reward is used as a conditioning factor by most Christian churches to create a control that is internal to a person. This internal control is called a conscience which the churches teach is an inherent, natural phenomenon, meaning we are born with it. As long as Catholics in this country were predominately working class and had little education such a belief acted to convince many of its rightness. However, second and third generation Catholics have become highly educated and have consorted with people outside of their ghettos and many have come to recognize the distinction between conditioning and conviction. The Christian leadership accounts for the variety in consciences by 1) their inherent defect on account of our fallen nature; and 2) their further degeneration from consorting with sinners, and developing habits by allowing our fallen natures to guide us in our choices, a disposition referred to in religious jargon as hardening of the heart. The churches attempt through indoctrination to infuse into the minds of their members the notion of an omnipresent, omniscient God constantly scrutinizing human behavior and not allowing even the smallest infraction to slip by unnoticed.

The control through fear that is the main feature of this method may have been successful in the past with masses of uneducated people, although that is questionable, but whatever effectiveness it had is rapidly being lost. In an age when survival requires continuous learning in order to survive, fear makes "it difficult to gain the detachment necessary to treat new materials and tasks in their own terms, free of the compelling preemptive context to which they have been assigned" (Bruner 1968:138). The most unintelligent aspect of this moral scheme, besides the fact that it inhibits learning and does not seem to work is that even if a person's concern is with obtaining the reward rather than avoiding the punishment, it requires an intense me-centeredness that contradicts the basic gospel message.

I doubt that anyone today would question the fact that since we have produced the modern equipment of war, notably nuclear devices and the rockets to deliver them to any target in the world, that the survival of humanity is at risk. Cardinal Ratzinger has labeled moral relativism as the greatest threat to the church in our time (John Thavis NCR 18 Oct. 1997 p.12). If he refers to a moral relativism according to which all values are equivalent the danger is to all of humanity not just the church. If, however, he refers to dissent and the questioning of church beliefs it is an institutional problem since the People of God are nothing if not diverse. We live immersed in a sea of pluralism and relativism which should be no problem for anyone who lives as Jesus lived, including those who either do not believe in Jesus or do not know him. Jesus is our anchor in the flux that can only increase during the new millennium.

One of the basic assumptions of this study is that any behavior that affects at least one other person, negatively or positively, has a moral quality to it. Compare this with Aquinas who says, "Those acts of a man [sic] which have moral value are those which advance him in the direction of his final end" (O'Connor 1968:38). With our globalized trade and communication, and everyday relationships with the people around us it is difficult to do anything that does not affect others in some way. If, for example, the threat of global warming is real, then people who buy automobiles that get 12 miles to the gallon of gasoline are making decisions that adversely affect all of us, including themselves. A final end (heaven) is meaningless to large numbers of people in the world with whom we must hold conversations to achieve consensus about a proper morality, hence survival (Churchland 1997). Even people who believe we can act to advance ourselves "in the direction of [our] final end" face a problem of how this is possible when orthodox teaching has it that we cannot merit heaven. It also tells us nothing of what we need to know so that we may survive.

The response of many people to religious talk that has become meaningless has been to give up religious morality as well as the church and a church can only give guidance to its own members within its present parochial context. I believe there is a value in trying to salvage church institutions but with a new kind of consciousness. The job of reorganizing the world on the basis of a proper morality will take more than a few activists. Church institutions can influence an enormous number of people.

We are in a new kind of Babylonian captivity in which we are free to go where we want to go, be what we want to be, and do what we want to do. Our problem is that the choices offered by these alleged freedoms are predetermined for most people by our grand myth of winning and losing whether religious or secular. Myth points to what is of value to a culture (Thomasma 1990:61). It is in fact our truth. In its secular version it is promoted in every way through the media by those who stand to become winners as a result of people buying into the myth. One would think that the Christian churches, which teach that Jesus is "the way, the truth, and the life," would offer alternatives to this idolatrous myth. Try imagining the reaction of parents who are told by a Catholic school principal, or the president of a Catholic college that their children will be prepared for renouncing fame, riches and power, just like Jesus.

Ever since the first person conceived of the first god the hope has been that appropriate behavior would elicit a sign of approbation, either a net gain in what one valued or the prevention of a net loss. Nothing has changed. Despite the occasional dispersion of the Jews apparently for violating their covenant with God, despite the lessons of Job, despite Jesus being quoted as saying how hard it would be for a rich man to enter heaven, the prevailing belief among the people in Christian cultures is that God will bless us here and now if we act right, and that the blessing will be in some tangible form.

The obverse side of this myth would have us believe that we have some control over divine favor through prayer and sacrifice. For the Jews this meant an elaborate ritual of sacrifice using the best of what they had, sheep and other livestock as well as fruit and grain. The concept of quid-pro-quo in human relationships with God has been a persistent form of idolatry for as long as humans have had a concept of God, as the record we call the Bible amply demonstrates.

This aspect of our myth is a distortion of the terms of God's covenant with his People. The terms of the covenant provided that if the Jews acted as a family they would prosper as a *people*. This truth still holds. If we act together we will prosper as a people. The reward is simply a natural consequence of people acting as a community. Hosea put the question of sacrifice in proper perspective for all time when he proclaimed as spokesperson for God: "I desire compassion not sacrifice. People are still appropriating the idea of divine reward for right behavior by individuals except that now the idea has become almost thoroughly secularized. We see it at the gaming tables of Las Vegas and Atlantic City and among the people who play state lotteries, especially when the prize approaches 100 million dollars.

Traditional morality has not dealt adequately with changes that result from technology. Technology at present may seem to be an engine that drives itself, but originally it was simply the way humans responded to an awareness of their contingent status. With our present division of labor, technology may solve a problem for one group while simultaneously generating problems for others. Moving manufacturing plants to a third-world country from the United States results in employment opportunities in the new host countries while forcing the people left behind to find other ways to earn a living. Also the new industrial sites in undeveloped countries tend to be unprotected from pollution by laws and official will. Thus major moral decisions affecting millions are being made daily, decisions made on the basis of cultural norms rather than a proper morality, which we have yet to devise.

Humans are necessarily social but unlike bees and ants we do not come precoded with the knowledge of how to be social. And unlike wolves, baboons and chimpanzees who are also social, what we must learn in order to be social is vastly more complex, at least in our own time. Undoubtedly the earliest humans with their simple lifestyles had not much more to learn than non-human primates. What brought on such vast changes? Whatever brought us to the present state of complexity has to have been a part of human nature. I suspect that "something" is a sense of time--past, present and future, especially the future. At some point the creatures that became human developed a sense of contingency about the future. Perhaps the resulting anxiety is what made the proto-human primate a human primate. Instead of just living from day to day as did the other primates they could have begun to project their needs into the future where they could not be solved. The only option would be trying to solve tomorrows problems today. Initially that could have been any number of technical developments--weapons for hunting, finding or building shelters, preserving food, domesticating animals. However the process got started we can readily see how one change would lead to another. Building a shelter, for example, would change a group's lifestyle. Hunters would go out and come back instead of migrating continuously. The group would suddenly be in the position of having a place and things to protect. The point is that for every contingency resolved, new ones would be generated. Nothing has changed. We are still looking for a way to end our contingent status. But now change is so rapid our future is more contingent than ever. Anxieties about our needs and wants (they become harder to distinguish) can put us at odds with others in the human family when the context within which we operate makes us adversaries, competing for what we perceive as the same limited resources. We have no global-scale plan for fair sharing. Some will win; some will lose. Why should it be us?

At first, pleasing or appeasing the gods for the sake of survival would be a separate issue from human morality. If someone besides the Jews brought the two together we do not know. We only have the

Jewish record of a God, the chief God, taking a personal interest in the welfare of humans leading to the conviction among the Jews that while there was nothing inherently wrong with inequities among humans, all family members had to be cared for, at least minimally under orders from God and under the threat of human and divine sanctions. In addition there were rules to minimize friction among tribal members.

The inadequacies of traditional Christian religious morality began to show up centuries ago leading many people to reject it completely, particularly during the Enlightenment. The focus of morality on otherworldliness did nothing to relieve the suffering arising from oppression and the great inequities among humans and the broad sense of family extended in space and time did not survive in the transition from Judaism. For most of the time since Jesus walked the earth, one of the staples of religious thinking had been that the inequities among humans was divinely ordained. Kings were kings and slaves were slaves because God wanted it that way. For over a century the Vatican has addressed the question of social justice in several encyclicals but these ideas have mostly remained on the level of words because the leadership sees its own task as administering to people's spiritual needs and staying out of politics and business. Leaving the problem of justice to politicians and business people results in tacit support for the status quo and does nothing to prevent the ravaging of the earth by our material culture.

If cultural norms or a transcendental morality were our only choices the race to survive is already lost, especially when one considers the problems inherent in human nature. But people will generally do what is in their best interest when they know what it is and there are many who are concerned. These people may feel overwhelmed by the immensity of the problems humanity faces. They need to deal with it on a level within the scope of their skills and talents. Certainly we should feed the poor, heal the sick, clothe the naked and be mindful of all the needs of the marginalized and oppressed, and lives devoted to such tasks can be fulfilling. But this is not where most of us are in the United States. Most of us work in jobs far removed from homeless shelters and soup kitchens. Most of us are married and raising families, and if statistics are to be believed, half of us are failing in our committed relationships. From a purely human point of view, Dr. Aaron Beck reminds us that "Love is never enough" (1988) to maintain such commitments, while the churches have little to offer beyond generic morality and it is also not enough.

If we are going to develop a global morality, I am suggesting that the best way to accomplish this goal is through an experimental and creative interaction at the level of pairs of individual and small groups. We all have ideas of how we would like to be treated specifically as individuals and through mutual self-disclosure we can better determine how our intimates should be treated then apply what we learn to our larger group and to groups beyond that until our thinking has encompassed most of the human family. An important result of such thinking is the realization that we are dealing with human satisfaction in real time, not in an afterlife that even the Christian churches will admit is beyond the possibility of our achieving. For any reward or punishment to be truly effective among humans the consequences must be right now or in the foreseeable future not in a life beyond this one, which clarifies the attraction of money, power and fame. We do need some way of knowing if our lives are on course in real time. By focussing our attention on how the human family can survive we will know what decisions we should make and when we should make them. For example, we know that the goal of humanity's survival requires that we not pollute our air and our water, that in general we husband our finite resources. Also, we must reject any system of thought that results in winners and losers whereby the losers are afflicted by a crushing poverty. There will of course be winners and losers in the sense that some will be better off than others. But the survival of everyone, including the winners, requires that everyone's minimum needs be met.

We will generally act in our best interest insofar as we know what it is and the best way to find out is through an openness to learning from our experience with others. One of the characteristic of the wisdom we need is that it leads us to make choices that do not close off other choices as for example in suicide. The wisdom from any source should be examined for what it offers but we must make the final judgment. When the Pope and the curia say that they know what is in our best interest their words carry conviction only for those who depend on authority to do their thinking for them. Their numbers grow fewer each year, especially in countries where people have become increasingly educated. A humanistic morality coincides with Catholic dogma in one respect rather than going counter to it. We cannot by our own efforts gain eternal salvation. So when church officials speak of pleasing or displeasing God they are not talking reality; it is a poetic way of speaking. Being pleased or displeased are emotional responses proper to humans. The task set for us by Jesus is community formation involving everyone with a particular concern for the survival of those who live on the edge. Leonardo Boff writes, "the Reign of God translates into community of life with the [Trinity] in a universal communion of brothers and sisters in solidarity with one another in the use of `the fruit of the earth and the work of human hands'" (1988:36). Also,

> From its point of departure in the anguish of the poor of the world, the whole biblical message emerges as a proclamation of liberation. Only from this point of departure among the humiliated and wronged does the gospel appear as good news (1988:26).

Eternal survival, whatever that means, can only be a gift from God, not something we need concern ourselves with directly.

Acting in one's own best interest is true wisdom, the ultimate form of intelligence. Like morality, wisdom comes in different versions. According to the grand myth of our culture, wisdom directs us to get into a top-rated school to increase our chances of getting a high-paying job, in other words to become a winner. Can a family member become a winner at the cost of making a brother or sister a loser. Humans gain the kind of wisdom promoted here through an openness to learning from experience, and from other humans, not indoctrination, and wisdom has no necessary connection with education. The educated as well as the uneducated become addicted, commit suicide and have difficulty forming intimate alliances. A formula for behavior is to wisdom as paint by numbers is to art. Other people's advice based on their own experience and the collective wisdom of our group certainly should be taken into account when we are determining our value system, but the wisdom of others cannot be accepted uncritically. It must be tested in the light of our own needs and experience. One size does not fit all. Humans are built to learn a certain way. Roman Catholic methods of passing on its wisdom, which is directed toward saving our immortal "souls" sometimes does violence to the way that humans learn. More importantly it has done violence to the way people live. It has encouraged people to be passive in the face of oppression because justice would be done beyond the grave. If our children were taught language the way church officials want religious morality to be taught, our children would become stutterers if they learned to speak at all. The Roman magisterium, as they call themselves, says we must act in certain ways whether or not we understand why or we are in danger of going to hell. This is not how Jesus taught. He repeatedly drew analogies from common experience to teach us: build a house on sand and when the big rains come the house will fall. Traditional religious morality has not depended on people being convinced that the rules are reasonable and people are finding many rules, e.g., the ban on contraception unreasonable. It is hard to believe that God made a rule that so clearly violates what is a survival response for so many people. We will better understand human behavior instead of making moral judgments if we remember that the primary natural law is survive, the response to which can lead to good or bad behavior. People generally act, to survive or to enhance survival as they perceive it.

At one time surviving was physically difficult for most people but did not require a great mental effort. Now life has become more complicated, even for people living in areas that lack industry, because the globalization of industry feeds off the unindustrialized. In the developed countries the uneducated are helpless before the onslaught of technological changes. An uneducated, technologically displaced person has few resources to call on. We should not be surprised that a high correlation exists between poverty and crime which is one kind of survival response to life's contingencies (see *Crime As Work* Letkemann 1973).

Under the Jewish dispensation the rules focussed to a great extent on what people had to do or not do to maintain community. Many of the positive rules the Jews had to follow--circumcision, diet, sacrifice of animals--seem arbitrary but they gave the community a special identity and served to distinguish them from their neighbors. Similarly, before Vatican II Catholics were distinguished by not eating meat on Fridays, going to confession, and attending Mass on Sundays and holy days. Such distinguishing marks are historically and culturally conditioned and do not necessarily fit other times and places, when our primary concern should be for the poor and outcasts although having marks of family solidarity can serve a useful purpose. Jesus made it clear when his disciples plucked grain on the sabbath that the need to survive superseded certain religious rules. He came with a positive message of what we must do to create a worldwide community, not just to maintain a community within tribal boundaries. Before Jesus came we were not supposed to kill tribal members because killing had a large negative effect on the tribal community, but just to refrain from killing does not in itself connect us. The law of the new Covenant turned things around. Now we were not only supposed to not kill, we are supposed to promote life--feed the hungry, heal the sick, clothe the naked, and so on, and not just those of our own tribe, rather the whole human family.

With this new kind of thinking we do not have to concern ourselves with what will destroy community because we are engaged in building or maintaining community. Jesus has lifted from our shoulders the onerous task of reflecting on what negative behaviors to avoid by promoting our engagement with life in an entirely different direction. This is not the direction our religious leaders have taken us. By making personal salvation our central concern they have managed to reestablish the legalism that had become the norm before Jesus came. Although they deny it church officials have made the rules of morality a formula for salvation. When the rich young man who asked, "How shall I gain eternal life?" Jesus responded with, "Keep the Commandments," A statement the church interprets in the context of its own belief of personal salvation, but in the context of Jewish belief it mean "Maintain the community by not doing anything to break the bonds." Jesus was not making proscribed behavior central to life as our leaders in Rome have done. Keeping the Commandments is minimal Christian behavior not its *sine qua non* as it appears to be in John Paul II's *Veritas Splendor* (1993).

In referring to "`fulfilling' the Law" he claims that "not even the most rigorous observance" can succeed in accomplishing that. He defines "`fulfilling' the Law" as "acknowledging the Lord as God and rendering him the worship due to him alone" (p.19). This is not the way Jesus taught. In the chapter on the commandments we will see how trying to "fulfill" the commandments has nothing to do with rigor. It is, rather, an easier way of keeping the commandments. John Paul II comes close to the gospel idea of fulfillment only in connection with the fifth commandment. He writes, "`You shall not murder' becomes a call to an attentive love which protects and promotes the life of one's neighbor" (p. 26). But the commandment reads, "You shall not kill." There is a significant difference between the two, the implications of which we shall examine in chapter six.

The rules people have for acting with, for or toward others generally fall into one of three categories, those of the sociopath (me against them), the tribe (us against them), the human family (all of us for all). But morality takes on an entirely different meaning when we enter into an interpersonal relationship, such as a partnership of equals. Under the old style of partnership wherein the man was the head of the household each partner was expected to fill certain roles. The rules determining these roles belong to the set of trivial rules by moral standards studied by Goffman and Garfinkel (Gouldner 1972: 378, 396). Unless these rules were transcended by the partners the connection resembled a business arrangement more than an interpersonal relationship. The Roman Catholic rules for man-woman relationships were, in the past, geared more to relationships with role expectations than to the interpersonal style that is the current ideal. The rule that used to tell women that they must always submit to their husbands sexual demands under the pain of mortal sin when added to the ban on contraception created a condition under which women could be subject to endless pregnancies.

The Pope's and curia's insistence that the prohibition against contraception is an absolute rule laid down by God is a major reason that Catholic officials currently have a credibility problem with the laity because it is so contradictory to what people have learned from experience. The ban on contraception violates a principle laid down by Jesus himself, viz., that the rules were made for humans, not humans for the rules. The Catholic hierarchy's use of the Onan story to support the ban on contraception in addition to the ban on masturbation actually supports neither. Onan violated the spirit of community by spilling his seed on the ground. He was acting against his brother in particular and the whole community in general by not being willing to conceive an heir for his brother. Moreover the truth in the story of Onan, like so much of the Bible, is about the importance of community, not about how a wrathful God might nail us if we break a rule. The basis for the absolute ban on contraception is not divine revelation but the so-called natural law, as the magisterium perceives it, which means essentially that since animals apparently have sex just for procreation, so should we. This teaching elevates biology above human intelligence.

Roman Catholic sexual morality, to the extent that it is adhered to, may prevent the close, interpersonal relationship that humans today generally accept as the most satisfying relationship possible. Worse than that, strict obedience to the rules promulgated by Rome becomes the ultimate in moral behavior instead of seeking the moral refinement proposed by Jesus through fulfilling the commandments. Compare the absolute, unchanging morality of Rome with Daniel Maguire's prescription for the way intimate partners should act with, for or toward one another. He writes: "The final judgment of the fitting way to [act in a relationship] will be based on an immediate intuition and on a sympathetic sense of what this concrete situation requires" (1979:305). The reference in this case is not some external rule but the interior requirements of the two persons in a relationship. So far from harming one another, by engaging in a dialectic and coming to know each other intimately they will have promoted the well-being of each other in ways that the Roman hierarchy cannot even begin to imagine having distanced themselves from the possibility of such relationships.

The ills of the modern world will not be solved by following rules, according to which people are types or play roles rather than act as free, creative beings. I believe that a global community can only result from a sufficient number of satisfying human connections at the level of pairs and small groups. We know enough of human psychology to assert with some assurance that if our interpersonal connections do not provide the kind of satisfaction our intuition tells us to expect, we carry this dissatisfaction with us into our relationships in the world at large. Given the difficulty we have in expressing our bad feelings, and the dearth of persons from whom we could get consolation for our problems, we are likely to either foist our bad feelings on those around us, especially children, subordinates and strangers, as e.g., in road rage, or else turn against ourselves and act self-destructively with the comforts offered by food, sex, alcohol or drugs. Bad feelings passed on to our associates will generally be passed on to their associates further negatively affecting the chances of creating global connections. Only those wise enough not to take personally what others do or say can escape the negative currents that flow from flawed interpersonal relationships.

Achieving satisfying interpersonal relationships is probably the best way to learn the most intelligent ways of acting with, for and toward other humans as the means of destroying each other become more potent, a task of increasing urgency as we create a global civilization through commerce and media but lacking the sense of community. Starting with a strong emotional commitment to each other, two people can more readily overcome the difficulties inherent in all communication between humans. Also, the closer bond thus achieved will not result in bad feelings spilling over into the rest of the world. The failure of the Roman bureaucracy to tap into ordinary human experience to learn what is required to establish a global community will ultimately force the People to do the job themselves. This is an awesome task for a people who have depended for centuries on having a leadership to tell them what they should be doing. This lack of leadership results in a great deal of experimentation, often with unhappy consequences.

Learning from experience in empirical matters differs radically from learning in the non-empirical world. The world of gravity, fire, sharp objects and so on, provide lessons which if we survive lead to changed behavior next time around. Non-empirical experiences have no built in guarantees of making us wiser. If we have a problem communicating with a partner, prior experience may lead us to get another partner instead of working with the current partner to solve the problem. Swapping partners by itself teaches us nothing. Reflecting on our past to find the sources of our differences can lead us to a larger reality which encompasses the smaller worlds of each partner.

The rules of Roman Catholicism forbids the swapping of partners through divorce and remarriage. The rule contains a bit of wisdom, but the wisdom is negated by the reason for the rule which is that it is a divine edict, hence is absolute. This way of presenting the rule does not inform us of what we need to know, viz., the necessity of solving communication problems to keep an interpersonal commitment going, nor does it instruct us in the value for ourselves and the world community of keeping the commitment going. Lacking the external sanctions of neighborhood, village and ethnic enclaves, keeping a commitment to avoid hell or gain heaven provides little motivation for staying together. Those who move on to a new partner anyway, if they become open to learning, may realize that nothing is gained by moving on again. They will have learned from experience but in a way that was forbidden by Rome and they must begin to practice a life-long celibacy if they wish to reestablish a relationship with the church. Compare this with staying in a relationship that is an armed truce to avoid going to hell.

By keying morality to survival and making the term generic I hope to avoid the morass of widely divergent opinions as to what morality is. We can also more readily discern the relative significance of any given rule by examining its contribution to survival of individuals and the species. As a generic term morality can be the basis for rational discussion with people of every persuasion. Your morality might not be my morality, nor his or her morality, but each of us could agree that our own beliefs concerning how we should act with, for, or toward another person is what constitutes morality for ourselves. We should also have no difficulty seeing that how we treat each other ultimately affects our chances of survival. Communication has to begin with some agreement on the subject of discussion, or it does not begin at all, and we need to communicate if we are ever to evolve toward a proper morality, one whereby the survival of any person or group does not require putting other individuals and groups at risk of not surviving. Nor would a proper morality require conflict and competition on the level of basic necessities between individuals and groups resulting in disaster for some. Such conflict and competition ultimately puts everyone at risk. Those who feel robbed of their necessities, as some already have, may decide there is nothing to lose if they try to take what they perceive is theirs from those who have it. Also, there is the acting out with which we must contend from people who are hurt and angry because they feel deprived.

It would seem that a proper morality in addition to involving us in the attempt to provide minimum requirements for everyone's survival, would also promote the optimum development of everyone's intelligence and creativity. The human species cannot feel secure that it has enough knowledge to meet all future contingencies. One of the contentions of this book is that one of the better ways of achieving this

goal is to enhance the possibility of intelligent interpersonal relationships, the part of survival that is of greatest importance to most of us.
I will try to show in later chapters that connecting in a significant way
with at least one other person is our most important need. Achieving
the ideal of intelligent interpersonal relationships involves overcoming
a number of seriously entrenched difficulties. The rules we use in
everyday interaction are established by observation, non-verbal inference and imitation. We usually cannot articulate these rules, whereas
the formal rules for relating taught by religions seem unconnected to
the problems of relating interpersonally except in a general way.
Imagine thinking, I will not kill my beloved. Judging from the results, the formal rules have not, do not and will not promote success
in interpersonal relationships, nor do they promote the long term
survival of everyone. For this we must look to the new way of seeing
the Law as revealed by Jesus. While it is ridiculous to think in terms
of not killing one's beloved it makes the greatest possible sense to
think of promoting her life and well-being. Since religious rules as
taught by church officials have as their primary purpose maintaining a
relationship with God to save our souls, relating to humans, including
one's mate, is a distant second.

Morality's connection with earthside survival is lost sight of when
the rules are viewed as the means to connect with God, i.e., when
they have been transcendentalized. There are several reason why
divinizing the rules generates difficulties for humanity: 1) If the rules
come from God they tend to become absolutized, and ideals that
humans should perhaps strive for becomes what they must do now or
risk eternal damnation; 2) changing "absolute" rules becomes highly
problematic long after it has become obvious to everyone except
church officials that they should change; 3) humanistic reasons for the
rules are lost sight of and the reasons for following them becomes,
"Because God says so" or, "We say so as spokespersons for God"; 4)
many of the rules promote tribalism and the boundaries are such that
members may find themselves outsiders at anytime; 5) persons who
become outsiders, having associated the rules with church membership may drop the rules even though some of them actually have a
bearing on survival, i.e., they are a real part of collective human
wisdom, a fact that the churches have not taken the trouble to emphasize.

Our feelings seem as natural to us as breathing, so we are generally not aware of having acquired them through a process of conditioning. Our feelings are for us unquestionably true (whether objectively
true is another matter). If we trace what we believe is true back to its
source we will find an unprovable presupposition which is why our

belief in what is true can change, especially when we come upon contradictory feelings in persons close to us, as we inevitably will. We cannot be completely rational, and we should not want to be. Feeling is the basis for all creativity, whether artistic, humanistic or scientific, We do not normally question our feelings but we must when we experience conflicting feelings. Our experiences of such conflict generally arises out of interpersonal relationships. For example, certain behaviors may arouse in us negative feelings until someone for whom we have strong positive feelings exhibits that behavior. Such situations provide us with clues that while feelings seem so true for us, they cannot be unquestionably true. When we can question our feeling knowledge we manifest the open-mindedness required for survival, whether physical or psychic. If we never question the appropriateness of our feelings, we simply accept or reject ideas according to the "truth" as we already know it, whether we are philosophers or farmers. The difficulty we experience in changing any belief generally results that belief being an item within a structure of beliefs we perceive as isomorphic with reality, our personal myth. *Myth* as used here refers simply to the way our knowledge is structured into some kind of coherent whole, our sense of the way the world really is. I agree with Ryle that a myth is

> not a fairy story. It is the presentation of facts belonging to one category in the idiom appropriate to another. To [change] a myth is accordingly not to deny the facts but to reallocate them (1978:10).

Myths are for us the truth around which we organize much of our lives. We should not be surprised if we find it hard to see from a different perspective than the one offered by the myth we live by. An alternative would seem at first to be an element of chaos. Believing that the world conforms to our sense of it must be held tentatively or else envisioning reality in another way will be difficult. Being able to re-envision reality helps in not being at odds with others; i.e., it makes pluralism acceptable, a must if we are to survive together. If our beliefs and feelings seem unquestionably true to us, we must either conclude that the same holds true for others or that everyone who does not think as we do is incredibly stupid. Because we encounter differences in feeling knowledge one person at a time we may not discover that we hold our truth as invincible when it cannot be.

The fact that we live by feelings makes solving certain problems difficult for us. The most rational among us must put aside rationality when we adopt premises for building a rational case. We have our "reasons" for accepting certain premises as true but they ultimately rest on faith. Only those who share our faith will agree with our premises. For thousands of years philosophers, theologians, poets and others have been trying to define what is good for humans. They all build rational cases; they all build them on arational bases (Efran 1987:23). Preconceptions of which we are unaware are problematic for everyone of us. These preconceptions, if we could make them explicit might seem to be self-evidently true to us; they are grounded in our personal understanding of what is really real, how the world works, in other words, our personal, grand myth.

Everyone recognizes the need for some kind of social organization for us to get on with the process of living, even those whose interests are destructive of that organization. Crooks for example depend on a body of honest people who will work to produce and acquire that which can be stolen. Social organization requires rules, some codified into law, many more implicit in the norms and customs of a culture. The most important ones (the object of this study) should be negotiated among intimates. The issue of how intimates should treat each other is not, as our religious leaders believe, absolutely and finally laid down by God. Rules vary in a number of ways besides being explicit or implicit. The sanctions for maintaining the rules range from capital punishment, through ostracism to gossip, to the breakup of interpersonal relationships. But whatever the importance of the rules or the degree to which they are enforced all of them have in common that they inform us how we should act with, for or toward other persons. When the rules by which two people relate to each other are perceived as negotiable by both parties, sanctions are not needed because the rules can be made to fit the requirements of the persons involved. Sanctions have no place in an interpersonal relationship. This directly contradicts the idea of many formal Christian religions that the rules people must follow come from God and are absolute and unvarying. In later chapters we shall further examine why this doctrine is misfocused and ultimately destructive, or as Bateson would say, "lethal" for humanity.

The founders of the United States were the first to build a legal wall separating religion and state. The diversity of religions in this country made this codification necessary so no religion would become dominant and force everyone to adhere to a parochial morality. The problem with most religious morality then and now is, as mentioned above, its transcendental focus. It prescribes how we should act with, for and toward other persons as a means of establishing a relationship with God. From a humanistic point of view transcendental morality is inherently flawed. Relationships with persons, including spouses become secondary to saving one's immortal soul. Also, our inability to communicate with God directly forces us to rely on the clergy as intermediaries, men as fallible as the rest of us.

The possibility of spending eternity burning in hell can arouse fierce emotions, so that people with conflicting moralities find themselves in conflict with each other to the point of killing one another as God's agents right down to our own time. Our own constitutional tradition has turned religious fundamentalists away from securing conformity to their moral convictions by means of physical violence to attempting to secure it through laws and constitutional amendments such as anti-obscenity laws, the Volstead Act and recent attempts to pass a constitutional amendment outlawing abortion, and so on.

From the foregoing we should see that adopting a pluralistic attitude will help us in our effort to maintain the open-mindedness necessary in our search for an intelligent morality that humanity needs for survival. No matter how broad our thinking we are always going to find ourselves in some kind of intellectual box due to our tendency toward closure and the tentativeness of all knowledge. But people in other boxes have something to teach us. I am suggesting that we may move continually to other boxes that better serve human purposes. "Truth" is communal (Piaget 1954:407; Efran 1987:38). We cannot connect through private truth. We simultaneously affirm our truth and connect with other humans if we are disposed to change and to being corrected through shared experience. Human purposes are *our* purposes, here understood to be those that promote community without sacrificing individuals. By pursuing an intelligent morality we direct our lives toward an open future, reason enough to study the suggestions made here. These essays are not offered as *the* truth. Consequently, unqualified assertions are never intended to mean that this is the way it is; rather, that this is a way of looking at the subject under discussion, i.e., views from my own box. While examining the social psychology of survival and the possibility of progressive moral evolution on a social and individual level I will unavoidably speculate on how we might continually learn to create a more humanistic world, one in which we recognize that we are necessarily social, and that this necessity extends beyond our family, tribe, city, or nation to all humans. These speculations are rational extensions of ideas some of us already accept. The proposals here are primarily intended to provoke thought so that we can begin the conversation necessary to bring our family, if not together, at least within tolerable limits.

We cannot be required to be intimate with everyone but Jesus said, "A person who is not against you can be counted for you." We need to keep in mind while searching for a proper morality: 1) the inherent flaw in transcendental morality with its effective suppression of free choice; 2) the divisive individualism inherent in the transcendental project of saving one's soul; 3) the occasional progress in moral evolution from humanity's beginning, a process that has proved to be an advantage for non-Greeks, non-Roman, non-Jews, slaves and all non-elites, a process that virtually came to a standstill during the domination of European society by the Roman Catholicism; 4) the necessity for experiment if we are to have a progressive evolution of consciousness. Moral pluralism provides many individual voices, the only way to have success in any stochastic process; 5) the purpose of a humanistic morality is survival of individuals as well as the species which can do very well without anyone of us; 6) finally, and most importantly, a morality on the level of society can only point out the rights and responsibilities of individuals in the most general way, and that in the form of an external code, hence the need to develop a different kind of moral code for interpersonal relationships through a dialectical process I call *moral refinement*.

We cannot avoid the question: How shall we relate to one another? If as I contend morality is basically the rules for survival we should have no difficulty discovering that we survive best by acting together. The only issue remains whether we can limit our togetherness to our tribe. Morality is grounded in biology and intelligence cannot be separated from values. Since every act that affects another human has a moral quality we are in a moral relationship with every other human on earth because what we do affects everyone to some degree whether we know it or not. Until recently we could not see our connection with Chinese peasants, Bedouin herdsmen or even the people across town. But the results of human behavior such as acid rain, the meltdown at Chernobyl, the destruction of the ozone layer over the poles, fish kills, the poisoning of our aquifers, the accumulation of toxic wastes and other ecological disasters are making us conscious of our connections to others no matter how remote, not only in space, but given that most of us will have descendants, also in time. As C. Wright Mills put it: "The history that now affects every [human] is world history" (1967:4). We have an obligation to question how we think and feel because our lives and the quality of our lives depend on transcending our present ways of thinking and feeling.

All of us evolve all the time, that is, we change. Whether this change is progressive is another matter. Many of us in the United States think of personal progress in terms of lifestyle, as in accumulating things and we measure social progress by advances in technology. By these measures we are progressing. However, if we use as a measure solutions to interpersonal and social problems the diagnosis is less optimistic. Our technical achievements may give us the illusion of social progress, but the problems of divorce, war, hunger, homelessness, and all the other factors that divide us speak otherwise. When crime statistics are less this year than last we do not have a clue as to the cause of the drop. We are not likely to see the connection between crime and the failures in interpersonal relationships but that is perhaps the most significant reasons for antisocial acts. When people feel alienated, especially children from their parents, they tend to act out their sense of disconnection. Not knowing why we are hurt or dissatisfied and not knowing how to find relief, we are going to unconsciously let people know how we feel by demonstrating hurt or dissatisfaction. If we were conscious of all this, and if we had the communication skills to let others know how we feel without acting out, those who care for us might offer some remedy. Acting out only aggravates the problem and produces more dissatisfaction for everyone involved.

As someone put it, science has given us nuclear capabilities while our overall morality seems not to have advanced much beyond the Neanderthals. This is not actually the case; circumstances keep changing so we continually adapt. The slow pace at which personal and social morality progresses is, I believe, in part attributable to the unconscious way we acquire a morality. Parents and other adults get children to memorize moral codes, but the children do not for that reason become personally convinced, and without conviction or fear of external sanctions humans "will drift (not leap) to where the gratification is" (Gouldner 1972:327). What this tells us is that unless we derive satisfaction from being convinced of a moral requirement and from acting according to that conviction we very often act in contrary ways. We have to depend on trust when children might have problems understanding reasons. We start with their trust so we must learn how to remain trustworthy to them.

There are certainly people who have sufficient faith in the possibility of eternal life to act according to the moral codes taught by various religions but there are more people for whom the reward is unreal by reason of its remoteness and the lack of empirical evidence. Also, the conviction and consequent behavior of those adhering to religious morality frequently leaves untouched the socially divisive prejudices that prevent the movement toward a global family morality. I have in mind particularly those religions that find a biblical basis for exclusion by race, and the homophobia that the leadership of many Christian religions deliberately promote, protests to the contrary notwithstanding.

Some individuals and small groups seem to have fewer problems in achieving moral progress. But society as a whole is apparently stuck in a rut of divisiveness and conflict. The larger society apparently cannot evolve progressively through social reform and mass movements. Nobody seems to know what causes anything. If religious leaders fail to lead us to adopt a global family morality we can expect even less from our political leaders who are tribal to the extreme and whose tribes are not necessarily the public that puts them in office. I am suggesting that moral progress will be accomplished from the bottom up or not at all. Individuals must first solve problems of personal conviction in moral values, and resolve conflict and division at an interpersonal level. If enough people manage this it will add up to progressive evolution at the level of society when individual and small community progress passes a certain point, when quantity turns into quality. The search for an intelligent morality is the search for ways to achieve this, starting with discovering the obstacles that stand in our way.

In addition to the failure of our political and religious leaders, who seem more locked in by larger social structure than the rest of the population, among the more serious obstacles we must overcome in our quest are the problems we experience in trying to communicate on all levels particularly at the interpersonal level. Social organization, whether of two persons or two hundred, depends on communication and the problems are particularly crucial at the level of interpersonal relationships. When these relationships go bad the negative effect reverberates throughout society. Consensus on survival values is not possible unless these problems are solved and without a certain degree of consensus everyone's survival is at risk. To achieve consensus the People must be convinced that solving interpersonal problems in the context of a global family morality is in their best interest.

CHAPTER III
THE SOCIAL PSYCHOLOGY OF REVELATION

Quite evidently the gods have not revealed everything to mortals at the outset; for mortals are obliged, in the slow course of time, to discover for themselves what is best. . . .Xenophanes

The church teaches that revelation has a specific content, that it is complete and closed since the death of the last Apostle. This teaching is contradicted by another orthodox teaching which says that God is truth. To have the truth that is God would make one God. Obviously what we have is something less than God. The most important characteristic of human nature is that we are learning animals. Is the church saying that we have no more to learn? That revelation is over and done with must inevitably suffer the death of a thousand qualifications. Our task is to reflect on some of those qualifications. We must therefore bracket what the church teaches so that we can learn.

If we believe that God's being is in some way manifested to humans we have to believe that this revelation is ordinarily limited by the human capacity for understanding. We also have to presume that God operates with nature and within nature in developing a relationship of disclosure with us. What this means primarily is that revelation is for humans a learning process that occurs in three stages: 1) What we learn about living together; 2) Our response to what we learn; and 3) Our reflection on our learning and response. The third element is the most significant. It is further revelation. Learning to count and identifying geometrical shapes are first steps on the way to learning the calculus. Similarly, if God is instructing us, there are first steps and subsequent steps making revelation inherently evolutionary. We will understand this learning process better and the steps that must be taken if we have some idea of what revelation means, where we are in the learning process, and where we are headed.

We need a certain amount of experience and knowledge before we can begin to understand why we have to go beyond church teaching to fulfill our destiny as learning animals. There is little point in telling a child who is just learning to count, about the calculus or even algebra. This is the case for communities as well as for individuals. If revelation is a learning process the implication is that we must be actively engaged, or at least open-minded and disposed to learning. The idea of learning also implies community which is minimally two persons. We learn from others and with others. This means is that if we have an insight or get an idea by ourselves it must have value in community, even if it is just with a partner, or its value is questionable . Charles Davis writes, "Truth is not reached by the individual in isolation." We attain "truth only in relationship with others" (1967:51). This is how the process works in science, except that in people relationships we are dealing with more complex situations and the attribution of causes tend to be oversimplified as when people identify the source of human problems as Original Sin. When an insight is experienced and we share it with others their experience can act as a corrective which points up the value of living in a diverse culture. The possibilities for correction is limited in a homogeneous culture. This explains why the great learning centers are generally urban.

Scripture can be thought of as inspired by God but not in any simplistic way. The more fundamentalist Christian churches believe that the Bible is direct, divine revelation, i.e., as though God dictated the words inscribed by human authors. There are too many blatant factual errors other complications for that kind of attribution. The Catholic church has a more complex view of revelation. It recognizes that revelation has been affected by the historical situation in which it occurs, and the literary and cultural conditions affecting biblical writers. As Philip Hefner tells us

> Even those religions that speak of divine revelation must acknowledge that revelation happens within nature, and that it is received, understood, and interpreted through the thoroughly natural structures of a natural animal, *Homo Sapiens* (1993:40-41).

Still, as presented by the Catholic magisterium revelation is, at least in part, direct, divine intervention in human affairs. We find in the *Catholic Encyclopedia,* a statement from Vatican I, that "human knowledge is of two distinct orders: natural knowledge-- reason--and supernatural knowledge--revelation" (1967 Vol. 12, p.441c). The magisterium claims that not all scripture writers were "immediate recipients of revelation," i.e., "supernatural knowledge." Obviously then some writers were. When they further claim that, "Some merely wrote down what they had learned from experience or from the testimony of others" (p.442), they are attempting to explain away what cannot be attributed to God.

I suggest that Occam's razor, the rule of parsimony used by scientists, is also appropriate for use with religious knowledge, including revelation. That is, our explanations should take the simplest form possible. This means that we should not explain with divine intervention that which can be explained naturally. Obviously God is not limited by our concept of what is appropriate. But if we accept the Bible as divinely inspired we should be able to give a consistent explanation of how this is so without having to explain away contradictions and certain events inconsistent with God's goodness, thus compromising credibility. Did God order violence against women and children (Num. 31:15-16; Deut. 20:15-19)? Did God approve Hosea's sin (Hosea 1:1-11). We should not have to attribute bad biology to God (Gen. 30:37-43) and even worse psychology (Num. 5:29-30). We need a consistent explanation of scripture. If we had such an explanation it would be superior to the magisterium's account which requires miraculous interventions in the minds of at least some scripture writers, and explaining away what cannot be attributed to God.

Sister Sandra Schneiders asks regarding scripture

> whether there is a way to understand text and interpretation which allows us to acknowledge honestly what we cannot deny, namely the moral problems inherent in the text, and continue to claim this text as normative and liberating for the Christian community (1991:55).

The blatant errors, the patriarchy, the moral biases and problems with which she is concerned reveal better than any other source, humanity's progressive, cognitive (read moral) evolution. If this is God's word, God is telling us that humans are learning and they are very slow at it. Humans have groped for truth numberless millennia and will continue to do so. The New Testament reveals further groping; we find there a preoccupation with a life beyond this one and a subsequent need to shape Bible stories for that purpose. So the answer then, to Sister Sandra's question, is "Yes," the text is "normative and liberating" understood as a record of humanity's progressive moral evolution, a process we are to engage in if we would share in the liberation promised to us. Because the Bible records this cognitive evolution we should not try to create an inclusive Bible that some of my brothers and sisters wish for. We need to keep before us the evidence that human responses, the second stage of revelation, have indeed been flawed. In many respects we are always at a third stage with regard to some revelation whereby we can reflect on the first two stages and better understand what and how God has been disclosed to us.

Clearly God has revealed that this is a human document. Changing the Bible to suit modern tastes would conceal the important revelation of what kind of creatures we are. Knowing this should prevent us from becoming fixated on what we know and the way we know. By viewing the Bible as proposed here we need not make excuses for anything in this very human document nor for interpretations once accepted as truth but are now open to question or simply rejected. I think we have to agree with Corbishley who describes revelation as "simply a statement of divine truth in terms of human experience" (1964:39). Human experience is an ongoing project with no foreseeable end. We are indeed learning animals. In addition, "Bible stories are secular not about God" (Greeley 1983:72-72). Obviously what we call "divine truth" can never be the fullness of truth given our finite capacity for knowing. We can only continue to learn.

Does God talk to humans, get inside their head and manipulate their thoughts and send messengers as intermediaries? If we believe in God we must admit that these and any other method of revelation are possible. But if we accept the Bible as revelations that have occurred to others, the evidence points strongly to the Bible as having emerged from human experience.

Thus, Jewish scripture is a record of what the Jews learned from experience, their responses to what they learned, and the subsequent accumulation of human wisdom at various points in history up the third century B.C.E. rather than any direct communication from God. The inconsistencies, contradictions, flawed human responses, the attribution of violence to God, and outright factual errors make human intuition and cumulative wisdom the most viable explanation of scripture's source. God's involvement in the process is not difficult to understand if we accept that God dwells within us, i.e., is immanent. A naturalistic explanation of scripture offers the advantage of opening up the wisdom inscribed there to persons who have problems with miracles and divine intervention in human affairs. The issue of sacrifice illustrates as well as anything how slowly and unevenly humans learn. When human genius first conceived of a chief God among lesser gods they carried forward the belief in the need for sacrifice. Clearly God does not need anything that humans might sacrifice. When Hosea and later Jesus declared that God desired compassion rather than sacrifice, the idea of sacrifice was still carried forward into Christianity. Viewing Jesus' death as a sacrifice for humanity's sins is simply a failure of human imagination.

There is a way to interpret his death that is more consistent with both what Jesus taught--turn the other cheek--and the caring father of humanity that he portrayed throughout his mission. Implicit in the interpretation of Jesus' death as a sacrifice is a denial of his teaching. Everyone knows that we cannot go around turning the other cheek; he could not have meant that literally, right? If he had actually meant that then instead of executing murderers we would have to feel compassionate toward them rather than engage in--let's call execution by its real name--human sacrifice. If this saying is too hard, let us admit that we are not yet ready to follow him to the cross and beyond.

Christians can think of revelation as the self-reflexive movement of the immanent God toward God and that such learning is under the influence of the Holy Spirit. For Christian or atheist a new idea of how we can live together requires a response on our part. This is where our freedom is exercised, which explains how our responses can be less than Godly.

An example of how revelation and response works is the realization by the Israelites that associating with pagan idol worshipers, particularly the women, had a destructive effect on their community and their commitment to the God of Abraham and Isaac. At their stage in cognitive evolution they could see no alternative to genocide, i.e., killing every man, woman and child as noted above. If we believe that God wants us to love everyone, including our enemies, this particular revelation and its human response demonstrates the type of difficulty we encounter in attributing scriptural revelation directly to God unless we see it as stages in the process of revelation as learning. Scripture clearly teaches us what kind of creatures we are, but not as commonly thought, that God is giving us explicit instruction on what we are supposed to know.

Revelation as described above may be viewed as a purely natural process. We learn because we are built to learn. We are truth questers. Religiously inclined persons may wish to believe that God created us in this way, whereas atheists and agnostic might claim that we just evolved this way. Either explanation fits the facts; we are the what we are. Those who posit God as the cause have to recognize that since creation would have occurred in the remote past we do not have to imagine God intervening daily or hourly in human affairs to make things turn out a certain way. Imagining such an inefficient God is idolatry. The problem calls for Occam's razor again. Either way, we have no basis for arguing with atheists and agnostics. God and creation are matters of faith not subject to proof. Thinking this way has the advantage of putting all of us on humanity's side with respect to morality, hence survival, and getting on with the business of living, especially by building a global community.

We humans must figure out for ourselves how we are to survive given the present condition of the world. Atheists and agnostics as well as Christians want reasons for acting or not acting in certain ways. We all want to act in our best long-term interests. Understanding scripture in this manner clearly points to the fact that we are responsible for making the world turn out the way it must be for all of us to survive. For example, praying to God to stop wars may be commendable but, "What are we doing to end wars?" is a question an atheist will ask and rightly so.

The third stage of revelation, reflection, opens up for us a whole new way of being conscious. The Bible itself is a written record of the progressive evolution in human consciousness. The passages that seem to contradict God's unconditional love for humanity and the bad science are not mistakes; they are stages in the evolution of human consciousness that have been attributed to God. We have already noted the evolution of morality. The Bible bears witness to the evolution of all human thinking. Orthodoxy has it that Adam and Eve and all their descendants could die because Adam and Eve sinned. The more likely explanation is that humans could sin because they became aware that they could die. The awareness of one's contingency had to have generated a self-consciousness unavailable to the creatures from whom humans descended. One might say that in fact that the thought of a personal death may have been the primary cause of a specifically human consciousness. The individualism arising from such self-consciousness could enable creatures with it to think of themselves as detached from the group and attempt to survive or derive various satisfactions even at the expense of the group. Having become human, as Sartre so aptly put it: "We are doomed to be free."

Further evidence in support of this explanation is the current state of humanity. We can witness different stages in the evolution of human consciousness among contemporary humans. Some humans seem to be technically proficient apes who do what they feel is necessary to survive or to find satisfaction of various kinds regardless of the cost to other members of the species. Others are concerned for the well-being of their own tribal members. Still others demonstrate a concern for the fate of all humans. If the process of revelation can be explained naturalistically, there seems to be little point in making it appear that God whispered in the ears of the prophets. It would seem to make more sense to say that we are learning animals and that our learning is cumulative. Without the Bible we could not know as clearly the moral path we are on and that is an important reason for calling it the word of God. It is a partial record of the growth in human wisdom.

Some revelations are more significant than others. At the top of the list are the revelations by Jesus. In a church that teaches that our destiny is eternal salvation we tend to forget Jesus' humanity. Jesus had to learn like other humans. He was not God masquerading as a human, a problem supposedly solved at Chalcedon (Robinson 1963:65). But despite the definition of Jesus' dual nature, when it comes to what Jesus could learn and what he could know there is a natural tendency toward confusion. If God knows everything how is what God knows kept separate from what Jesus knew? The answer is simple but not easily grasped. When we speak of God knowing, we project our manner of human knowing onto God, more idolatry. We not only do not know what God knows, more importantly we do not know how God knows. Perhaps Jesus had to suffer and die as he did primarily to establish his humanity. Clearly he gave evidence of being a religious genius the way Mozart was a musical genius. It also makes more sense to think of Moses, the writer of Job, the writers of the New Testament, and so on as religious geniuses rather than divine secretaries.

From what has been said so far it does not seem likely that God reveals what we need to know about ourselves and others while we are in a passive state. Revelation in this way would seem to contradict our essential freedom. Baum tells us that "Dialogue with others and personal conscience is the locus of the divine word. Divine revelation is never extrinsic to the process by which men [sic] come to self-knowledge, gain the important insights, and lay hold of the true values" (1971:35). When others speak to us there is no necessary abridgment of our freedom to accept or reject as would be the case in a direct revelation by God. Humans come "to be through dialogue with others. . . Consciousness is not a given; it comes about through conversation--being addressed and responding" (p.41). The kind of learning that changes us requires our full participation.

Some humans, for example, Theresa of Avila and John of the Cross, have claimed an immediate and direct revelation of God's self.

Such a revelation does not involve knowledge about God because God cannot be an object of knowledge for humans and as God's free gift such experiences are not obtainable by human effort. Such experiences, if they are real, are more aptly described as Communion rather than revelation, a true, unmediated experience of two persons (I call this a Primary Experience, of which, more later). Obviously then the revelation I described as a learning process is a different order of revelation from what these saints experienced, but it is also different from what the magisterium calls revelation. It has to do with ordinary humans and community formation. Even private revelations need to be shared with a spiritual director or someone who can help a person discern if the experience is illusory. The immediate revelation of God's self to an individual is beyond talking or writing about, so our discussion must be confined to revelation as learning by ordinary mortals.

As we learn we change. Baum calls this change, conversion and tells us that this is an event that must occur over and over. But if we are actively involved in the process we should reach a level of learning when the process becomes constant, i.e., we will have learned to learn (Bateson's Learning II, cited in previous chapters). At that point there should be a continuous, progressive evolution of consciousness. Most of us are capable of learning what others already know, while a few are capable of breaking new moral ground, i.e., gaining new insights into how to act with, for and toward one another. When the magisterium teaches that revelation was closed with the death of the last Apostle, that can only mean that the basic message given to us by Jesus is complete. This basic message is to love one another as he has loved us, especially by caring for the poor, the sick and otherwise marginalized persons, but it does not tells us all that we need to know to act with, for and toward others, especially in the rapidly changing circumstances with which we live. In that sense revelation must be a continuing process. Baum writes, "Divine revelation can no longer be regarded as something that took place only in the past" (1971:34).

Clearly we are continuing to learn. Perhaps no lesson has been more significant than that we are not born free; rather, we are born to become free. Aquinas taught that the will is a faculty of the soul, hence is free because it is unaffected by what affects the body, but our studies of genetics, socio-biology, and social psychology demonstrate that our behavior is to a great extent determined by genetic disposition and early experiences, hence the need to become free in the same way that learning a language frees us to communicate. Furthermore, our freedom and spirituality do not depend on a separable soul. Without constant, critical reflection on our behavior we cannot be free, and the gospel is nothing if not a call to freedom. Science has become a source of revelation that now supplements scripture by teaching us first that some of what we thought of as revelation is bad science and that all knowledge is tentative. What we know must pass the test of our experiences together; truth is ultimately validated in community.

Until relatively recent times we could not have expected anyone to say with any hope of being understood that a progressive evolution of consciousness is what life is all about. This progressive evolution in the purely material realm is so obvious from the plethora of human inventions that we need not labor the point. In the case of revelation as learning, progressive evolution may seem anything but obvious. A case can be made for the opposite because the continuing evolution of consciousness leads each generation to think that it has witnessed a moral decline during its lifetime. An example of how such thinking occurs may be seen in our move to big cities where we are no longer constrained to follow rules because of social sanctions. But what is the value of being good when we are coerced? In the larger picture there is sufficient evidence in history and especially in scripture to warrant the conclusion that progressive evolution in our thinking has occurred. We have only to think of the end of slavery, the rise of democracy and its acceptance by the Vatican bureaucracy, and more recently, their declaration of the freedom of conscience of individuals. Still, each generation must find wisdom on its own, starting with conventional wisdom.

Each generation begins anew with its own problems to face. Young persons, at least in the West, do not have to consider the question of slavery having been born into a world where slavery has been outlawed, but they have other injustices to deal with such as discrimination against ethnic minorities, blacks, women and homosexuals. Wisdom is acquired differently from ordinary knowledge. It is not a subject with well-defined borders; nor is it taught like math or history. We can assert with confidence that for each person wisdom is not just acquired differently it is actually different. What constitutes wisdom for a person hinges directly upon a person's value system, particularly that person's supreme value. If accumulating money is more important than anything else in a person's life, what constitutes wisdom for that person will differ radically from the wisdom of a person who conceives of going to heaven as the ultimate value. The wisdom of both of these persons will differ from the person whose values and efforts are primarily directed toward promoting the life and well-being of everyone. Ultimately, true wisdom, the one we can all live with and that seeks a proper morality, must bring us together, or at a minimum be non-divisive.

The disagreements among theologians on the nature and function of revelation are legion. The variations range from a pure subjectivism such as we find in Kierkegaard's "leap of faith," and certain of those theologians who subscribe to revelation as "inner experience" (Dulles 1992:68-83), and a crude objectivism, the one-time position of the Vatican, that views revelation as expressed entirely in formal propositions. Dulles delineates five models which do not in anyway exhaust all the variations. One might say that there are as many variations as there are people who speculate on the subject. The five models represent major concepts around which a number of theories may be clustered. Revelation as learning, the basic premise of this study, is primarily an intersubjective or interpersonal process which closely resembles model five and certain aspects of model three in Dulles' study.

However it happens, this learning experience we call revelation, that is God's self-disclosure, and an appropriate human response is possible for everyone regardless of a person's orthodoxy. Baum tells us that Jesus "summons his followers to brotherhood [sic] that transcends the boundaries of the Church" (1971:32). This can only be the case if by "Church" Baum means the institution. If the Church is the People of God, as the bishops at Vatican II declared and as presupposed in this study, then anyone who lives by the values Jesus taught and exemplified by his life is one of his People. It does not matter if someone is an atheist or non-Christian. As Baum himself notes, "What counts, ultimately, is [a person's] engagement in life" (p. 12). Theologian Jon Sobrino, S.J. also tells us that "any orthodoxy is radically insufficient" (1985:31). He means that subscribing to a set of propositions, no matter how lofty, cannot take the place of living "the Way." The institutional church does not control the movements of the Holy Spirit, and I doubt that the Holy Spirit is concerned about getting credit for what happens. We cannot conclude that revelation is some once-and-for-all-time divine utterance. Otherwise we would have all the revelation we need at this time, a claim made by Evangelical Protestantism because the Bible is a finished book, while Roman Catholic officials base their claim to the completeness of revelation on the tradition that revelation ended with the death of the last Apostle.

Clearly we do not know all we need to know in the way that we did not at one time know that slavery is wrong or that free consciences are required for free behavior. Whether God actually inspired scripture writers is not an issue for us. We want to know what scripture has to say to us concerning our present human condition; what wisdom does it have to offer us so that we can get on with living together. Scripture seems in some ways to tell us how we should relate to God, but with the teaching and example of Jesus it very definitely tells us how we should relate to one another. We have to recognize the difficulties involved in pursuing a relationship with a transcendent God, a non-problem for masses of uneducated people in earlier times who lived in world of magic and were convinced that they could speak to God and that God responded with rewards or punishments in this life. Relationships require communication of some sort. If we are going to talk with God and not just to God it will have to be God as immanent in our brothers and sisters. Moran writes, "Between two persons. . .there is no deeper communion than a relevatory one, that is, a continuing and free, giving and receiving of personal knowledge" (1966:181).

Although the Jews had a very complicated system of rules for relating to God the emphasis was always and still is upon relationships with one another. They were a people and acting as a people was their most important way of relating to God. We have good reasons to believe that the kind of revelation we need has not, and probably will not come to an end. We have not developed to the point where most of us are asking when a decision is to be made, "What would Jesus have us do " Jesus is not only the ultimate example of God's revelation, but more importantly from our perspective, he demonstrated the ultimate response.

As a People we have reshaped our experience in the light of what has worked for us and what has not, we have accumulated wisdom first through oral tradition, then oral tradition plus writing. As we have more and more experience our fund of wisdom seems to progressively evolve. This knowledge of how the world works is most easily discovered and passed on in the case of our empirical experiences. We readily learn that fire burns, what gravity does to us, and so on. The effects of poison are empirical but learning from experience can be lethal, so we lock them away from children until they are ready to take our word for it that they are dangerous. Most of the people in the world learn about God and religion through oral tradition. Even the books they read tend to be popular repetitions of oral traditions rather than studies on the frontier of the search for moral wisdom. In other words most people take somebody's word for it that God and God's requirements are such and so, and that certain behaviors, including thoughts, are bad and others are good, and because they are God's requirements the assumption seems to have been that we cannot question what we are taught. This is the locus of the problem in trying to transmit humanity's accumulated wisdom. The transmission of this wisdom is attempted by people who are not themselves convinced of what they have been taught by the church's magisterium. If they were convinced they might have the arguments to make what they say believable. In a world where free consciences are the norm the church has only persuasion to work for it.

A major reason for this lack of conviction is the magisterium's own teaching that we are guaranteed to fail. The basis for this teaching may be the passage in Romans 7:19 where Paul writes, "For the good that I wish, I do not do; but I practice the very evil that I do not wish." Even secular philosophers have similar thoughts. A.C. Ewing writes, "We often hold a belief quite genuinely and yet because of some strong desire which carries us against reason we do not act as if it were true" (1962:115). Contemporary lay persons say, "I know it's wrong but I do it anyway," which is total nonsense. If we are really convinced that behavior is wrong, meaning that we really know that it is not in our best interest to act a certain way, e.g., drinking poison, then we will not. It will not do to argue that people smoke knowing that it is not in their best interest. What smokers get from smoking outweighs the risks; even suicides believe they are acting in their best interests. The magisterium does not emphasize personal conviction. Instead, it emphasizes the conviction that we can put absolute faith in what it teaches, and what it teaches is that we *will* fail. We could hardly ask for a clearer warrant for doing what we feel like doing rather than what we are told we should do.

The guarantee of failure will be confirmed by human experience for many. They have it on the word of the magisterium which finds support for this in St. Paul's words and in the pessimism of St. Augustine. Another reason to reclaim religion from the church. This is not what Jesus taught. If we can trust the words attributed to Jesus, he issued a call to "Be perfect as your heavenly Father is perfect" (Mat. 5:48). For us, this can only mean to act with compassion toward all members of the human family, especially the poor and otherwise marginalized. That Paul is not the ultimate in revelation we know from his own words and what he says concerning women and slavery. We also know that the institutional church has not been without error both in what it has said and what it has done. The faithful are not the only ones who must be open to learning.

Children will take our word for what is supposed to be the truth, but as they grow and learn and share experiences with their peers, other adults, and parish priests, the wisdom they have been garnered will not always be useful in their real-world experience, especially the experience of seeing adult behavior contradicting what has been taught. If children have been frightened into believing that there are bad, long-range consequences such as hell, they may try to conform to avoid the punishment, but they will often fall short, as in fact has been predicted, a fact that tends to confirm the truth of what has been taught, viz. that we are somewhat helpless when it comes to being good, and that we need massive graces from God and lots of practical assistance from the clergy such as frequent absolution. The term for this in sociology is "self-fulfilling prophecy." The question that calls for an answer in our time is: How do we teach convincingly without the carrot of heaven and the stick of hell? Part of the answer is clear from what has been said. We must be at least convinced ourselves so that our behavior corresponds with our teaching. This requirement raises the big question: How do we become thoroughly convinced? This brings us back to the disposition necessary for learning, a readiness to change based upon experience and conversations with others rather than an absolute trust in what we are taught by authority, even authority of undoubted holiness. If we are truly committed to learning, if we believe that working to bring about the reign of God means forging bonds with other humans, that is, community formation on a global scale, then we can trust our collective consciences and our experiences will inform us of what does and what does not work toward that end. This process works especially well between committed couples.

There is one common thread that runs through all the various theories of revelation. Given the fact of revelation there will be a human response, and being human it is difficult to believe that such responses are not inherently flawed. Barth tells us that our response is always vitiated by sin. He further claims that since religion is a human response to revelation "even in a Christian context, [it] is to some extent a perversion of revelation" (Dulles 1985:95). This is a sort of restatement of Paul, and is of course, standard church teaching, which until Vatican II was not applied to the church itself. But what are the practical consequences for us? The idea of sin and sinfulness is not revelation for us unless it results in a change that helps us connect with other humans. We have to keep in mind that truth derives from communal experience. We will learn later that even under the best of circumstances, communication of any significance, as say between lovers, is inherently problematic.

What has not been clear from the magisterium's teaching in the past is the important distinction between sin and sinfulness. The assertions by Paul and Barth, as well as the magisterium's teaching on sin has sometimes obscured the distinction between sin, which is something we do, and sinfulness which is a condition we live with. Sin has already been described as a breach of community that we can understand by asking the questions: "Who is harmed?" "What is the harm?" According to the distinction made here, Barth's "vitiated by sin" should be read as vitiated by sinfulness. Sin, as previously noted is not acting in our own best interest because our best interests lay in connecting with others and creating community. Creation of an institutional church as a response to revelation is not of itself harmful to anyone but it is a human response, therefore likely to be flawed. Also, institutions are inherently tribal hence divisive. We have no certainty about what Jesus said but if the scripture we have is correct he either said, "On this rock I will build my institution," or "On this rock I will assemble my People." The Greek term *ecclesia* translates as either "church," usually taken to mean *institution*, or "assembly of people." The bishops at Vatican II clearly opted for the second interpretation. Knowing what is actually in the best interest of individuals and the community is not always easy to discern, but the best interest of one can never be destructive of the other, a principle that calls into question war and capital punishment, but not necessarily self-defense. Sinfulness, however, as a perpetual state of being means an abiding ignorance of what is in our best interest, both short and long term, a condition that requires us to always be learning.

In addition to the responses of Jesus himself we are told of one perfect response in history, that of Mary, Jesus' mother. However it happened, the birth of Jesus is an incontestable fact. Whether Mary's response to the conception and birth of Jesus was flawless we have no way of knowing. The Roman Catholic magisterium claims that we do know, but in the light of other claims by the magisterium that we know to be flawed, skepticism can hardly be sinful. Such a dogma primarily calls for a response of pious devotion and as with anything else has a value to the degree that helps us in community formation. There is no absolute requirement that we say the rosary or join the Legion of Mary. The magisterium's teaching that Mary never sinned has to mean that her every response to God's revelation was flawless, in the sense of always acting in her own best interest as well as everyone else's, hence the dogma of the Immaculate Conception. In fact according to the distinction made here between sin and sinfulness, according to this dogma neither act nor condition is applicable to her. But the basis for this dogma is the doctrine of Original Sin that had been deduced from the belief that Genesis was history instead of a mythological explanation of the human condition. I prefer keeping Mary human, and one of us, despite the one flawless decision she supposedly made with regard to Jesus' conception.

Revelation as learning requires some effort on our part to understand, especially by reflecting on our life story and the responses we have made. If we are on course in our spiritual journey such learning should serve to enhance relationships among all humans. The church will insist that we must be prompted by the Holy Spirit, but whether or not credit is given to the Holy Spirit it happens because we are all graced by the Spirit's indwelling. If we wish to bear witness to the Gospel among the non-religious we need to speak in secular terms, insofar as we are able. Thus it is better for us to say "learn" instead of "convert" and ignorance of what is best for ourselves and everyone else instead of sinfulness. Let the Spirit do what the Spirit does in silence.

The revelations that occurred to others and recorded in the Bible are undoubtedly a major source of revelatory learning. Some of these events are more significant than others. We have to put in a very special category what we learn from Moses, for example, that our care and concern for family must extend indefinitely in time and space, from Job, that God does not operate on a quid-pro-quo basis and from Jesus that we should love everyone including our enemies, which is an extension of Moses's revelation about family to everyone in the world. Some of what we learn from the Bible has more to do with illustrating the flawed responses of the humans to whom they came than in what we can appropriate directly as God's teaching, except of course, the revelation that our responses tend to be flawed, based as they are on ignorance of what constitutes our best long-term interests. To illustrate: We looked at evidence of the Israelites' flawed responses to the revelation that they (the men) would be tempted to idolatry by associating with pagan women. But from what we know of God from Jesus we would not expect that God revealed to the Israelites that they should kill anyone. Such a response contradicts the New Testament teaching that God is the God of everyone.

Through our experiences, especially from our reading and reflection on the Bible, God has revealed to us that morality evolves progressively, that what was right at one time is not necessarily right now, e.g., the purity regulations concerning a woman's menses, polygamy, no work on the sabbath, and so on. The Jewish scriptures and the New Testament contain many examples of this progressive evolution of human consciousness. Knowing this introduces us to the context of learning how to read and understand the Bible, which is learning on another level. Bateson introduced us to the concept of "Deutero-learning" or learning to learn (1972:167-173). In popular parlance this is "catching on" to how something works, in this case, the process of learning itself. When the magisterium teaches that revelation ended with the death of the last Apostle they are probably referring to those revelations of the past which can be a source for us, but that are not revelations for us until we have pondered them and have learned something of what it means to be human in community in our own time and under our own circumstances.

We may legitimately ask why, if in fact morality has evolved progressively that we do not seem to be any better off, why there is so much conflict in the world, why marriages are less stable, and above all why we live with a threat of extinction from nuclear weapons and environmental degradation. I think the answer lies in the fact that although we have been given more we have acquired more responsibility. Marriages, for example, in the past were tied together by circumstances beyond the control of the marriage partners such as social sanctions and economic necessity. In our own day we expect marriages to be partnerships of equals. Marriages must now be held together by choice and we are not always choosing well, partly because many of us are operating under the old assumptions regarding marriage. It is a problem of transition. We are not accustomed to the freedom we now have and have not made the corresponding adjustments. Many of us know of young persons who were goody-two-shoes at home, who upon being thrust into the freedom and responsibility of being on their own at college made choices that they might not have made had they learned how to be free by being given freedom and responsibility early on. We come "to be through dialogue with others . . . Consciousness, is not a given; it comes about through conversation--being addressed and responding" (Baum 1971:41).

Jesus' teaching encompasses everyone in the whole world. Therefore his witness as how to act freely with, for and toward other humans is the ultimate revelation and cannot be transcended. However, the insights and illumination that enable us to work toward the ideals he established for everyone continue to come to us. For example, we are told to love everyone. What this means and how we are to accomplish it are relatively unique problems for each of us. By first discerning what the problem is for ourselves and reflecting on how we may solve it, we are participating in the search for revelation and the corresponding higher consciousness accompanying it.

The Christian churches say our goal is eternal life, or as they sometimes express it, to save our souls. This is not a reality many of us can relate to anymore than an ordinary first grader can relate to algebra. Heaven and hell probably made more sense to the primitive imaginations of people with less education, who lived in a world of fairies, elves and witches and other manifestations of magic. Belief in the traditional teaching concerning heaven and hell was also possible even for people with more education but who had faith in what the churches had been teaching. However, the bishops at Vatican II made three declarations that liberated Catholics: 1) The primacy of indivi-

dual consciences, meaning that we must act according to our consciences whether they are right or wrong. 2) The Church is the
People of God, not the pope and the hierarchy, not the institution,
rather the People. 3) We are a pilgrim Church, meaning the church is
not a perfect society, protected from all errors by the Holy Spirit.

Although our consciences are free we still have the responsibility
of learning, not as under the old rubrics where this meant memorizing
and accepting on faith what the institutional church taught whether
one was convinced or not. If we violated a rule we had to report it in
confession to keep from going to hell. I cannot speak for others but I
bought the terrifying lessons we were fed. We need not dwell for
long on the subject of an inerrant church. The church history we
were taught in high school bears little resemblance to the way it really
was, as say written by Paul Johnson (1976). What we learn when we
get beyond propaganda generates a credibility gap for many Catholics. The publication of *Humanae Vitae* plus the liberation of Catholic
consciences probably did the most to make Catholics distinguish
between faith in God and faith in church authorities (Greeley 1998:8-
11). Once having begun to think for ourselves and analyze what the
magisterium teaches we discover numerous inconsistencies and contradictions. Are we, for example, composed of body and soul? Or
are these abstractions left over from Greek philosophy? Gabriel
Moran writes

> A more radical kind of thinking and a different style of living
> are needed to rediscover the unity of man [sic] that precedes
> any distinction between body and soul. If [humans are]
> divided at the start, then all attempts to restore unity by
> bringing the parts together prove fruitless . . . the common
> presentation of such distinctions in catechism and theology
> manuals is at variance with revelation (1966:154).

Still the church speculates about the disembodied existence of
people who die, of the suffering souls in purgatory, and various
characteristics proper to a soul, matters about which no one has a
clue. It is all speculation. Humans have characteristics, abstractions
do not. Furthermore, the magisterium teaches that eternal life and
resurrection belong together, that we cannot save ourselves and that
eternal salvation (whatever that means) is wholly a gift of God. We
read in *The Silence of God*

> the theory of immortality slipped into Christian speculative
> thought in the earlier centuries, it is not a biblical teaching

and can be supported by isolated quotations from the Bible only by a dreadful forcing of the text. This theory has its origin in quite different soil, that of the Greek philosophers. I am sure that our proper theologian would stress the fact that immortality is a state that cannot be reconciled with the biblical understanding of resurrection. For one thing, he would explain, resurrection is strictly an act of God. All references to it in the New Testament are in the passive mood: Jesus *was raised* from the dead, *we shall be raised* from the dead. It is a matter in which we are uncompromisingly dependent on God (Carse 1985:95).

If we are indeed meant to be resurrected there is no need to posit an immortal soul. The problem seems to be one of the time needed to cleanse the soul from the stain of sin, as magisterium expresses it, as though God needs time. I suspect that Plato's "soul" is necessary for people who cannot imagine how the transition from this life to the next could take place without an interim substance. This is a human requirement, not necessarily God's. We would be better off just admitting that we do not know.

"Not knowing" in this case would be a difficult admission for a church whose primary product is eternal salvation. In our weakness and ignorance we would all like some assurance that we are being taught is the truth. For those whom eternal salvation is important the church has to lay out some criteria for the faithful to follow so that they will have assurance of being on the right path. But as we have seen the criteria carry little conviction because the behavior of the faithful, good and bad, allegedly creates effects in transcendental realm from which there is no feedback. The church interposes itself between God and humans and supposedly acts as the feedback mechanism so we can know what kind of effects we are creating. What assurance do we have that church officials are credible? Apparently we only have their word for it. They can point to tradition and supporting texts in the Bible, but they created the tradition and the canon of the Bible. The overriding fact is that their own orthodoxy tells us that we cannot directly earn heaven and that there is in fact no way to know if we are saved or damned. If there is such a thing as eternal salvation it may be the byproduct of some other effort on our part.

Much confusion arises from the fact that many of us have not completed the transition from magical to empirical thinking. Some would say from mythical thinking to scientific thinking, but that appears to make mythical thinking synonymous with magical thinking.

In popular thinking myth is the opposite of realistic thinking, whereas in our so-called realistic thinking we are simply dealing with the best myths available. Bultmann's proposal to demythologize the Bible could be more accurately expressed as "remythologize the Bible." Scientists, many of whom have faith in their freedom from myth, continually create new mythologies. We can see this if we reflect on the scientific thinking of previous centuries that has since been super-seded. The theories of Johannes Kepler, Isaac Newton, Niels Bohr and others were not wrong, just incomplete, a stage in the evolution of our empirical myth making. Similarly our thinking about God, religion and morality have grown out of earlier religious myths. Our current perceptions of reality come from the myths we live by, whether religious, political, economic or scientific. We should think of myth as an assemblage of many ideas into some kind of meaningful whole that are not naturally connected

Myth refers to our understanding of how the world works, particu-larly our folk psychology. It is a set of ideas pervading all aspects of life, that defines what is bad and worse, good, better, and best. It prescribes our most fundamental values and explains what life is and should be. It tells us how to relate to other creatures, human and otherwise, and to God or the gods. We might think of myth as a philosophy that has not been, and cannot be made totally explicit. Because of this inexplicitness a number of inconsistencies and contra-diction can coexist without disturbing the believer (Lakoff 1987:92-96). The advantage in attempting to make our myth explicit by remythologizing, or converting it into philosophy, is that we are better able to examine it critically, especially in relation to other aspects of what we believe. Also in communicating with others about such important matters we will further clarify for ourselves what we know and believe, and engage in the mutual revelatory learning we need.

Thus *myth* is appropriately applied to the theories, hypotheses and explanations of religion as well as the natural sciences. The so-called facts of natural science can only represent a small part of the dynam-ics of what we call matter. In brief, science is a much more creative enterprise than is commonly believed. As Bateson put it, in the world of things, "...there are no maps, no names, no classes, and no members of classes" (1988:21; see also D'Amico 1989:121). All such entities are ideas in our heads or in some form of media. Scien-tific theories are created explanations for things and their relationships just like ordinary myths. Karl Popper explicitly calls them myths (1968:127), while Kuhn, in *The Structure of Scientific Revolutions* uses *paradigm* to serve a similar purpose. What scientists discover when they look at the world is determined by the model of the world, paradigm, or conceptual scheme that is currently in vogue. Parts of the model and relationships between the parts become the categories. In assigning groups of objects and relationships to these categories scientists first focus on similarities, and ignore differences; for example, they see stars before noting the unique event that each one is. Next they formulate ideas about how items in a category relate to each other, or whole categories relate to other categories. They then test these ideas (called hypotheses) against the current myth or perception of reality. If history is any guide current perceptions of reality will be superseded. This kind of myth transcendence occurs in all subjects of interest to humans, including religion and theology. A significant difference between religion and science is that fundamentalist religions are more often than not explicitly committed to not changing, whereas science, while not committed to change, is unavoidably subject to change because, as Polanyi tells us, there cannot be a central control to the process on a global scale.

So where are we in the learning process we call revelation? What we have learned regarding morality is instructive at this point. A morality that exists as a code "out there" is highly ineffective. For a proper morality, one that works for people, we need rules, or better still principles from which we can derive the rules, for acting with, for or toward one another that we are convinced are in our best interest, especially our long-term interest. Without this conviction motivation has to come from an extrinsic source which is bound to be unreliable. For example, the hope of gaining heaven or the fear of eternal damnation are so remote that they can hardly compete with whatever illicit behavior attracts us at the moment. In our relationships with people we will treat well those we like or who treat us well and respond negatively to those we do not like or who do not treat us well. Revelation resembles morality in that respect. It cannot be something out there. If we are brought up in a Christian church we have heard the words ascribed to Jesus many times, but only when they become internalized leading us to change our lives can we speak of being touched by a revelation of God. Avery Dulles in reporting on theologians who looked "to the religious experience of the believer as the point of insertion of God's revelatory activity" (1992:68-69) criticizes this view of revelation on the grounds of its being too personal and private. But this kind of revelation is akin to the "consciousness" or "new awareness" model and like any revelation, including the revelation that is Jesus, it must meet the test of helping to bring about the Reign of God, which from a human perspective can only mean in our day a global community.

We may have heard in preaching or in a reading of the Gospel

"Seek first the kingdom of God and his justice and all else will be given to you besides" (Mat. 6:33). Then at some point in time this statement becomes meaningful in such a way that we see our past in a different light and we are driven to a different kind of future than we would otherwise have had. This is a knowledge beyond knowing as we ordinarily understand it. The way that Gabriel Moran expresses it is that "revelation is not only knowledge: it is encounter" (1966:182). When revelation is a reality for us we have been touched by the Holy Spirit. When that happens something is not just known in the head. It is something that affects one's whole being, similar to the experience of St. Theresa of Avila mentioned above. A commandment such as "You shall not steal," is just information until that day when we encounter the Holy Spirit. Then one sees one's brothers and sisters in a new light, and so far from taking what belongs to them one becomes respectful of everything anyone has. On that day the things one possesses become trivialized except as gifts.

This can happen many times in our lives because we cannot come to the end of learning. If we learn to learn, change can occur continuously. The transformation in us brought about by a new awareness of what a particular set of words mean such as those just described may later result in further transformation by the realization of the inadequacy of our previous response to the enlightenment we received, maybe even to the point of giving everything away. Thus revelation can be a process of deepening as well as widening. From this we can infer that one of the characteristics of divine revelation is that it calls forth a response from us leading us toward a life that connects us with others. Only then does the Bible or any other source become revelation, but the narrow view of revelation offered to us by the magisterium does not encourage us to look for revelation within ourselves which is the only place that matters and a process beyond their control. They seem to be more concerned with our orthodoxy, which as Sobrino pointed out is inadequate. As a consequence the magisterium does not teach us to recognize revelation when we encounter it, i.e., anything that brings us closer or binds us to one another. The church fears a rowdy subjectivism which leads it to promote a static view of revelation as expressed in doctrinal propositions and scripture. Doctrines of the church and the Bible which record revelations that others have experienced are only sources until they becomes personal. Clearly many people have heard and read church doctrines and the words of the Bible without being affected, including the words and examples attributed to Jesus. Can we speak of revelation when there is no effect? I submit that we cannot.

What kind of effect should we look for to say with assurance that revelation has occurred? The criteria seems obvious--a life has been changed to more closely resemble "The Way" as witnessed by Jesus' own life, or community bonds have been fostered, an interpersonal relationship has deepened to the point of communion. The countercultural ideal witnessed by Jesus' life does not appear to be for everyone, and until recently that is what the church has taught. We were told that because of the effects of Original Sin we were not able to avoid sinning. But what is Original Sin? It is an inference from an alleged act of disobedience by Adam and Eve. Whatever truth the story contains, we know the story to have been a fabrication not history, what are we to do with an inference derived from a fictional story? The possible meaning of Genesis will be presented in chapter four. But what emerges from what has been said about revelation thus far is that our ideas of what it means to be the People of God has undergone a progressive evolution and more awaits us.

Without this record we call the Bible we simply would not know. The past would be subsumed by the present, the way that mid-twentieth century Catholics thought that the church they were born into had always been the way they found it because mostly they were not students of history. But if our consciousness is evolving toward a greater understanding of humanity in relation to God then because God is infinite there can be no end to the process. If God is truth, on what grounds can anyone claim to know the truth? This does not imply a superiority of people now over those in the past. The people of earlier times could only be responsible for the perspectives (read revelations) available to them at that time. We do not call a first-grader stupid for not knowing algebra. Also the responses to revelation possible at any given period are limited by the culture in place at the time. Thus when the Jews began to think of human sacrifice as wrong, the leap to no sacrifice at all would have been too great to comprehend. Apparently sacrifice of one's goods to appease the gods or to curry favor with them had been around for a while. The response to this revelation was to sacrifice to the one God and to forbid the pagan practice of sacrificing humans. God does not need sacrifice. In both the Jewish scriptures and in the New Testament we find the expression, "I desire compassion not sacrifice" (Hos. 6:6; Mat. 9:13, 12:7).

A sacrifice can be *pro forma*, i.e., made regardless of how one feels, but compassion must come from the heart. If nothing else, measuring ourselves against the ideal of loving everyone, including our enemies, should promote in us the virtue of humility. Our moral failures and the recognition of our abysmal ignorance about the meaning of life suggests an alternative path to the progressive evolution I call moral refinement throughout this study. Each of the five ways of looking at revelation recorded by Avery Dulles has some validity. The one that best describes the view consistent with the thesis of this study is the one referred to as "the new awareness" model. Those who hold to this model describe it as "a breakthrough to a higher level of consciousness as humanity is drawn to a fuller participation in divine creativity (1978:115). "...it is seen as a divine summons to transcend one's present perspectives" (p. 187).

On this perspective, as revelation becomes personal we should change how we act with, for and toward our sisters and brothers, i.e., our morality. Revelations about morality are clearly distinct from the morality that we generally accept. Aside from the morality of socio- paths, we can say that a purely human morality tends to be tribal, and in our present world tribal morality, besides contradicting the gospels, is inevitably anarchic because tribal boundaries exclude. It is difficult to imagine that we could have figured out on our own that we should be concerned with the life and well-being of everyone, including our enemies, the extension to all humans by Jesus of the family morality of the Jews. However, once the idea has been expressed by some religious genius and we reflect on it we can see how such thinking would promote and ultimately enhance everyone's survival, including our own. The idea is reasonable even if we could not have reasoned to it. Because of God's unconditional love for all of us an intelligent morality becomes the primary focus of revelation, not eternal salva- tion, about which we can do nothing. Next in the evolution of our consciousness, revelation should lead to moral refinement but for it to function that way it must, as with morality itself, be seen as reasona- ble. Even if we are unable to act according to this "new awareness" the realization of our inability is itself a form of higher consciousness, elsewhere referred to as the recognition of our sinfulness, or perhaps the virtue of humility.

If there is any meaning to the idea of eternal survival, the startling fact is that, according to scripture, the moral requirements are the same as for earthside survival of the species. It hearkens back to Jewish family morality, the purpose of which is to promote and maintain the welfare of the community rather than just the personal survival of individuals as it became under Christianity. Except that now the family must be seen as global in scope. This has not always been apparent because the connections among the people of earth have only within this century become so close, for good or ill. At the beginning of the 20th century the trip that took several days between Europe and America can now be accomplished in less than two hours by missiles, and the fact that we have missiles tells us something about the morality we have been living with. The emphasis on community may sound as though the value of the individual has been diminished. Actually, everyone must be concerned with the well-being of individuals for community to function as it ought. Anyone treated as a cipher will have difficulty acting as a proper member of a community.

The clearest lesson we have about how to live is Jesus himself. Given that God is both immanent and transcendent our task is not to create a relationship with God. We already have one. We can understand from this why Jesus said that what we do for others we do for him, but we have to develop a consciousness of what we are, what we have and what we do. We are not born with it. Self-knowledge is the most important aspect of the higher consciousness we are supposed to be developing. If God is immanent in me, then God must be immanent in all my brothers and sisters. It is hard to imagine a bigger test of my faith, because when I look at my brothers and sisters, especially some of them, they do not give much evidence of the Holy Spirit being immanent in them. But then looking at myself honestly I have to ask: Am I giving evidence of the Holy Spirit being immanent in me? Like the fact that the earth moves, we ordinarily cannot experience God's immanence directly in ourselves or others. I know it because I have been told and I trusted the people who told me until, that is, I found reasons of my own for believing.

If as the church claims God has been revealed to us, and if as it further claims God is infinite can there be an end to revelation? According to the Catholic magisterium revelation ended with the death of the last Apostle. Obviously much depends on how revelation is defined and who defines it. By claiming sole authority to define what the sources of revelation are and what revelation is, the church has only closed arguments for those who have faith that church officials know what they are talking about. Credibility suffers when we find contradictory claims. William Marshner, a Catholic theologian, "takes the view that revelation and dogma are one and the same thing. Dogmas he would say, not only faithfully reflect the word of God, but are themselves the word of God" (Dulles 1992:xii). We immediately encounter a difficulty with this claim when we ask how the dogma of the Assumption and the Immaculate Conception fits into the context of revelation having ended with the death of the last Apostle. The magisterium tells us that such dogmas were implicit in scripture and tradition. What this means is that there is some basis for having drawn such a conclusion. As their thinking goes, if Mary is the mother of God she must have been born without Original Sin, which leaves unanswered the prior question: What is Original Sin?

In *The Church* (1967), Hans Kung's agrees with the magisterium about revelation being closed. However, he writes, "This revelation is inexhaustible" (p. 264), presumably meaning that we can garner new insights from it forever. Are the new insights new revelation? The idea of a closed revelation in addition to being based on the assumption that God's manifestation to us was completed at the death of the last Apostle, leaves the institutional church as guardian, interpreter and protector of these truths. But if, as I have maintained, the Bible reveals the evolution of human consciousness, the church's view of revelation is too narrow. We know that the various writings that we now call the New Testament were not written by the Apostles themselves, that the gospels were written some time after the death of the last Apostle. We can also be fairly certain that much of the gospels are imaginative reconstructions. However, we should not have difficulty with the idea that the gospels present us with truth under those circumstances. We can find truth in Genesis with far less basis in fact than the gospels (See Chapter 4).

Still, we are left with two questions that have not yet been answered satisfactorily by church authorities: What is revelation? What are its sources? Aside from the possibility of an unmediated, private revelation of God's self to an individual (about which we can say nothing) without going into specifics we can answer the first question broadly. It is knowledge of God in human terms and of God's People and the relationship between the two. This knowledge of God is not, of course, information. A better analogy would be the "knowing" of intimacy we read about in connection with Adam knowing Eve. As for sources of "the new awareness" we have the Jewish scriptures, the New Testament with the teaching attributed to Jesus, the test of reasonableness, all the commentaries that have been written on these sources, and finally ordinary human experience. We do not know for certain exactly what Jesus said and we cannot rule out direct inspiration by God for some of what we know, but if God operates with nature and within nature then I suspect that the parts of revelation that most of us could not have figured out for ourselves can be attributed to religious genius, like geniuses in any human enterprise-- Mozart in music, Einstein in physics, and so on. Most of us, for example, could not have figured out that the divine economy does not operate on a quid-pro-quo basis (prosperity as a reward for good behavior), the lesson of Job and the repudiation by Jesus of the belief that a man could be born blind because of his sin or his parent's sin (John 9:2-3). Job had been part of the Jewish tradition for 300 or more years yet the disciples of Jesus were astounded to hear Jesus say that the rich would have difficulty getting into heaven. "Then who can be saved?"

they asked (Mat. 19:23).

When the bishops at Vatican II identified us as the People of God they did not create a new concept. The Jews acquired that title when they made a covenant with God. Under the new covenant with Jesus we also became the People of God except that the title was no longer restricted as it had been with the Jews. Standard church teaching is that Jesus came for everyone. Until recently Roman Catholic officials interpreted its own teaching narrowly, meaning that if Jesus came for everyone, the benefits could only be had by becoming a Catholic. The Catholic church has till recently been an exclusive club with rules specifying who was in and who was out. In short, it manifested a tribal mentality.

To some extent it is still that way except that now allowance is made for our "separated brethren" who presumably are not entirely outside. The title People of God can be understood in four ways. One is all inclusive; i.e., every human is a member simply as a biological fact and as a creature of God (Dulles 1978:58). There is no self-recognition under this title by members of this group which includes atheist, polytheists, pantheists, panentheists, animists and so on, and no particular morality follows from these facts. God's Spirit dwells in all and we may assume that all receive grace, but because the title is all inclusive it explains nothing. The second way includes those who are God's people in a special sense, all humans who recognize them-selves as a member of the human family and treat other humans accordingly regardless of their belief concerning God. The third way is even more restricted. These would be people who specifically be-lieve in God and who fulfill the requirements of a people in the second sense for religious reasons; i.e., they see themselves as acting according to God's will by being a member of a Christian sect or denomination. The fourth kind of People of God distinguish them-selves from the second and third way by living according to a tribal morality that does not recognize all humans as members of the same family, and any person who is not a tribal member may be viewed as an enemy of God unless that person is a potential convert. This group may feel that they are doing God's work by punishing or even killing those who do not meet their tribal standards.

Religious officials, including many who called themselves Catholic, at certain periods of history exemplify the fourth concept when the feeling prevailed that forced conversions and burning witches, here-tics and infidels were viewed as doing God's work. These are not actually People of God. They are more accurately described as people of the institution. Each of these ways of defining the People of God presents us with different premises from which we will come to different logical conclusions, hence leading us to different ways of acting with, for, and toward other humans, i.e., our morality. This study is based on the second view of the People of God. By using this premise the ecumenical task is already accomplished. There is no need to engage in attempts to convert non-believers, members of other Christian denominations, or people of any religion who are feeding the hungry, clothing the naked, healing the sick and so on. Atheists working this way are not witnessing for Jesus, but we can recognize in their behavior the morality and principles that Jesus taught. We need not ask more of them. If there is anything special about being Catholic, since the hierarchy considers the church to have the fullness of truth compared to other churches, then its members, including the hierarchy, perhaps especially the hierarchy, must have a special responsibility to bear witness to "the way, the truth and the life" of Jesus by acting accordingly.

When those called to proclaim the gospel, the leaders of the various sects and denominations, are themselves disconnected from each other, those outside the fold are not likely to miss the contradiction between words and behavior. Under these circumstances the primary message of the gospel, to transform the biological fact that we are a family into a proper family and everything implied by that will not make sense to those who do not yet subscribe to the idea. Failure to operate from conviction that we are all one in God manifests us as liars. Without resolving our differences we have failed before we begin.

Some of the various denominations and sects are trying to solve the problem of their disunity. Anyone experienced in solving problems knows that the first step in solving a problem is to correctly define it. By seeing the problem as one of unifying the various institutions they have tackled a difficult if not impossible task. They are operating from the premise that the institutions are the Church. The Roman bureaucracy's claim has been even more restrictive. By their reckoning, at least in the past, they alone are the true Church. The others are imitations with degrees of validity based on how closely they resemble the church of Rome. By using the premise on which this study is based, that the Church is the People of God in the second sense described above, unifying the institutional churches becomes a non-problem. In fact the People of God are already unified by their manifestation of caring for their brothers and sisters, no matter the denomination or sect to which they belong, or whether they belong to a non-Christian religion, no religion at all, and even if they are atheists. Jesus identified his disciples in very simple language. He did not require a test of orthodoxy. They did not need to be able to quote scripture or tradition. He asked only that they treat one another as family, with special concern for the poor, the sick, the imprisoned and other marginalized persons belonging to the underclasses. As the liberation theologians teach, orthopraxy is more important than orthodoxy. We should remember that the hero of the "Good Samaritan" story is a heretic.

Orthodoxy is less important to the People of God than to institutional leaders. Persons who claim leadership roles should certainly know where they are leading the People under their care, but for that purpose all orthodoxy does not have the same value. Humans who are feeding the hungry and are generally caring for family members who are unable to care for themselves should not have their work or their persons disvalued because they do not believe in the Bible as divinely revealed. Judging from what has happened during the past two millennia Christian officials and clergy need to clarify their job description, starting with the fact that they are the servants of the People of God. Jesus is alleged to have expressed many ideas. What is his basic message? What could possibly be as important as that basic message? The institutional structures built atop his basic message have by their very nature distorted it. Our servants have become our lord and masters, particularly Catholic officials, and among them, notably the Roman bureaucracy. Fortunately the Spirit is at work in his Church, the People of God, and not just among the hierarchy, except as they are the People of God.

The Spirit among the People of God enables them in our time to be aware when they are taught falsely. They realize that specific teachings do not always befit us as humans and family members, hence they are not from God. As we learn from Baum, "The locus of the divine is interpersonal" (1970:58). This is one reason why the People of God rebelled against *Humanae Vitae*, one of the more obvious contradictions of the People's experience, and this from teachers who, because of celibacy, are absolutely committed to not having such experiences. The magisterium presented the reproductive behavior of non-human animals, not just as ideal but as an absolute requirement for humanity. However the error became an advantage for the People of God. It had the effect, along with the liberation of consciences, of raising the consciousness of the faithful. It was an unqualified revelation. At that point many realized that they must accept responsibility for their own spiritual development and not be totally dependent on what comes out of Rome. Since that event, in connection with the liberation of consciences by the bishops of Vatican II, the faithful have discovered the questionable nature of many church teachings, especially the way the church teaches about sin.

CHAPTER IV
GENESIS REVISITED: Homo Stultus

Man's nature must be held to include what he may become. Max Otto

In our effort to reclaim religion from the church we must reexamine the Genesis myth in the light of what we know from history and contemporary social psychology. The church's magisterium would have us believe that humans are inclined to evil because of the fall from grace by Adam and Eve. The biological origin of humanity will likely remain forever shrouded in mystery but the origin of human evil can be discerned in today's humans. It remains the same as it would have been in prehistoric times. The massive ignorance with which we are born has not changed. We require the care and concern of other humans to survive infancy and early childhood and the education we receive toward this end comes from people who still carry the burden of ignorance and of faulty knowledge that I call ignorance II. The most important aspect of knowledge one would expect to passed on is how to survive. Much of this knowledge is implicit and is not passed on consciously in our society where we do not live on the edge as in say Chiapas, Mexico. Still, virtually everyone recognizes our dependence on other humans in the matter of survival, hence families, tribes and larger groupings. However, only in our own time have we become conscious of threats to life from weapons of mass destruction and destruction of the biosphere.

To fashion a proper morality, one that will enable us to survive individually and collectively, we need to understand what kind of

100

creatures we are. The obstacles to understanding come with the knowledge we absorb from the culture within which we are immersed. We start with a massive ignorance and we learn a great deal that is flawed or just plain false. Thus our basic ignorance is compounded by what I called Ignorance II, knowledge that prevents us from learning. Contemporary social and psychological sciences, though not as clear and unambiguous as the sciences of physics and chemistry, still provide valuable insights into human nature, insights that far from negating the wisdom of past ages, enable us to put that thinking in terms that modern humans can understand. Genesis properly interpreted, for example, reveals important truths for us about what kind of creatures we are, especially after it has been relieved of some of the theological baggage it has been made to carry. One of the great lessons it offers comes from learning how myth shapes our thought and behavior.

Another obvious truth is that humans have had a problem from the beginning. The story even says explicitly. "Man [sic] was evil from the beginning," (Gen. 6:5). The idea of "evil" as used here makes it sound as if there is some occult quality to our behavior. If we accept that evil behavior (sinning) is not in our best interest, the statement should be read, "Humans were ignorant of how to act in their own best interest from the beginning." This would apply whether a person's primary concern is earthside survival or eternal survival and remains the case till this moment. "Evil" has other-worldly connotations, ignorance is a human quality we should be able to understand and work at resolving. The second kind of ignorance we noted earlier is more difficult to deal with. The ignorance I call Ignorance II, the faulty knowledge that stands in the way of knowing, e.g., the idolatrous belief that God rewards and punishes in this life for our behavior, a belief contradicted throughout scripture.

Genesis, read as an explanation of how we came to have this problem of ignorance, or how life might have been different and presumably better had Adam and Eve not "sinned" provides us with no useful information. Such thinking was developed and expounded among Western thinkers when Genesis was almost universally regarded as history. Theoretically the message in the story telling us what we need to know has always been available. All of us are born ignorant of how to act in our own best interest and the best interest of everyone. This condition expressed in theological language is known a "sinfulness," a condition that is generally more of a problem for humans than sin, but "sinfulness" like "evil" carries a penumbra of occult meaning that we must get beyond if we are to deal with it. We can see that in trying to develop a proper morality, if we talk about ignorance, (not knowing how to act in one's own best interest) it would be more acceptable to most of earth's inhabitants than if we talk about either sin or sinfulness. If we resolve that aspect of our ignorance that permits us to arrive at a conviction of how we should treat other humans we will simultaneously be acting in our own best interest to the best of our present knowledge. We may continue to make mistakes and learn from them but operating this way we need not concern ourselves so much with "sinning" and there doubt will be no doubt about who is responsible.

Non-human animals are not likely to be aware that they will die. Becoming aware of the possibility of death has to have been a stage in the process of attaining the kind of consciousness humans have. Awareness of their contingent status would have made humans anxious about their food supply on the morrow and other requirements for staying alive, leading them to act in ways that would keep them from having to think about it all the time. In that respect the Genesis story contains wisdom that is as modern as tomorrow: We cannot resolve human anxiety once and forever. Also some paths are evolutionary dead ends. The lesson is taught more clearly in the New Testament. Jesus says "Do not be anxious then, saying, `What shall we eat?' or `What you shall we drink?'. . . Your heavenly Father knows that you need all these things" (Mat. 6:31-32). In contemporary language, he might have said, "Don't worry. The earth is bountiful enough for everyone," which we must now qualify by adding--"given a proper stewardship."

We are learning animals and we are self-created (May 1991:29; Fagan 1979:62). The behavior illustrated by the story of Adam and Eve trying to resolve their anxiety forever in one act is the expression of a common human wish. All humans at least some of the time and some humans most of the time would like have all their problems done with for good. However life does not work that way. As learning animals we learn primarily by trial-and-error. Sometimes such lessons can be painful and even lethal. The flaw we are supposed to have acquired as a result of the sin is in part what would have led to the alleged sin. Choices made in the hope that we can resolve our sense of insecurity arising from the ignorance of what will happen on the morrow is self-destructive.

The Bible is replete with stories that follow the same pattern of choices that go against the evolutionary potential of human nature, for example, the Israelites and the golden calf opting for a visible god, and in the New Testament, Peter at the transfiguration saying, "Lord it is good for us to be here. Let us make three tents, one for you, one for Moses and one for Elijah" (Mark. 9:5). Peter, according to the story, manifested the desire we all have at times to become fixated at a certain stage of development instead of remaining open to further development. Jesus tells us to live with the sense of ignorance with which a child is born because unless we accept the kingdom of God like a child we will not enter it at all. In another place we are told that the kingdom of God is within. Taken together these verses tell us that the kingdom of God is a metaphor for our destiny which as I read it means continuously evolving toward an ever higher consciousness. This higher consciousness for humans is the recognition that ultimately our best chance of surviving and enhancing survival for one and all is in community. In our circumstances this means a global community.

In the New Testament we find another lesson related to the same problem, that is the obstacle to learning posed by riches (Luke. 18:24). Rich persons have resources that may make them feel secure, i.e., not needing anything, perhaps not even people, thus failing to become aware of their greatest need which is to create themselves from moment to moment in connection with others. A rich person may lack the anxiety that promotes such creative effort. We may think of anxiety as being the locus of creativity.

A more subtle lesson on the same subject occurs when Jesus, near the end of his mission, says, "I am telling you the simple truth when I assure you that it is a good thing for you that I should go away. For if I did not go away, the divine helper would not come to you" (John. 16:7) The divine helper, or Holy Spirit is the immanent God. There is no actual coming; rather, there is a growing awareness of the resources we carry within, for Christians, the immanent God. Like Peter at the transfiguration, the Apostles tended to become fixated on Jesus, live and present. Jesus told them they had to be on their own in order to experience the insecurity that would keep them growing toward fulfillment of their potential.

This analysis of human nature is a long way from the centuries of speculation on Genesis, Original Sin, Adams extraordinary gifts before the Fall, the consequences to us of Adams sin, and so on, as laid out by Augustine, and more recently, Henri Rondet (1972). One of the more pernicious lessons derived from Genesis is the belief that God micro-manages human affairs by rewarding and punishing in the here and now. Orthodox teaching denies this but the teaching is ambiguous, perhaps because the tendency to believe this is either part of being human or it flows from the fear of our contingent status. We see it in the story of Job when Job's friends assume that his losses are a result of some sin. And again when Jesus told his disciples that riches had a way of limiting human growth and development (Luke

18:24-26) his disciples were astounded. As with many people before and since, believing that personal prosperity was a sign from God of personal righteousness is still common. It is significant that the disciples were not just surprised but actually astounded. There is a certain truth to the idea of reward and punishment in this life for our behavior, but these are built-in consequences of our behavior, e.g., a sense of satisfaction from feeling that our needs are met, peace and joy when our behavior is in accord with our natures, anxiety and alienation when we feel disconnected from others. One of our problems is that what gives us satisfaction on one level of existence may destroy the possibility of satisfaction on another level. We can connect with one person sexually and enjoy a primary physical experience while simultaneously destroying relationships or the possibility of relationships with several people, hence of Primary Experience of a more significant kind that creates and promotes connections among all of us.

If the churches have seemed to focus too much on sexual sins we must recognize that they have been operating on the basis of how destructive sexual activity can be. That is the limited truth the church offers while neglecting the larger truth that leads people to that greater intimacy of the mind where the ultimate Primary Experience takes place. If people believe that physical bonding through sex is the ultimate experience, we must ask where and how they could have learned differently. When children and adolescents experiment with sex their consciousness has generally not developed sufficiently for them to imagine experiences that could transcend sex. The result is faulty knowledge which I have labeled Ignorance II, a condition everyone finds difficult to escape. How shall we prevent such experiments? Threats of dire consequences, temporal and eternal, will no longer serve. In addition, the opportunities to experiment abound. This leaves only persuasion, particularly by example, as a way for the church to deal with this problem. Since the churches lack a theology of intimacy they have little to work with. The best hope for preventing unreflective sex among our children is for children to discover the joy of non-sexual bonding with parents. Children may never discover experiences that transcend sex unless they discover them with parents. Frightening children with the fears of pregnancy, disease, shame or eternal damnation has lost whatever effectiveness it had and trying to control young lives with curfews and access to certain people, places, and media is difficult if not impossible in this age of the world wide web.

Recognizing non-sexual Primary Experiences can be a first step. To discover in a book, for example, the clear expression of a thought for which we had groped unsuccessfully we may experience an explosion of enlightenment that we carry with us all of our days. Keats records such an experience in "Ode on a Grecian Urn." In contemplating this piece of art Keats revels first in the pure sensual enjoyment of the scene depicted there. Then he begins to think about what he is seeing. The lad pursuing the maiden will never catch her but she will always remain fair. Then although the figures remain static from a purely visual perspective Keats begins to imagine what happens off scene and his thinking becomes an artistic event in itself allowing him to declare in ecstasy, "Beauty is Truth, Truth Beauty, That is all you need to know."

Keats experience exemplifies the kind of consciousness toward which we should be evolving. This is not what the churches are teaching. It is certainly the case that the mass of uneducated persons do not seem destined to repeat Keats' experience, but I have to believe that the possibilities for imaginative experiences and creative responses exist in all of us on some level. Most people, at one time or another, experience a highly satisfying, non-sexual relationship with another person. Unfortunately they are mostly accidental events and are not actively pursued. The churches, while promoting stable marriages should also be promoting the pursuit of of intimacy that transcends sex. Church history, however, reveals that marriage has been for the better part of two millennia a license to sin instead of the occasion for a progressive evolution in consciousness. The failure of the churches makes it imperative that lay persons assume the responsibility for learning then teaching each other and their children what makes for the most satisfying kind of life because such a life coincides with what it takes for humanity to survive, reason enough for reclaiming religion from the church.

Modern biology and the other sciences that study humans have made it easier for us to understand some of these lessons from the Bible. It is anachronistic to think that anyone should have perceived these lessons about human nature long ago. Certainly church officials whose job it is to teach us could not have known. Actually we should not look to the hierarchy for innovations in human thinking. This is the job of prophets--Francis, Clare, Luther, Erasmus, More--persons who do not have a vested interest in maintaining institutional structures. The tension that exists between a church bureaucracy and its prophets ultimately results in the communal evolution toward truth. After an idea has been tried and tested in the well of human experience, a point is reached where we can say, "Yes, this works. This is the truth, at least for now. So we should not be surprised to find the Vatican bureaucracy apparently putting obstacles in the way of what some of see as progressive, cognitive evolution.

When in *Humani Generis* Pius XII came out against polygeneism in the face of growing evidence for the reality of human biological evolution he was attempting to salvage the biblical idea of a single set of parents for humanity which is required for the doctrine of Original Sin (Rondet 1972:241). Pius XII's job was to keep this before us because he perceived Genesis as telling something about ourselves that we needed to know. The church's explanation tells us that we have a problem about which we can do nothing; in other words we are victims of a fault committed by an imaginary set of parents from whom we are all supposed to have been descended (Rondet 1972:265).

We do not know for sure how humans originated but the empirical evidence favors polygeneism, i.e., belief in the multiple origins of humanity from creatures with a common genetic makeup. The evidence for polygeneism is still all around us in the unevenness of our current state of cognitive evolution. If we can speak of pre-human primates they no doubt exhibited the same patterns of dominance and submission that we witness in contemporary nonhuman primates, patterns which to some extent have remained a part of our human heritage. The patriarchal-like social structure we see in non-human primate societies, with the physically superior male leading the group is ideally suited for both social stability and passing on the best genes to the next generation. However in the evolutionary transition to human, bigger is no longer necessarily better because of changes in the brain. Although the coding for survival of the group probably remains genetically the same on one level (bigger is better) the emergence of creative humans (polygeneism) here and there among the various groups would demonstrate the superiority of brains over brawn for the sake of survival, for example, in the invention or improvement of weapons for hunting, or the domestication of plants and animals.

The beginning of technology and innovative strategies for survival very likely contributed to our becoming recognizably human because of their destabilizing effect on the group. which no longer depended entirely on physically superior males. Any kind of destabilization tends to produce anxiety (the need for closure) to which humans generally respond with fear or creativity. This is a crucial time for keeping the whole of the natural law, i.e., "survive" and "together". Even a creative response can neglect one half of the law, for example in planning a bank robbery. While focussing on survival the "together" aspect of the law is neglected. Technological innovation continues to destabilize society by making certain jobs obsolete while creating others. The resulting anxiety may be responsible for prevalence of the various ways people choose to escape--alcohol, gambling, TV, the internet and various other addictions. In any case technology eventually led to a division of labor and contributed to differentiation and individuation of the species. The resulting increase in human productivity has not, however, been used to increase the survival chances for all of humanity.

Among nonhuman primates the group acts as though it were a single entity, each part contributing to the survival of the whole. Under such a system a single, dominant head makes sense, as does impregnation of the females by a superior male. In the transition to humanness, superiority is not so clearly defined. As a result of this analysis we can imagine where evolution seems to be headed or, given the tendency for humans to seek closure at any price, I should perhaps say where it ought to be headed. Survival as a group is still a priority. If the group does not survive neither will the individuals in it, but the concern of most has been bound by the limits of the tribe. However, with a global economy and instantaneous worldwide communication we need to transcend tribal loyalties to deal with threats to survival of the species. The original primate coding of bigger is better will not serve us well in our present situation when the best chance for survival of all requires the cooperation of most of us. With everyone promoting the life and well-being of everyone else, or at least not placing obstacles in the way of that objective, the chances of everyone's survival increases, and not just basic survival, but an enhanced survival. Thus the third phase of human evolution should move us from brain quantity, i.e., simple increases in the ease and speed of information processing to brain quality which is the kind of wisdom that enables us to make life sustaining choices for the human family, the ultimate in intelligence.

Another possible reason why creatures began to emerge as individuals may have been the decline of the estrus cycle in females. With the increased availability of sex that resulted, dominant males could become satisfied with one or two mates thereby allowing subordinate males to pair-bond with a female of their own. When we consider that increased brain capacity meant that the size of the dominant male no longer signaled superiority and would no longer by itself guarantee access to any and all females, this kind of pair-bonding would reduce the potential for conflict while promoting individual identities.

If we look around us today we can recognize individuals at different stages in the evolution of consciousness toward the ideal state of viewing all humans as members of a global family. We need not search far to discover that some humans have not evolved much beyond the other primates, while others appear to be as evolved as far as we could expect, using as a criterion, promoting the life and well-being of everyone, including the unborn. As with other human phenomena the greatest number of persons are probably somewhere between these extremes.

The potential for learning and self-creation in the direction of the ideal human are what really distinguishes us from other primates, and promoting this ideal should be a major function of community, the ultimate beneficiary. Christianity only pushes this kind of self-creation incidentally since our primary purpose on earth is seen as eternal salvation, an idea that has been a tradition for so long we should not expect it to change any time soon. Our best hope is in giving more emphasis to ideas that are now marginal. That is why I believe that the best chance for changing the larger structures will come from changes at the level of committed pairs and networks of such pairs. At the present time this hope seems as farfetched as any scheme for changing the world given the divorce rate. Moral revisionists are proposing that the church relax its ban on divorce and remarriage. Perhaps they are right, but this is not the locus of the problem. The church needs to revise its whole concept of committed interpersonal relationships. The issue of marital and non-marital intimacy will be dealt with at length in other chapters, particularly six, eight and nine. In this chapter I only want to link interpersonal relationships with the problem of closure, a characteristic of human nature, actually of animal nature, which for humans is both a curse and a blessing.

We know that the Jews were not the only ones who imagined a golden age when humanity was without troubles. The Greeks, for example, had Pandora. This phenomenon continues right up to our own time. We can always find people who can remember when the world was much better than it is. The church Fathers were not exempt. It led them to speculate on what we lost through Original Sin, the name for the alleged act of Adam and Eve. This doctrine was propounded with great passion by Augustine, Bishop of Hippo. Some of his more exotic proposals would have us never getting ill and in the end not dying but being assumed directly into heaven at the end of our allotted time. Also, he thought human nature changed as a result of the sin. But as we shall see, two related aspects of human nature which are the real sources of problems for humans existed prior to the alleged sin. One is the need for closure, part of our mammalian heritage and the other, and perhaps later, depending on where we mark humanity's beginning, an awareness of life as contingent. Closure is an automatic tendency of the mind to find order in

the world or answers to disturbing questions, and having found them
to lock on them (Maslow 1971:118-119). Sometimes our need for
closure is satisfied easily as when we see enough information to fill in
the missing pieces as in the partial letters below.

There is little doubt that this tendency is biological, because we
share the process with other creatures, and we apparently cannot not
perceive patterns. When we lack enough information to achieve
closure, however, the result may be some degree of anxiety and the
problem for each of us depends on our ability to tolerate anxiety. The
result could be acceptance of incorrect answers. We could, for
example, have been brought up in a culture in which people generally
believed that God punishes and rewards here and now. With such a
belief if things go bad we can usually find confirmation in reflecting
on our most recent misdeeds. Living with the tension that arises from
this need for closure can lead to creation on many levels, but it is a
problem for most people and extremely difficult for some. And as
indicated above in the case of criminals, we may respond creatively
while neglecting the social aspect of surviving. Most of us have a
tendency to adopt the quickest and easiest solution, the traditional or
conventional answer. The attempt to escape from anxiety can take
many forms, from believing in a guru who will furnish answers, to
drug addiction, to suicide. But once we know that Genesis is not
history our problem assumes a human shape rather than the mysterious affliction known as Original Sin. Our ability to create plus the
built-in potential for an evolution in human consciousness should lead
and in fact has led us away from blaming two mythical creatures for
our problems to searching for the true nature of our problems and for
ways of dealing with them.

Whatever we think, say, or do implies a theory of what it means to
be a human being. "Each one of us has a theory of human nature, or
tacit assumptions about human nature, whether [one] is conscious of
them or not, that permits [one] to navigate in the world" (Becker
1971:116). Our idea of what is human determines how we treat
others, how we respond to them, how we train and educate our children, what we need in order to maintain our self-esteem, and what is
perhaps most important for us, our theory will determine how we
approach the development of a committed relationship. Our theory of
human nature and our morality are two sides of the same coin. This

is the case whether, as for most of us, we have adopted unwittingly a theory from those around us, a church group for example, or have fashioned a theory of our own. For each of us the theory is made up of many elements, not all of which are accessible for conscious examination. There is, therefore, no simple way to describe this theory for any particular individual, much less for a group. We must agree with Max Otto that whatever humans may become is also part of their nature (1949:33). In fact we might say that human nature ideally is a work in progress. As Heidegger expressed it, "Being is becoming." Malleability and the possibilities for becoming are two of our most important characteristics, another way of saying that we are learning and self-creating animals. Much of this becoming is relatively automatic as we absorb the culture into which we are born. As we encounter the world of differences in other humans we continually change. We live "In a world of flux, everything is always changing. . . . Change is the automatic and inevitable byproduct of interaction" (Efran 1990:56-57). But there is a very large difference in not wanting change and welcoming change, also in having it occur unconsciously vs. consciously pursuing it. In the first instances we are forced into change with no possibility of control. In the second we will be going with the flow and may have some measure of control. Life is a bus or tram according to Bateson (1988:167-168). But he notes that, "change is typically made in pursuit of some *constancy*, some previously defined goal" (p. 46). If the "previously defined goal" is to remain unchanged we will change anyway with unpredictable and perhaps undesirable results.

Survival demands constant adaptation. Persons who expect change and accept change as a matter of course or who pursue it will be more comfortable with the process of living. Authentic existence according to Heidegger requires freedom from the past and openness to the future. Fixed ideas about human nature, particularly the negative ones, focus our attention on limits rather than possibilities, and it is among the possibilities that we may find intelligent ideas to replace the bankrupt ones now current, such as the idea that killing groups (war and terrorism), or individuals (murder and capital punishment) can solve human problems. Intelligent ideas will elude us until we recognize that the subtlety and complexity of being human translates into subtle and complex human problems. We have only to look at our tendency to think in stereotypes to realize that our disposition for closure leads us to simplify to the point of oversimplification. The ignorance and neediness with which we are born results in a life-long series of contingencies, which in matters of importance often assumes an urgency that may make us act foolishly--Does she love me? Will I get the job? What will my parents do when they find out I'm pregnant? Will that country attack us? What will I eat and what will I wear tomorrow? And so on. We do not find closure for these kinds of problems as easily as with the incomplete letters above.

We tend to confuse nature and culture. Our unconscious adoption of culture makes it feel natural. When a trait exhibited by a person is not common to all, as it would be if it were natural, it is likely to be the product of culture. For this reason we must exclude from the list of characteristics we attribute to human nature, at least in the simplistic way these traits are sometimes presented, Lorenz's idea of aggression (1971) which is only one way of dealing with frustration, and Ardrey's idea of territoriality (1966) which is one way of responding to our sense of contingency. We are not all aggressive, and territoriality has radically different meanings for different people. Mazur and Robertson contend that the territorial "instinct *diminishes* as we move from lemur to man" (1974:158). Some humans do not find 2000 acres enough, while others are satisfied with what we call personal space or zone of privacy. According to Hall (1969:157) Arabs apparently lack even a concept of personal space. Also, persons who tend to be aggressive do not necessarily direct their aggression against other humans in harmful ways. They may sublimate them in sports and other activities such as satire. Lorenz's and Ardrey's theories as they are sometimes used belong to that class of oversimplified extrapolations from the study of non-human animals that do not fit all or even most humans. In defense of Lorenz's position, I should add that perhaps his overemphasis is to make a point against an overspiritualized view of humans which emphasizes saving one's soul instead of surviving here and now. We may infer this from Lorenz's affirmation of his student Wickler's (1973:281) comparative studies of humans and animals. These studies can shed light on human nature, but must not be pushed too far.

Imagining a human without some sort of culture is difficult. Maybe this is why some sociologists go one step further than Max Otto and contend that human nature is acquired. Stories of so-called feral children are cited in support of this idea. Unfortunately such a concept may lead to the belief that functionally and congenitally defective humans may not be considered persons, hence not entitled to our care and concern, a concept amply demonstrated by the Third Reich. Given our strong tendency toward ethnocentrism, we may decide, as in fact some of us have decided, that there are others who are subhuman since they differ from us, e.g., convicted criminals in most cultures, the Jews in Hitler's Germany, blacks in the U.S., heretics and the unsaved wherever fundamentalist Christianity is in power, and infidels in certain Islamic cultures. When the definition of what is human is determined by the ethnocentric ethics of a culture, those who are not the right kind of people are in danger, given large differences in power with no moderating structures. The survival of everyone is at risk with such a policy. The group having the power to eliminate others today, may find us reprehensible tomorrow. But from the perspective of this study differences in culture between persons in committed relationships should be our most important concern. When couples from different cultural backgrounds experience difficulty achieving a common closure, communication problems will generally be found at the base.

Historically there are four generally accepted categories from which inferences may be drawn concerning what it means to be human: 1) Human nature is basically corrupt, or naturally inclined toward evil, as taught by St. Paul, St. Augustine, John Calvin, Freud and others. 2) Human nature is basically good and becomes corrupt through bad institutions, an idea whose chief proponent was Jean Jacques Rousseau. This is the *tabula rasa* theory of human nature; i.e., it is entirely the product of the environment. 3) Raw human nature is unimportant, neither good nor bad in itself. It is wholly determined by genetic and environmental forces, such shape being appropriate or inappropriate to its own culture. Calling this human nature good or evil is a subjective judgment based on parochial concepts of good and evil, and these concepts are relative since they vary over time and from place to place, arising either from the culture or as a reaction to it. 4) Human nature is viewed as mostly determined by genetic and environmental factors, but there are opportunities to gain some measure of control over the process by using our knowledge and understanding to promote those aspects of the environment and genetics that empower us, and to transcend those aspects that limit us. In other words human nature is subject to creative, progressive cognitive evolution. The school of humanistic psychology led by A.H. Maslow (1971) supports this fourth view of human nature, as do existentialists such as Sartre (1965:263-268) and Heidegger (1961:132), also certain advocates of Eastern philosophy such as Watts (1967), Pearce (1980) and Ouspensky (1974).

Each of the four views proposed were intended to help us understand human nature as it really is, and to liberate us in some way, also to aid us in surviving. St. Paul's purpose was to keep us from being victimized by drives and tendencies about which we might be ignorant, but his main concern was our transcendental survival. Calvin hoped to liberate us from anxiety about transcendental survival by teaching us that the matter was already settled through divine election.

Freud's idea was to free us from problems that originated in unresolved conflicts between the drives that we experience as children and the requirements of social order. Rousseau wanted to liberate us from the net that institutions cast about us for their own purposes. Left alone, he said, our own natural goodness would emerge and we would have a wonderful, peaceful world.

Scientific philosophers and philosophical scientists, proponents of the third view of human nature, want to retain the freedom from institutional control that Rousseau proposed, but without the naive belief that the world would automatically turn out all right, also to liberate us from the illusion of freedom where none exists, as in an exaggerated notion of free will. Our freedom is not so much "in controlling outward events. . . but in controlling the inward temper in which [we] face these events" (Collingwood 1956:36). The fourth view holds that some measure of self-determination is possible, but this freedom is not automatic. That is, we are not born free as most people believe but must acquire freedom. It is a skill of sorts. Learning the language of our culture, for example, frees us to communicate with members of our culture. Most of us are born with the ability to learn, but without a nurturing that most people do not get, this ability does not become the skill that leads to optimum freedom for humans. Perhaps this is what Jesus meant in bidding us to become like little children.

The fourth idea is the one adopted in this book, and it resembles that of certain secular humanists such as Paul Kurtz (1988:110-111). However, there are two important differences between the humanism of Kurtz and mine: 1) He teaches that religion is bankrupt as a means by which some persons may become free, and 2) that private, individual behavior is amoral, i.e., entirely without effect upon our relationships with one another. If as I contend, any behavior that affects one or more persons has a moral quality, either negative or positive, then Kurtz's judgment in this respect is seriously flawed. In many instances proponents of freedom--St. Paul, Calvin, Rousseau, Kurtz--fail to distinguish between "freedom from," that which enables us to minimize or eliminate behavioral constraints and "freedom for" which requires the acquisition of knowledge or skills that broadens our range of choices.

The importance of being connected to other humans goes beyond infancy and early childhood when total dependence forces us to be social beings. Some people reach a stage of development where they can say, "I don't need anyone." Only a few of us can be this idiosyncratic, however. There simply is not time, nor space, nor resources in the world for most of us to be alone and self-subsisting. The vast majority of us have to live cooperatively. Furthermore a person subsisting alone accepts a minimal existence which most of us would not find satisfying. Most of us look for and find a mate, and it is in this matter of mates where our understanding of the disposition to closure will serve us best. At one time people most often mated with someone from a similar cultural background. Now, neighborhoods, ethnic enclaves and small communities are disappearing and mates are chosen from a more diverse pool. This means that we can no longer go into a committed relationship with a set of rigid expectations of how our partner will act and expect the relationship to survive. Thus, if we want closure we cannot expect it to be the simple process of filling in with information we already have as with the letters above. We are going to have to deal and negotiate. I am not suggesting a trading game--"You give me this and I'll give you that." The dealing and negotiating I refer to has to do with self-disclosure. We have to complete for each other the sense of who and what we are. The current scandalous divorce rate is a consequence of not understanding this requirement for contemporary, committed relationships, or perhaps it is due to a cultural norm that makes such an effort seem foolish. Starting over with someone else may seem to be the easier option. Later I will explain the advantages of a three-way commitment--the partners to each other and both to the relationship itself. We must note, however, that the problems that result from diverse backgrounds is pushing us toward a more conscious kind of interpersonal relationships.

The issue of closure extends beyond the perception of patterns within immediate sensory details. Closure is also the biological basis for creative imagination when people can tolerate some level of anxiety (Gerard 1968:229). Once elements of knowledge exist in the mind they can be combined and recombined into numberless patterns. One pattern can be substituted for another, and patterns can be combined into systems of still greater usefulness and complexity. A couple were discussing the cost of their impending divorce, $1500, when one of them said, "We could go to Europe for that much." "The other responded with, "Let's," and they did.

The downside of closure is that although we can learn alternatives to patterns, there are, as for other animals, neuro-physiological difficulties. Also, the patterns we live by are not completely accessible to us. We cannot articulate reasons for much of what we do, but we can rationalize, i.e., create a plausible explanation. We have even less success in explaining the behavior of others because our explanations are drawn from personal thought patterns that we have probably adopted uncritically such as stereotypes and which we project onto others. We may, for example, explain the recidivist behavior of convicted criminals by saying that they are naturally bad, a theory that will never lead to the solution of our crime problem. If we start with the understanding that behavior is always in some way a survival response we may get a handle on the problem. If we look at what criminals generally do as a pattern of economic activity (Letkemann 1973), we can then ask ourselves what we can do to get people to pursue their wants and needs in more socially acceptable occupations. Then we can experiment. If the cause of crime is that some people are naturally bad, warehousing them in prison is entirely appropriate.

Once a pattern is grasped we assume understanding of what we perceive. "When the branches of the fig tree becomes tender and it puts forth leaves, you know that summer is near" (Mat. 24:32). Or we may note a weather pattern such as winds and clouds flowing from a certain direction followed by rain. Most of our knowledge, perhaps all of it, exists in the form of one pattern or another, or as an item within the context of a larger pattern. We also discover abstract patterns such as grammatical regularities in language and in explicated myths. This tendency to find order or see patterns is called "closure" because once a partial pattern is perceived we generally need to complete the pattern in some way, as with the partial "ABCs" above. We are not at first aware that the patterns we think we find are imposed on the world. Patterns seem to be apprehended directly, as when a three-year old says, "He hitted me," revealing a grasp of the pattern of regular verbs, but without any knowledge of verbs regular or otherwise. Large numbers of academic specialists-- linguists, anthropologists, psychologists, and so on--try to make us aware of rules and patterns that determine our behavior. The theories offered to us by academic specialists can be liberating in two ways: 1) they can help us to understand ourselves by making us conscious of the patterns we live by and how we got them, offering us the possibility of changing our thinking and behavior, a process Peter Berger calls "alternation" (1963:51-54); and 2) they can help us tolerate differences in others.

Our tendency toward closure frequently results in an inability to assimilate new knowledge when the new item is incompatible with our existing patterns of knowledge. Even when patterns of knowledge do not contradict the existing ones, a person who wishes to acquire new knowledge can be inhibited, as in trying to learn a foreign language. As with culture, the need for closure both liberates and constrains. Most people are convinced that they are in charge of their lives because they seem to be making decisions to do this or that, unaware of the constraints imposed upon those decisions by genetics plus the knowledge and training to which they have been exposed. They are like fish in water unable to take cognizance of the element within which they live because it is so all pervasive. The automatic process of closure that at first enables us to learn has now resulted in an apparent dead end. What we think we already know cannot be learned, Ignorance II, again.

This points up a major advantage in our time for people in committed relationships. The fact of having to disclose to someone, who and what we are just happens to simultaneously provide self-knowledge by requiring us to formulate such knowledge, no easy task as anyone who has tried it knows. According to the criteria established earlier the most intelligent idea of human nature has to be the fourth described above by which we overcome in some measure the determining effects of genetics and environment through a creative engagement with others. The process of disclosing ourselves to an intimate has a liberating effect by making us more conscious of what drives us. We enjoy more freedom to disclose ourselves to an intimate partner because we may presume a sympathetic, compassionate listener. This kind of creative engagement will be treated extensively in chapters eight and nine.

Although we are limited in many ways, the limitations on what we can think, do, and become are not absolute. The possibilities for creativity can arise from our sense of contingency even though it is at the same time a major source of our problems. The anxiety produced by a sense of something incomplete prompts us to act. A trivial example would be seeing a picture on a wall canted. Most of feel compelled to align the frame with the other lines in the room. The danger is in the tendency we might have to adopt the quick, easy, or traditional solution to more complex problems without reflection. We have no guarantee that our plans will work out the way we intended. Bobby Burns expressed it poetically: "The best laid plans of mice and men gang agley." It may very well be the case that we are wholly determined by factors beyond our control as some scientists and philosophers would have us believe, but to accept this without question may induce in some persons the same kind of passivity that results from the conviction that we are already free, that there will always be wars, that humans are inherently evil, that we are already saved, or whatever. We do not pursue what we already have or what we think we cannot possibly find, and we generally will not try to change the unchangeable. Participating in the pseudo-conflict, freedom vs. determinism is unintelligent because it is unresolvable in that simplistic form. Finding our limits and trying to transcend them is intelligent. There is no question of total control. We cannot control our genetic makeup, yet, and we become culturally conditioned in many ways long before we have concepts for that process. The task of finding and transcending limits is made more difficult by the muddle of variant views postulated to define the problem, its causes, and its possible solutions. Spiritual descendants of Calvin, for example, deny absolutely the possibility of a spiritual freedom that can be used to save ourselves. If God knows everything that will happen, then our salvation or damnation is predetermined. This is not to say that every particular event according to this system of thought is predetermined, only the final outcome. It is a closed system, like a tree. The acorn is destined to become an oak, but the configuration of its branches and its size are not predetermined.

When certain religions teach what they call "absolute truth" about human nature, they do so on the grounds that they are in possession of the God's word either from the Bible, the Koran, some other holy book, tradition, intuition or some combination of these. The Bible is a record of human, cognitive evolution. The ideas of God and morality show a definite and considerable progressive evolution from beginning to end, which is evidence for the Bible being the way humans understand God and morality rather than God's explicit revelations. If the Bible expresses absolute truth as alleged by some this is faith contrary to evidence the Bible itself provides. How would we account for the paradoxical idea that our ideas are absolutely progressively evolving? Our understanding of "truth" seems to be a discontinuous process not simply the acquisition of a set of final answers. As we gain knowledge we seem to stop at fixed points along the way, individually and collectively. Then because of closure the pattern gets set and we have to transcend what we know in order to grow, much the way that a snake or bug outgrows its skin and has to shed it in order to move to the next level of growth. Like Peter in the story of the Transfiguration: we want to hang on to what we know to be good and never have it end (Mark. 9:2).

Human nature according to the Christian tradition was supposedly altered by the sin of Adam and Eve, the two major alterations being that we have to work for a living and that we would die. This altered human nature, as the story goes, is the one we inherited, but given our knowledge of evolution the "Fall" attributed to Adam and Eve very likely did not happen. Human nature on the contrary seems, rather, subject to being elevated, despite our propensity for wanting, as did the mythical Edenites, what we cannot possibly have, e.g., certain knowledge and the elimination of contingency, ("You will be like God" Gen. 3:5). Another example of human foolishness is the belief that either there is no way of resolving the issues that divide us, or that if our side, church, country, the Western alliance, the Communist, etc., had its way, that is, had enough power to force its views on the other side, then the issues would be resolved.

By focusing our creative efforts on life's contingencies for ourselves or our tribe instead of the global community so that everyone would benefit, we pursue technical solutions that provide "freedom from" instead of "freedom for." This kind of response also tends to pit us against one another for what we perceive are scarce resources. We are continually changing the name of our insecurity, and redefining what will relieve us. We know how to store food and keep ourselves warm in the winter and cool in the summer. We have lengthened the lives of many, but we still must die, and the extra years do not automatically become better, only different, and we continue to have many of the same problems as the people we read about in Genesis.

Religious tradition since that time has interpreted the story of Genesis as an all-encompassing dependence upon God. Most concepts of deities imply a dependence. The Jewish innovation lay in conceiving of dependence on a chief God, one in charge of everything, instead of fertility gods, weather gods, household gods, and so on. Whatever human nature is, the theological concepts of human helplessness and dependency upon God serve no practical purpose, and may be one of the most destructive ideas that humans have retained from early times. When humans become convinced that some task is beyond doing the result is likely to be apathy. We need ideas that encourage us to push on and keep searching for ideas that promote the kind of consciousness that truly liberates us. This is ostensibly the purpose behind the theological enterprise. However, the Catholic magisterium teaches us that if we admit our helplessness and dependency, perform all of the required rituals, and obey the rules of the group, we will prosper, however prosperity may be defined. Some persons have undoubtedly found hope and encouragement in this formula, but as in most human enterprises, foolishness prevails all too often. Rituals tend to become meaningless motions, and rules become formally observed or ignored without an understanding of their purpose. If we ask a clergyman why we must obey a particular rule that does not have an observable effect upon us or on our relationships, e.g., Sunday worship, the response is generally, "Because God says so," or "We say so." We can find good reasons to gather for worship on Sunday or any day. "Because God says so," is not one of them.

Theological concepts of "good" and "evil" as the church teaches them are not helpful with either our genetic dispositions or environmental forces that determine our behavior in some ways. There is no way to have a direct experience of what relating to a transcendent God could mean. If we adopt a humanistic morality based on global family values we will not have to refer to something outside of ourselves to know whether what we have done is right or wrong. The other person or persons will let us know in some way, or if we are capable of learning from experience we may realize our failure after the fact, perhaps long after when some unrelated incident triggers reflection. Our concern should be with liberating ourselves from any absolute concept of what we are, ought to be, or ought to become. The only possible way of avoiding victimization by genetic, environmental and authoritarian factors is to question the shape given to our lives by these forces, and to ask what if anything might be done about it.

Living in a society, as we all must in the beginning, liberates us up to a point. It gives us language and ways of thinking and acting that free us from the more difficult aspects of living, but what it gives with one hand it takes with the other. In addition to giving us patterns of thinking and acting there is also a strong tendency to force us to conform to given behavior patterns. A variety of sanctions that range from mild disapproval to death are used to this end. Then there is the ever present tendency toward closure which inhibits learning. A forced conformity can be justified only on the grounds of a real and present danger, for example, not letting children play with knives. More frequently, however, enforcement is based on the belief that the enforcers are in possession of *the* Truth.

When people are obsessed by the belief that they know how God wants us to act, they assume that people who act differently are not only unnatural they are also offending God. This belief compels them to act in God's interest by enforcing conformity on other adults as well as children by banning "dirty" books and movies and whatever else is seen as morally dangerous. We need to protect children from predatory adults for the children's sake not for God's. Unfortunately we cannot act directly to save children from indoctrination by adults who believe that the children must conform to the wishes of a supreme being that cannot be seen nor heard by anyone. Adults who act as though they know with certainty what God wants have been given this assurance by their respective clergy, but all adults, including clergy, share the same limitation as their children--an absolute inability to communicate directly with a transcendent God.

When we examine interpersonal relationships we will see that God as immanent can communicate with us through other humans when we permit it. The clergy may argue that they have God's word in scripture and tradition to act as mediators between God and humans, but their arguments fail to take into account that Scripture needs interpretation, and not all clergy are blest with adequate understanding of even the interpretations they have been taught. History reveals a progressive evolution of morality from the abysmally stupid practices of earlier ages--the torture and burning of witches and heretics; the crusades to kill infidels, notably the children's crusade; the deep involvement of Church officials in politics after the fall of Rome; the canonization of Greek philosophy, and so on.

The world is evolving toward ethnically, linguistically and religiously pluralistic societies. In many countries, even in parts of the United States, people are no longer arrested for so-called deviant sex offenses, and at least legally people's life chances are not as completely limited by race and ethnicity as they once were. The death penalty has been abolished in many countries and some states in our own country. The religious and nationalistic fervor which sustains hostilities between peoples still survives in many places but is increasingly seen by many of us as barbaric and futile, if only for economic reasons. Although the trend toward progressive moral evolution is slow we are no more likely to reverse it than we are to reestablish the divine right of kings.

The hierarchy of human worth once thought to have been established by God is still with us but the idea has changed from ascribed or inherited worth to its being acquired. As humans become better informed they stop accepting their subordinate roles passively like other animals. We do not generally find baboons and chimpanzees sneaking up behind the dominant males to do them in. Nor do we see their females staging mass rallies and protests over the way they are treated. Male baboons may, when the dominant male falters, challenge him according to their custom, but they seem otherwise accepting of their position in the hierarchy of the group. Humans, however, seem to need a sense of dignity, some reason for self-esteem, or whatever label we may attach to the need. In societies where a hierarchy of social classes is accepted as the norm some dignity may be attached to whatever role a person may have. In such cases contentment may be found in being a good butler, shoemaker, nanny, or in whatever role a person may be cast. But in our society (U.S. 2002) people are not supposed to have an ascribed value, nor do they have a value in themselves, despite what our Declaration of Independence says. One's class, hence one's personal value, is theoretically earned. Actually it is determined according to occupation, wealth, skin color, and a host of other status indicators, some of which are acquired while others are ascribed. Among people who have not yet "arrived" there is some value attached to striving for upward mobility, so that so-called good students have a value. Homeless people, those on welfare and other marginal types out of the pursuit have little. A good bit of the crime in our culture, especially white-collar crime results from the pursuit of status indicators--good clothes, fine automobiles, the social approval of wealth, and so--by people unequipped or unwilling for whatever reason to fit into the socially proper economic system. The idolatry of believing that God sanctions a world of winners and losers has not changed since Job.

My experience in trying to teach morality to students between the ages of twelve and twenty-five, male and female, is that they have poor notions of right and wrong apart from what they have been told, especially when what they have been told is not consistent with the behavior of the adults who have taught them. Invariably they utter nonsense such as, "I know what's wrong, but I do it anyway." Anyone with a personal conviction of some behavior being wrong, i.e., not in their own best long-term interest, would avoid that behavior. The "wrong" behavior that people "do anyway" is generally a violation of a rule espoused by adults for which the perpetrator lacks understanding and conviction, especially if the violator is not caught. In other words they are referring to a code that is external to themselves.

If conscience is a part of human nature, it is not a little voice in our heads inerrantly telling us right from wrong. Perhaps the best that we can say of conscience in relation to human nature is that we are born with a need to live among other humans, and our need to be social means there are certain behaviors that will enhance living together and promote harmony while others are divisive. In other words every conscience starts with the same first element, "Survive!" What specific behaviors are required to survive remain to be determined by the humans who have to live with the rules they make. Briefly we may state that what people regard as sin in one place may not be so in another. Since we are born without specific survival skills other than a few reflex behaviors (sucking, coughing, sneezing) the requirements of survival have to be learned, such as avoiding extremes of temperatures, the dangers of breaching the skin, what is toxic if inhaled or ingested, the effects of gravity and so on. From the need to learn to survive and our absolute dependence upon others, all oughts have emerged. Even in those religions that view conscience as the means that will enable one to attain an afterlife, the moral codes primarily serve to maintain peace and harmony within the tribe. The problem with such codes is that they can pit tribes against one another.

The future of humanity depends to a great degree on how we train and educate our children. What we do to them, with them and for them and the examples we set will establish the patterns they generally follow throughout their lives. If history teaches anything it is that if we persist on our present course the current mess will be carried forward into the next generation, perhaps magnified many times due to the larger number of people involved, the technological rape of the planet, and the massive intrusions of media in our lives. Therefore, the theory of human nature we use as a basis for educating children is significant. The Roman Catholic magisterium, having canonized the Thomistic philosophy, is in the inflexible position of having to teach that human nature does not change. Consequently, they deal with the world's problems by rationalizing why we have them, e.g., Original Sin, and cannot get rid of them instead of proposing practical solutions.

There is also the matter of our use of the world's resources. The rules by which we will survive must generate peace and harmony among people, or at minimum be non-divisive. Such rules will help us to establish and maintain bonds by the way we act with, for and toward one another. Since much of what we do affects other humans, near and far, present and future, much of our behavior has an inescapable moral quality. Therefore we need to develop a global consciousness to have a proper morality. We have to become more knowledgeable because our problems have become more complicated.

Unraveling basic human nature from the culture in which it grows and develops is no easy task despite some very obvious distinctions. It is natural to eat, but what we eat, how we prepare what we eat, and so on, is cultural. Speaking seems natural, but our language, like our food is cultural. Our culture feels natural to us, and so the culture of others feels unnatural, except in those areas where it resembles ours. For good or ill, the concept people have of human nature is more significant than what human nature might actually be. Whether we regard humans as created directly by God, evolved from nonhuman creatures, or some combination of these two ideas, we are here, and being here puts us face to face with certain problems that have plagued humanity from the beginning. We may choose not to deal with these problems, but the problems persist in affecting us. We cannot escape a moral stance. We are obliged to respond to the age-old question: "Am I my brother's keeper?" but hopefully in non-sexist way.

We call our species Homo Sapiens, but we seem to have overstated our qualifications. If intelligence is for survival, in comparing ourselves with other primates we appear to be intelligent because we can survive under a greater variety of circumstances. But the validity of this judgment obviously depends on what we mean by *intelligence* and *surviving* because surviving is not a one-time event. The other primates are more dependent for their survival upon what the environment offers, as was the case for humans at one time. Now we are dependent upon our technology in order to create livable environments such as large cities far from food sources. If the creation of such technologies were strictly for the welfare of all humans it would indeed be proper moral behavior and we could call it intelligent, i.e., behavior that is in humanity's best interest, but there are serious questions concerning whether we can, as a people, say this of our behavior.

The most important rule for being morally intelligent is to be constantly aware that what we think is in our best interest must remain tentative at best. Gouldner speaks of a "view of science [that] emphasizes man's vulnerability to error [and] the wisdom of the past" (1971:266). This is the kind of intelligent disposition everyone needs. There will always be more factors involved in our future than we can possibly know. We have to ask ourselves if pursuing the demands of a lifestyle that generates so many losers on a global scale can be in our long-term interest.

We would be hard-pressed to find individuals who did not believe that they ordinarily act in their own best interest. Even people who commit suicide believe this. So do murderers, rapists, drug addicts, and child molesters. This means that for humans, intelligence is a possibility rather than a fact. The other possibility is Ignorance II, as noted in the Prologue, a condition in which faulty knowledge effectively blocks our ability to learn. With this extreme kind of closure a state has been achieved in which a person is inhibited from learning either by prior learning, or the belief that the person already has certain knowledge. Most of us, for example, are ignorant in this way about foreign language. Our prior knowledge of our own language inhibits the acquisition of another language. To learn a foreign language we need to establish new neural pathways, and overcome the strong tendency to slip into the old ones. Ignorance II as the opposite of intelligence can be overcome; it requires becoming aware of our profound ignorance, meaning the depth of our ignorance, and accepting it, thus providing us with a greater opportunity to learn. With this criteria it seems that much of what we learn in religion and especially the way we learn it, results in Ignorance II. Any knowledge we have must forever remain tentative.

Because of the problems resulting from closure, belief in our own open-mindedness is inherently suspect. Very few of us doubt our ability to learn from experience. Faith in our open-mindedness results from the way experience seems to confirm what we know instead of teaching us. Vision is generally our most trusted sense. We even have a saying, "Seeing is believing." So we would expect that if we could learn from any experience it would be visually. But optical illusions belie certainty in visual experience. Knowing that a stick is straight does not keep it from appearing bent in water. In a drawing, the line that appears shorter may actually be longer. An intellectual awareness that the world turns does not change our perception that it stands still. There are some kinds of misperceptions that experience cannot help.

Time or distance between a behavior and its consequences is another problem. When most of us touch a hot object the immediate burn translates into a learning experience. We may burn ourselves on another object, or even the same object at another time, but we usually learn caution. Some consequences are so remote that it is hard for us to make the connection between the behavior and the dire consequences--smoking, drinking contaminated water, not protecting one's ears from loud noises. Missing opportunities to learn in or out of school because we see no use for what is being offered can also have long-term consequences. Passive and conforming students may be preferred to the creative and challenging ones by our overworked teachers (Getzel and Jackson 1963:160) but learning anything of significance requires active, critical participation.

Challenges by students to the current system of schooling are responded to by rationalizations rather than reasons. When students ask, "Why do I have to take..." this or that subject, what teacher is wise enough to know what any particular student needs? Unfortunately most students do not know how to ask troublesome questions, and they learn early that most adults, not just teachers, prefer passivity and conformity. The best answer to why anyone should take a course is that the system requires that the course be passed if one plans to continue schooling, which begs the question of how it might meet the personal needs of any individual. The idea that a person needs schooling in order to survive economically (i.e., "get a good job" as it is sometimes expressed) is part of our culture's mythology. If a person has to learn in order to survive economically, there may be more efficient ways of doing this than through our current system of schooling. Students do not generally know this, nor do they learn it from the experience of schooling itself, because in our culture the ideas of schooling and education are considered synonymous. When at the beginning of every new class I wrote on the board, "Don't let school interfere with your education," the statement seemed strange to most students. How many students think of school as a "sorting mechanism" to separate the winners from the losers (Gatto 1991:56)?

Except for the prohibitions of violence against persons and the destruction or taking of property, the possibility of moral consensus in the matter of specific rules is receding, consequently a workable, nondivisive pluralism must be our goal. The fact that we subscribe to different moralities is evidence that human nature does not come with a pre-formed conscience as suggested by some religions. We have to find or create whatever morality we will have. Even the one rule we can count on being built-in, viz., *survive*, is nonspecific. Later we will examine four moralities that can be reduced to two, 1) save one's self, cooperating with others when it provides an advantage, disregarding the consequences to others when no harm to oneself is perceived. 2) Save oneself as a member of a community, acting to promote and sustain a system that provides an opportunity for all members to survive, including a system of support for those who are incapacitated, mentally or physically. Exclusive, limited communities belong to the first category. They have a tribal morality, while those who believe in a global community belong to the second. Theirs is a family morality extended to everyone.

Part of our claim to being more intelligent than other species rests on our ability to survive under a variety of conditions, including those where we could not survive in a natural state such as under the sea or above the atmosphere. By focusing upon economic survival we seem not to notice that we do not "live by bread alone," that we have aesthetic needs too. These aesthetic needs, like the need for food or shelter, is to a great extent shaped by the culture, hence by the grand myth and various lesser myths of the culture. We live with a kind of picture, to use a metaphor, of the way life should be, and how all the parts that make up the picture should be. When the big picture lacks coherence our feelings may range from discomfort to seriously disturbed. This may explain why infants and older persons are reported to have died from lack of attention, or why losing one's fortune can lead to suicide, or even why a person will gamble away money needed for food and shelter in the hope of winning a fortune. There are many patterns of behavior in our culture that are self-destructive, hence unintelligent to various degrees, yet like traditional schooling they are standard parts of our apparent survival package.

The various senses we use to put us in touch with the world are part of our human nature, but they are not distinctively human. We share these capabilities with other animals who seem to be better equipped than us in many respect--birds see better, dogs smell better, cats have a better sense of balance, and so on. However, if we had better sense equipment we might be less human. Part of being human means being less dependent upon our senses for survival and more on our wits and on each other. Our knowledge of what counts as being human has reached a point at which social evolution could progress in a conscious manner. We have a number of progressive ideas available to us, but we cannot bring them to bear on our problems because they contradict our dominant myth in its secular and religious versions, particularly in the matter of winners and losers. This myth rests on the implicit idea of personal salvation, a scheme whereby a few are saved and many are lost. In its secular version, a few get rich and many are impoverished. A person would have to be stupid to be concerned with progressive social evolution for a global community while living according to such a myth.

Progressive evolution does not mean, as some have thought, creating superior biological specimens through eugenics, nor by creating a middle-class lifestyle for everyone through the spread of technology. Instead, we must be conscious of developing a global community for the best interest of everyone. We need a system within which at least everyone's basic needs could be met. Not everyone wants to be rich or even middle class, but our present system militates against poverty with dignity in highly industrialized countries. Because mobility is possible in our system, one's status is both "the penalty and proof of personal failure" when one does not rise (Potter 1965:105). The technologies that could enable us to provide for greater numbers of people are unfortunately not committed to the benefit of all humans. They are used to make war, to make profits, and a host of divisive and self-destructive uses instead of providing for the survival of everyone. This is not intelligent behavior even for the winners as Bonhoeffer noted (1976:11). Even when technology seems to have had the purpose of helping everyone to survive, e.g., immunization of third world people, regressive social policies have resulted in death by starvation for large numbers of those same people.

Whatever chance we have of gaining the freedom that matters, we must first get rid of the notion that we are born free, or that we are free when we reach a certain stage of consciousness, or that we are free because we live in a free society, or because according to St. Thomas our wills are a function of our "immortal souls." Freedom may be thought of as a narrow window of possibility opening at odd moments in our lives, particularly when we are learning and in times of crisis. The open window is not always there. Taking advantage of the opportunity when it arrives requires a mental readiness that begins with the admission of an abiding ignorance of what is in our own best, long-term interest, and an even grosser ignorance with respect to the best interest of everyone else. For if freedom comes from knowledge there is a certain kind of knowledge about ourselves that is essential, and this knowledge cannot be taught only learned, usually in a relationship. Most of our knowledge is transitory, uncertain, and relative, in part because life is contingent. We try so hard to eliminate contingencies by controlling as much of life as we can. We went from finding or catching our food and other necessities to the domestication of plants and animals, to the development of ways to store our necessities, to specialization, to the invention of money, and so on, and life still remains contingent for everyone and impossible for some. We have no way of seeing a future we would be better off accepting as uncertain even as we prepare for it.

The New Testament demonstrates an evolutionary leap beyond Jewish Scriptures regarding what is proper in human relationships, but the message has been transformed into one of attaining personal salvation. Faith can mean believing in the absence of evidence, but accepting certain Biblical statements as factual requires faith despite the evidence. There is little to choose between religions that teach that the only way we can be saved is to throw ourselves on the mercy of God and those scientists and philosophers who claim that God and free will are myths, and that human behavior is determined by so-called natural laws, as is everything else in the universe. A bit of the old Greek idea of Fate is evident in both views, although some atheistic scientists and philosophers seem to be more willing to take responsibility for what happens in the world instead of blaming or crediting God, or worse, blaming people who believe in God.

In any case we cannot ignore the contributions of science in the last hundred years to our knowledge of what it means to be human. The churches may not think so but this is also revelation. Most of the churches have accepted what science has learned about nature but are still dragging their feet on what we have learned about humans. Their position is not much better than popular notions of what is natural and human. If we want to know if a certain behavior is a manifestation of intelligence or its lack, we need more knowledge of its context than is generally available to us. We need, as Bateson says, two sources of information to know, the way that two eyes give us better depth perception (1980:79-81). We are usually limited to our own histories as the only relevant context we might possibly know. A dialectical sharing of knowledge in intimate relationships is one of the better ways for us to gain the dual sources of information Bateson describes that leads to better self knowledge.

Understanding and wisdom are not directly transferable from one person to another. Examples of what being intelligent means can be provided, but we cannot make another person intelligent, anymore than we can make another person happy. In the case of children we can provide barriers to intelligent behavior by confusing them and distracting them from optimum development, or by teaching them that making mistakes is bad instead of demonstrating that it is one of the better ways to learn from experience. In short it is easier to mess up young heads than it is to set them on the path of making optimal choices, which is what intelligence and freedom should be about.

Optimal choices can only come about by operating from those principles that lead to and maintain open-mindedness, the ultimate survival characteristic. These principles can be expressed in a number of ways: All knowledge is tentative. If what I know is adequate for today, it may not be for tomorrow. I must, therefore always be in a learning mode. We learn from our culture ways of functioning in the world that come to seem natural. Thus we become biased against differences in our own or in other cultures. Feeling knowledge is more important to us than so-called objective knowledge. All of these principles have one characteristic in common. They all require us to reflect seriously on the way we think and act, but the means for such reflection are not as a rule provided in our culture, and because of our apparent need for closure, the first pattern we grasp tends to become *the* pattern.

The need to organize our world into patterns and achieve certainty constantly comes up against the tendency of the world toward change that maintains our contingent status. This means that we cannot solve human problems once and for all time. The human mind abhors chaos and uncertainty but we do not deal with them intelligently by continually trying to prevent change. The tendency of the world to change means that our knowledge has to match the constant flux of reality. When we do not accept the fact that insecurity is part of being human we are likely to act self-destructively. The history of the world is littered with the wreckage of schemes designed to achieve absolute certainty, which may explain why in our contemporary world religions are beset by one crisis after another.

Religions exemplify the difficulty humans have learning from experience. We keep trying to put reality in a box, but it keeps slipping away from us. The attempt to produce certainty and eliminate contingencies has had the opposite effect of what we intended. Religious leaders invent doctrines such as "Original Sin" Then we learn that Adam and Eve are fictional characters. We invented agriculture and animal husbandry in order to secure our food supply. Then we invented farm machinery and strategies for creating surplus food, yet millions have died in recent years from starvation. We now experience more change in a decade than humans once experienced in a century. We live in a constant and rapidly increasing flux. Thus, ignorance of our species that drives us toward order (stable patterns), and the tendency toward closure that leads us to accept the first order that we find or create as *the* order aggravates our problems. Expressed in another way: the dominant aspect of our nature, the ignorance that drives us toward survival and provides an opportunity to become wise is countered by the bio-psychological tendency toward closure which renders us unable to learn if we accept the resulting knowledge as final or absolute. Instead of pursuing order we should pursue organization, i.e., how we might best connect with others to solve our common problems instead of seeking the secular equivalent of personal salvation. Organization can only come about through communication.

The answer to the question "What is human nature?" may be answered by saying, humans are what they become, and they have some small choice in the matter, though they may not know it and may not learn about it. The apparent disadvantage of being born without the knowledge of how to survive has resulted in a multiplicity of ways to survive, all of them good at various times and in various places. The theory of what it means to be human is ours to create. We need no longer be victims of the culture, hence, of the myth into which we are born. Passivity in learning and knowing is unintelligent because survival requires us to change to confront a changing world. Insofar as we can we need to make explicit the patterns of knowledge and behavior by which we live. The unconscious repetitive behaviors we call habits are hard to break because habits are items within a larger pattern, not the pattern itself. If we cannot break a habit then our choices are obviously limited. Habits have value only in those aspects of life which are trivial--which shoelaces we tie first, what we eat, what we wear, and so on.

Our people habits are especially pernicious. People are not things, and our responses to them must be based upon an attitude of learning from the experience of engagement, rather than reacting to them as though they were types. Among all the changing events in the world, there are none so changing as people. People are potentially the greatest source of the contingencies that can be so disturbing to us; they can also provide the greatest opportunities for the satisfaction we crave. As we grow and learn we enhance the intelligence with which we were born and hopefully attain optimum freedom. It will not do for us to see people as types and then react to the types instead of the persons. If our aesthetic sense is violated by our perception of another person, our perception may be at fault rather than the personality or behavior of the other person. People question their perceptions this way when they are in love, or are otherwise intimate. We cannot love everyone, nor can we be intimate with everyone. The fact of closure makes too many differences in others intolerable to all but a few. We can, however, develop an openness to others that will insure that we act with each person as intelligently as we are able and we never miss an opportunity to connect and to learn.

CHAPTER V
LANGUAGE, MEANING AND MORALITY

Traditional theology was premised upon language as transparent, unproblematic, capturing the objective reality and communicating it without bias. . . .William McSweeny

Words can only suggest truth; they cannot encompass it. Our thinking is historically conditioned and the words we use always come from some biased perspective. For nineteen centuries official church truth held that slavery was justifiable. This "truth" had illustrious proponents--St. Ambrose, St. Augustine and Martin Luther. "Augustine had rationalized slavery as being . . . part of divine retribution for the fall from grace" (Maguire 1979:230). Clearly, truth is not what we have; it is what we must seek. We are truth seeking animals, another way of saying that we are learning animals. Learning when it pertains to the survival of humanity is revelation. The doctrines and dogmas we have are various stages in that revelation or learning process. They may furnish hints and clues to the truth. They can never be the truth, especially not if, as the church teaches, God is Truth.

For centuries, the Catholic magisterium has taught as truth that the priest in the act of consecration during the Mass changed the bread and wine into the body and blood of Jesus, giving the impression that it was this way from the beginning. Protestants have strongly disagreed. They consider it a symbolic action. We now know that the idea of transubstantiation developed during the first two centuries of the Christian era. Also, the words of consecration used by the priest

131

cannot have been what Jesus said. Aramaic has no copulative. Jesus would have said, "This my body," and "This my blood," (Martos 1981:241). This could be interpreted as "This will become my body," and "This will become my blood"? By sharing the bread and wine the disciples would have participated in a symbolic act of communion. This interpretation does not deny the "real presence," and it fits the Protestant version of the "truth." If as Jesus said, "Where two or more are gathered in my name, I am there with them" (Mat. 18:20), the "real presence" becomes a non-issue. Those who believe the Catholic magisterium's interpretation and those who do not may both experience the "real presence." Interpreting the Eucharist in this fashion makes good ecumenical sense by making diversity non-divisive thereby contributing to the progressive evolution of human consciousness. Originally people gathered at someone's house to share a commemorative meal. There was no priest to consecrate a Eucharist. The meal was a sacred sharing that brought them together in a special way that can properly be called Communion.

We can no longer doubt that history reveals the progressive evolution of human consciousness. In the chapter on revelation we learned that an evolutionary perspective is the only one that permits a consistent reading and interpretation of the Bible without having to make excuses for factual errors, strange science and crediting God with violence. Up to now learning what kind of creatures we are has been unavoidably slow and erratic. We have not had an adequate base in experience to figure it out. The Gospels offer a loose but fairly consistent collection of ideas from which we can infer the kind of changes we should make in our thinking and behavior in order to continue the process of evolution, but except in science we have no social structures specifically promoting the progressive evolution of consciousness. Perhaps we have now reached a stage at which we can gain greater control over the process by finding the reasons behind the ancient prescriptions and proscriptions for human behavior. We can then discard what is irrelevant to the wisdom of the ages. By discerning what is reasonable within tradition people will be less likely to unreflectively discard the whole business which is what seems to be happening now.

In this chapter we will examine how language and communication simultaneously liberates and binds us in our movement toward a proper morality, one we can all live with. An analysis of language can help us become aware of the extent to which language affects and even determines our thinking so that we may gain some measure of freedom from the constraints inherent in language. For example, accepting the body-soul dualism in Christian thinking and the necessity of saving the "soul" part tends to distracts us from our proper concern, viz., working to establish the reign of God in this world. Although the magisterium teaches that we have a unitary existence, that body and soul are not two separate substances, they still claim a disembodied existence for our "immortal souls" at death. Recently John Paul II while affirming that humans probably evolved from lower life forms, wrote that we are required to believe that there were no humans until God infused a human soul and that each conception repeats the process. Imagining God operating so inefficiently is one more manifestation of idolatry.

Soul is a concept adopted from the Greeks, primarily Plato and Aristotle. Souls were needed by the church at one time to account for what seemed to be immaterial experiences such as intelligence and imagination. In addition "souls" appeared to be necessary to account for what happened between death and resurrection. The mystery of "souls" has served as an aid to the church in maintaining control of the faithful. At some point in our lives we all have the experience of being in the presence of a corpse. What this experience says to the unsophisticated mind is that something is missing. This "something" in popular thinking is a soul. Are there disembodied substances floating around somewhere? No one knows.

No one, not the pope and the college of cardinals nor any of the hierarchy, can tell us what happens after death. The theory concerning the afterlife on which church doctrine is based is an interpretation of certain Biblical passages that could be interpreted in other ways. If we are preoccupied with saving our souls we are directing our activities toward a goal about which we can know nothing in order to save an entity that may not exist. The church has permitted, when it has not actually encouraged, the idea of saving our souls to promote good behavior. All pre-Vatican II Catholics have been taught the necessity of saving their "immortal souls." In the context of personal salvation, "good behavior" means following church rules. Thus we may treat our neighbor well for the purpose of saving our souls rather than because that is good and satisfying in itself. Much of our failure to follow the rules can be directly attributed to the nebulous nature of that enterprise. We are conscious of being alive, but there can be no consciousness of having a soul. The morality offered to us by the church remains outside of us instead of becoming *our* morality because of its apparent disconnection from what is real. The temptation to break a church rule arises from the concreteness of what tempts us in contrast with the fuzzy unreality of the alleged rewards and punishments connected with church morality. Satisfaction has to come from within as a result of good behavior itself as it does with what is considered bad behavior, as in "revenge is sweet." I am not denying an afterlife. I merely wish to point out that our proper pursuit is here on earth and we do not know what awaits us beyond the grave.

In much recent writing about the church we find a distinction made between horizontal and vertical theology. John Paul II and the current curia seem overly preoccupied with the latter which Gary MacEoin (NCR Dec. 26, 1997, p. 18) describes as a concern with "an individual relationship with a Christ up there in the clouds . . ." Further back in time James Carney, S.J. saw the Catholic leadership insisting that the hierarchy stay out of political affairs and focus on administration of the sacraments, which is another way of saying that priests should attend to the problem of "saving souls" instead of trying to change the structures that oppress the poor (1985:289; see also Bokenkotter 1998:512). Such thinking is based partly on the assumption that injustice will be remedied in a life beyond this one and partly on the remnants of the theory that supported slavery, viz., that our station in life has been established by God. Such a perspective reveals a failure to recognize the *de facto* support this gives to the rich and powerful who are often oppressors. It also fails to take into account the great middle class in developed countries who do not feel oppressed, hence are not motivated to take certain aspects of church morality seriously because they do not require a redress of injustice in the next life. In other words the prospect of heaven does not have the motivating force it once had.

Prof. Scott Russell Sanders tells us that putting too much stock in eternal salvation is a species of despair. "Only people who are convinced there can be no relief in this world will fix all their hopes on some other one" (1998:36). The upper and middle classes are less likely to be motivated by a morality that does not provide satisfaction here and now and this can only occur if the Catholic magisterium and the various churches teach a morality backed by reasons that make sense here and now. Even the desperately poor, led by liberation theologians are beginning to look for relief of economic injustice in this world instead of waiting for God to make things right in the next despite John Paul II's declaration of liberation theology's irrelevance.

In the matter of sexual morality, if the church wants people to abstain from sex before marriage, they must present convincing arguments that sex outside of marriage can harm persons or have a destructive effect on community. Unfortunately for the church the reasons for abstinence are subtle, based as they are on the nature of true intimacy between persons. That it is wrong because God or the church says so carries little conviction. This is also the case with any moral prescription or proscription. How will the magisterium teach moral refinement, which is where progressive, cognitive evolution should be taking us, when it is unable to persuade people to keep the basic moral code of the church? I suggest a return to the basic teaching of Jesus in scripture where the primary emphasis is on a concern for our neighbors, a horizontal theology, and a challenge we can understand. St. John writes, "How can we love God whom we can't see when we do not love our neighbor whom we can see? By analogy, how can we be drawn to a community of saints in a heaven we cannot see when we are not drawn to a community of our brothers and sisters on earth that we can see. There are four good earthly reasons for adopting a morality that emphasizes community formation here and now instead of one that is supposed to get us into heaven: 1) We are necessarily social and connecting with other humans is its own reward, especially intimate connections that involve our whole beings; and 2) unlike trying to connect with God "up there and out there," this kind of activity falls within our competence; 3) it is the only way we will survive as a species; 4) if our behavior creates effects in a world beyond this one, how could we know what they are?

In the introductory chapter I suggested a definition of *morality* that most of us could agree on, at least for purposes of discussion, i.e., morality is the rules or the principle from which such rules can be derived that determine how we act with, for or toward other humans. A common understanding of morality is that it is the rules revealed by God and promulgated by religion, and is the opposite of immorality. Since each person's moral code varies somewhat, any discussion of the subject with a religious definition might immediately entail a conflict of judgments over whose morality is proper instead of starting as it should with an agreement of what is being discussed. There is also the fact that religious morality tends to be an external code to which the faithful are supposed to adhere. In such a moral system there are many failures (sins) because, 1) the faithful are not operating from conviction; 2) they are taught that it is impossible not to fail (Rondet 1972:165), giving them implicit permission to fail; 3) the rules sometimes seem to contradict experience, which is not supposed to matter because they are creating an effect in another realm from which there is no feedback; and, 4) the penalty for violating the rules, hell, and the reward, for keeping them, heaven, are too remote to be effective for an increasingly educated citizenry. The magical view of heaven has been more attractive to the poor and oppressed because until the development of liberation theology they have had no other source of hope in their desperate situation.

By linking morality to survival and distinguishing those items of morality that promote or reduce the chances of survival from those that have little or no direct bearing on whether we survive as individuals or groups, our chances of arriving at a consensus of what is in fact a proper morality are vastly improved. This scheme offers the advantage of leaving untouched parochial religious morality for those who retain faith in what their religions teach, provided they do not try to coerce others into living according to their morality. The standards arrived at by such discussions of what is a proper morality would have the merit of being directly linked to experience and would not have the negative and usually divisive effect of parochial religious moralities. Public nudity, for example, has no direct effect on survival of individuals or the species. It does however offend the sensibilities of those who think it is a sin. Since an important factor in the survival of humanity is social harmony, hence an important element in a proper morality, it is appropriate for those who want to be nude in public to have places for that purpose where they will be free to be nude and free from harassment by those who disapprove. Civil laws that prohibit such places force one group to obey the parochial moral code of another group. This contributes to social disharmony just as much as being nude where it will offend those who think it is wrong. From these considerations we can derive a basic principle of a proper morality: Coercion in moral matters that do not bear directly on survival cannot be part of a proper morality. The contending parties should settle differences through negotiation.

Stealing does not in itself kill anyone although some people are so attached to their possessions that they may want to kill. However, stealing in a culture of scarcity where what is stolen directly affects someone's survival has a different moral quality than in a culture of abundance. Since there are more people in the world whose lives depend on what they own, and since we can never tell from appearances who does and who does not need their possessions for their life and well-being, civil safeguards such as laws and police are entirely appropriate to enforce this aspect of morality because we can legislate morality when a consensus exists. In addition, stealing generates social disorganization whatever the circumstances. And so it is with many of the rules by which humans live, even some of the more seemingly arbitrary ones.

We should see from what has been said so far that some of these issues are easily resolvable while others are not. The necessity for public discussion should be apparent, making it important to understand how communication succeeds or fails. Up to now public morality has been decided by those with the power, which at one time meant the churches. Now, however, the power apparently belongs to the majority, but their coercive power is somewhat tempered by the court system (a form of discussion, although contentious) which was not the case when the church reigned supreme in society and in moral matters.

Our goal should be a code, or better still principles from which rules can be derived as needed, so that every individual is operating from conviction. A further requirement of a proper morality has to be that each individual must be prepared to learn from every person and in every situation. St. Thomas Aquinas described us as rational animals. A more accurate description would be that we are learning animals with some rational capability. Such talent for rationality as people have is often used for rationalizing (making excuses) than critical reasoning. The problem with reasoning, as has been noted, is that it must start with premises, not all of which are self-evident to everyone. This accounts for why Thomas' philosophy has been superseded in many respects. I suggest that we need a new kind of consciousness, one that can be found among those who are sufficiently evolved but which is not itself promoted by religious officials.

The moral significance of the problems we have in using language to connect with one another is primary because it is at the level of committed pairs and small groups that I believe the foundation for a global family morality will be established, and the language used for such connecting is precisely the language that is inherently problematic. Its problematic nature arises in part from the diversity of cultural backgrounds of the people trying to connect. It also lacks the kind of empirical associations which would make it unproblematic for us such as "chairs," "tables," "trees," and so on. Unless we become conscious of this difference we will act as if the language of morality reflects reality in the same way as empirical language. There can be no guarantee that our use of *love, God, beauty, sin* and the like will be understood by another person.

A different set of problems arise in the use of language to establish and maintain interpersonal relationships because couples come from increasingly diverse backgrounds. However, they generally begin with a strong motivation for resolving differences and when the greater effort required to understand each other succeeds it provide the most satisfaction that humans can have. This success benefits all of humanity. Connected couples provide the only basis for a global community. When individuals resolve their differences in a relationship they will not build up a fund of frustration and hostility to pass on to those outside of the relationship. And finally, the skill learned in resolving interpersonal problems is transferable to resolving differences with others. Unfortunately this communication skill--listening with the intention of learning, and speaking to self-disclose--is not what the various religions usually teach in connection with interpersonal relationships. The more fundamentalist religions, including official Roman Catholicism, have generally promoted wife/mother and husband/father roles rather than the development of intimacy between couples, a pernicious instance of the church's minimum standards. We are at a stage in our moral evolution where learning communication skills has become a necessity for creating a viable lifelong commitment to another person. We cannot enter these relationships with the expectations people had in homogeneous societies.

In developing an intimate relationship we have problems in addition to the lack of language skills and the lack of courage to self-disclose. Institutionalized social structures other than language that affect interpersonal relationships and roles that people acquire unconsciously contain serious obstacles to intimacy that are not likely to be overcome unless these structures and roles are to some extent made explicit so they can be dealt with. Social structures change slowly, probably from the cumulative effect of change in many individuals as, for example, the residual racism in this country (USA) clearly demonstrates. Consequently we must deal with these structures by understanding how they affect us so we can to some extent negate their effect within ourselves where these structures actually reside.

Once while discussing the origin of life with a doctor, I suggested that to say God created life is no more amazing than to say that it began by accident. He replied that scientists claim that it began by chance not by accident. Now, *accident* and *chance* do not express exactly the same idea, but they both imply that an event arising from either one is neither by choice nor design. The doctor knew as well as I did that these words have this characteristic in common. Apparently some unstated idea underlay his response. What it was I can only guess. Perhaps it implied a defense of his agnosticism. Although not intended, my reference to God could have been understood as supporting creationism in the sense that it is believed in by Christian fundamentalists. The presuppositions that led to our thinking differently were invisible hence our respective thoughts seemed natural to us but not to each other.

This anecdote illustrates one of the difficulties that needs to be resolved in our search for an intelligent morality, both on an interpersonal level, which I call moral refinement, and for larger groups. That is, in matters of importance we must negotiate meanings in attempting to communicate because an intelligent morality on the level of society must originate with connections between and among individual humans. If we take for granted that others hold the same meaning for words such as *creation, wisdom, God, intelligence* or even *survival*, misunderstanding is inevitable. Arguments over what is meant by such words may seem to imply that there is some objective reality that goes by the name. One or both sides may believe they know the reality corresponding to the word, for example what "God" means for an atheist or agnostic. Such arguments are futile. If we already "know," then we cannot learn. Our knowledge has become dogma, another name for Ignorance II.

All dogma is inherently problematic as a basis for communication except among those with faith in the same dogmas. This is the case whether the dogma is from science or religion, hence we are unlikely to connect with some persons through dogma. Intelligence enables us to survive by prompting us to gather sufficient information, interpret it in a timely fashion, and to act appropriately. The process may begin with recall, learning from others, direct experience, or by invention. To survive we must be constantly learning, as in looking both ways before crossing a street. The last time we looked is not adequate for this time. We can only learn if we recognize that we are ignorant in many respects, especially in regard to people. Survival requires that it be "together," and togetherness will more likely result when we regard our knowledge of person as incomplete and very likely flawed. When we recognize that another person's knowledge differs from ours, we are being offered a chance to learn. Ignoring the possibility is unintelligent and is ultimately a non-survival trait. Dogmatic knowledge can result in failure to connect with others. The negative effect of one such failure may be small, but all the small negative effects added together contribute to the kind of world we have.

There are many definitions of *intelligence* the one used in this study is understood to mean wisdom in the context of a global morality rather than the speed or ease of learning as it is conventionally viewed. In other words the choices we make that promote everyone's survival and promote our long-term interests are wise or intelligent choices, whereas, those that attenuate anyone's chances of survival are unwise, hence unintelligent. The knowledge required to make intelligent choices must be learned. There are no ready-made formulas, but three main criteria for a proper morality are: It promotes human connections; it preserves existing connections, and it is non-divisive. These criteria apply whether we are dealing with interpersonal morality or a wider, social morality. An interpersonal morality calls for a higher degree of consciousness and readiness to learn, which is why it is a paradigm for a global family morality.

The first requirement for using or gaining wisdom from any encounter with other humans is to understand what their words and gestures mean. We connect through communication. Our most important and satisfying connection is Communion which in its most evolved form may be to a great degree nonverbal. If my assessment of the dialogue between the doctor and myself, cited above, is correct, he added nothing to the discussion, because his assertion contained a contradiction, which could not have been the message he intended. There are two major obstacles we must overcome in determining what people mean. First, we must accept that even the most articulate among us have difficulty clearly expressing certain ideas in a way that anyone else can understand. Edward Hall cites the difficulties of "cross-cultural communication" (1963:10). We must treat all communication in non-empirical matters of significance as cross-cultural. This means we are on permanent call to be sympathetic and sometimes compassionate listeners. Our ideas exist for us whole. They are embedded in some larger context which determines or affects their meaning. For example, our attitudes toward capital punishment will be derived from our presuppositions about human nature, the model of justice imparted to us as children, our reaction to that model and a whole list of factors which are largely opaque to us, in other words our tacit knowledge (Polanyi 1962:70-71). Furthermore, communicating these ideas requires that we reconstruct them into a linear pattern out of pieces--words, gestures, voice tone, figures of speech, and so on--that only awkwardly correspond to our ideas; "it is speakers not statements which mean" (Sorri & Gill 1989:65; also Polanyi 1962:262). We all experience the difficulty of putting what we know into words.

> Between the idea
> And the reality
> Between the motion
> And the act
> Falls the Shadow
> T.S. Eliot

The meaning of nonempirical referents, particularly those that are the most important to us, can only be understood within the context from which they derive their meaning. Therefore, in matters of some complexity, understanding another person requires that we have to have some idea of the general context such as background assumptions of that person's thinking, then place specific ideas within that context. We can see from this how extraordinarily difficult communicating certain sensitive material about ourselves might be, and the greater difficulty of grasping what another person is attempting to

disclose. Without the dialectic that results from having a compassionate listener we might never make ourselves understood in trying to
disclose ourselves, hence might never succeed in formulating an
adequate self-knowledge. Journal keeping can be an approach to self-
knowledge; unfortunately most people do not write, so a connection
with other persons remains for most of us the best way.

At the time of my encounter with the doctor mentioned above I saw
only what I perceived to be his faulty thinking. I did not listen
sympathetically, thus failing to connect with him when offered an
opportunity. I did not realize at the time that his defensiveness was an
invitation to connect in his domain, i.e., agnosticism. If faith in God
is a gift as we have been taught, then agnosticism and atheism are also
gifts, not only to the agnostics and atheists but to Christians who
should feel especially responsible for bearing witness to global human
values before everyone. Bearing witness to the truth of what Jesus
taught involves not only the difficulties inherent in communication,
but for those of us raised as Catholics there may be an additional
problem of tending to see agnostics and atheists in a negative light.
Viewing persons this way puts communicating with them out of reach.
I should have said to the doctor, "We have to live as humans however
we got here, and this requires us to respect persons who believe differently from ourselves particularly when those beliefs do not obviously generate divisions." This or some other formulation could have
been worked out dialectically at the time to demonstrate that we were
on the same side, viz. humanity's.

If people have problems with ordinary exchanges having to do with
morality, consider the following:

> This turning away from God to the created world, to the
> powers of this world and to human strength, and the disobe-
> dience towards God's will and enmity towards God himself
> which follows. . . is what we mean by sin (Kung 1976:203).

This statement contains no useful information about morality for the
average, intelligent, educated person. This is found in one of Kung's
books that has the *Nihil Obstat* and *Imprimatur*, meaning the book is
free from doctrinal and moral error according to Catholic teaching. I
should add in Kung's defense that at the time he was still trying to
meet the Vatican's standards of orthodoxy. His statement about sin
while free from doctrinal error is problematic. What does it mean to
turn "away from God to the created world"? For that matter, what
could it mean to turn toward God and away from the created world?
At one time people listened to this religious language spoken to them

by the clergy and felt they knew what was being said. They had faith in the hierarchy who claimed the role of mediators between themselves and God. That time is rapidly passing. A transcendental God is beyond the possibility of experience for most of us, and I suspect for the hierarchy also. The most positive thing we can say about such statements is that they are poetic expressions of some hidden reality that remains hidden after the words are heard or read. If it is poetic, then the poetry is in the language and figures of another age and needs to be translated. How can we avoid that which we do not understand. Of course in other places we are told that an example of this turning away from God is in breaking the Commandments, an answer that begs the question of how God is affected by what we do. Furthermore, as we shall see in chapter six, the Commandments do not mean the same now as when they were first promulgated, despite the magisterium's contention that God's law does not change.

Properly understood, keeping the Commandments is not enough; we must fulfill them. This is the law of love, caring for our brothers and sisters, or at minimum not harming them because Jesus said that persons not against us can be counted for us (Mark 9:40). So in language that contemporary humans can understand, one kind of sin is hurting, or putting someone at risk for harm or neglecting someone we are obliged to care for. Another kind of sin would be creating negative effects for people we may not know as in causing ecological damage, and in general whatever negatively affects community. In terms of survival sin means not acting in the best long-term interests of ourselves and the rest of humanity. Or if we wish to express this idea in religious, poetic language that our contemporaries may translate for themselves we can speak of turning away from our brothers and sisters in whom God is immanent. Conversely we can be virtuous by turning toward this immanent God.

People in undeveloped countries generally suffered at one time without thinking of themselves as oppressed because they did not see a connection between their problems and the economic policies of the first world. When they come to understand the connection, as many now have, they may decide to seek justice for themselves, hopefully through non-violent means. Up to now many of the world's oppressed have accepted their lot as part of the divine plan, because when church officials have not explicitly taught this they let people believe that justice would be theirs in the world to come. Such ideas may only make sense in relation to hidden aspects of our knowledge, in other words, our myths.

I am not, of course, suggesting a conspiracy by Vatican officials. We are all learning, including church officials. I am merely describing the way it has been done and continues to be done, with an eye to keeping things as they are, but now with diminishing success. A priest in good standing can now write a book sanctioning Catholic dissent that at one time would have been put on the Index of forbidden books (Kaufman 1995). Much of what we Catholics have believed does not hold up well when examined in the light of reason. Chief among these beliefs is the transcendental morality that the church not only teaches but maintains is absolute and unchangeable. The only certainty Catholics have ever had that this morality is in fact absolute is that church officials have declared it to be so. With few exceptions there is no secondary confirmation from experience, nor is it likely that there can be. We have only the church's word for it, so it is solely a matter of faith in church officials, not to be confused with faith in God. We have little choice about faith in God. We either believe or we do not because we cannot experience God directly, at least most of us cannot. But to have this kind of faith in church officials we would have to know from experience their credibility and our experience of them has not always been of this sort. They have made many errors in many different ways. They have all the human failings we find in ourselves, except that their failings affect large numbers of people hence are more serious. The church's claim to inerrancy rests upon the idea that Jesus promised that his church would not fail, a logic that could only be valid if in fact the pope, cardinals, bishops and the rest of the hierarchy are *the* Church. Although they have claimed this title, sometimes implicitly, often explicitly, clearly they are not. The bishops during Vatican II declared that the Church is the People of God. More importantly, the errors of church officials, so evident in history, reveal better than anything their humanity and their capacity for error. Their failing however is to recognize that like all humans they are growing and learning and to see their knowledge at any point as a stage in that growth and learning. If they could do this they would have less of a problem admitting that what they once believed has changed and now they know better.

The doctrine of infallibility is the claim that the pope cannot err when speaking ex-cathedra in matters of faith and morals. Since the promulgation of this doctrine there have been only two ex-cathedra pronouncements: The first declared that Jesus' mother Mary was immaculately conceived, that is, without Original Sin. This raises the question: What is Original Sin? Given what we know of Genesis the answer provided by the church for nearly seventeen centuries tell us little or nothing because the answer is couched in an extension of the Eden allegory, which cannot be history for people who believe that dinosaurs became extinct approximately 65 million years ago.

The doctrine of Original Sin itself suggests a mysterious quality. The Catholic magisterium teaches that Original Sin inclines us toward evil and that it is a consequence of Adam's and Eve's disobedience in the Garden of Eden. We saw in chapter four that the verse, "Man [sic] was evil from the beginning" (Gen. 6:5), translated into non-sexist language becomes: Humans did not know how to act in their own best, long-term interest from the beginning. This is the case whether we think in terms of earthside survival or transcendental survival. This statement, by expressing the human problem as one of ignorance, takes it out of the realm of the occult (evil) and expresses it in a way we can deal with. We have no way of knowing what is meant by an immaculate conception (Jesus and his mother), or an unimmaculate conception (all the rest of us). Looking at the doctrine of the Immaculate Conception according to the redefinition of evil we have: Mary was born knowing how to act in her own best, long-term interests. The doctrine remains a matter of faith, but at least we have a handle on what it is we are supposed to believe.

Religion is shot through with these kinds of language problems which puts church officials in a box. They cannot simultaneously say to the educated faithful that they have been using logic improperly when they make inferences from Genesis as though the story is history, and to the uneducated that all along they have been telling the absolute truth, as when Pius XII wrote in *Humani Generis* that the law of God is written on our hearts. I cannot know for sure what Pius XII had in mind. Most likely it was a poetic way of expressing Aquinas's idea of the basic natural law, viz., do good and avoid evil. A more meaningful way of expressing the natural law is, "Survive," and since we are necessarily social we must add, "together." Every living creature is generally compelled to survive, and because humans are necessarily social, surviving is best done together.

Fundamentalist thinkers generate confusion when, following Aquinas, they try to show that we do not have to learn specific rules for forming our consciences, since they are already written on our hearts, rules such as the Ten Commandments. They tell us that when we do not find these rules in our conscience, our moral "decline is owed not to moral ignorance but to moral suppression." We aren't untutored, but `in denial.' We don't lack moral knowledge; we hold it down" (Budziszewski 1998:23). Unraveling the complexity of the idea that survival is the fundamental natural law is why public discussion is necessary. Survival is not just the natural law but when understood that it results from cooperation it is the primary message of the Gospels. We must act as human family members by feeding our hungry brothers and sisters, clothed their nakedness, heal the sick among them, and so on. Aquinas was correct in connecting morality with the natural law, but the way he expressed it does not make the connection as clear as when we understand the connection between surviving and fulfilling the Commandments (chapter six). The way natural law has been taught has had the effect of keeping the law external to us rather than convincing us that it is written on our hearts.

One of the reasons why the traditional teaching on natural law does not result in conviction has to do with the fact that even though "survive" and "together" constitute the whole law as a unit, the "survive" part is primary and anyone who feels that survival is threatened will be tempted to act alone (without or against others) to stave off the threat. Viewed from the outside what a person perceives as a threat may seem to be no threat at all, but we cannot make judgments about what a person thinks or feels. Jesus understood the emotional problem we have. He counsels us: "Do not be anxious for what you shall eat or what you shall wear" (Mat. 6:25). Next to love, fear is probably the strongest motivation to act that we experience. Unless we understand that we should give equal weight to "survive" and "together" we ultimately put everyone at risk, including ourselves.

The alleged "law of God" that Pius XII tells us is written on our hearts is sometimes called a conscience. In religious jargon we cannot tell for sure what *conscience* means because it is a variable depending on, among other things, our religion or Christian denomination. There is a lack of consistency between consciences. Persons who accept Catholic teaching will not use artificial birth control. Whereas, good Anglicans and Lutherans may. Is God writing different scripts, or is the problem that God does not write anything? Bok tells us that, "even for the well-intentioned, a conscience is unreliable as soon as matters of complexity and intensity must be weighed" (Bok 1979:100). This is easy to understand if we recognize that we are not born with a "conscience" as suggested by religious teaching. Consciences are formed as we grow from infancy to adulthood. Environment and genetics plus experience are the ingredients of conscience formation. And unless we want to introduce miracles into everyday life, any involvement by God would have to be so remote (mammalian beginnings) as to be pointless for us to consider. Conscience formation has in general one of three results: 1) sociopathology, wherein social behavior is dictated solely by what is personally advantageous; 2) tribalism, wherein behavior is limited by what is advantageous to tribal members; and 3) globalism, whereby persons act, to the extent that it can be known, to enable everyone to survive, including remote descendants, while immediately concentrating on aiding the most disadvantaged in the here-and-now. We are all mixtures of the three. The church attributes this variability to our fallen nature, a view that will be a long time changing.

The crux of the problem here is in "the extent to which it can be known." I noted earlier that our problem, in theological language, is not so much sin as sinfulness. In straightforward secular terms this mean we cannot always know how our behavior will affect others. We can imagine and empathize in some cases, for example, what it would be like to be raped, or be the victim of incest, but of course, any imagining will pale alongside the reality. However, people who victimize others probably do not spend much time trying to empathize. When Jesus was reported to have said, "Father forgive them; they know not what they do" (Luke 23:34), he could have been speaking for any victims who had a profound understanding of the problem that humans have. What has been labeled sin by the churches, specific acts such as murder, adultery, theft and so on, are actually symptoms of a deeper, more intractable problem, not Original Sin, a concept that provides no useful information. Our problem is an ignorance so deep we do not know we are ignorant, an ignorance that becomes complicated by false learning that deserves a concept of its own, Ignorance II.

We are all born not knowing how to survive and most of us learn how to survive with a tribal code which can be described with a metaphor from science as the displacement of entropy. In plain English we are prepared to survive even if it means others will not. We are not talking self-defense, rather, a disregard or unconsciousness of how others will fare, absorbed as we are with our own problems We are also not talking callousness. We are talking ignorance, a failure to understand how a system would work that enabled everyone to survive. There is a further complication alluded to earlier; i.e., the tendency people have to communicate their hurt by hurting others through ignorance of other means. Some of us intuitively understand these interpersonal dynamics and how we must survive together, a talent. Everyone else must acquire the skill. It can be learned from those who know. It is also possible to learn from experience, as say from having been victimized oneself and extrapolating one's feelings to others.

From this analysis we can see how confessing specific sins according to kind and number is not the way to solve human problems. And to be told that we will indeed fail, but keep coming back to be shriven so we can start again is to put people on a virtual treadmill of sin and repentance. Learning from mistakes is human. Repeating mistakes is not; it is rather, a result of having been taught bad psychology, of not understanding our real problem. If spiritual life is a journey, most of us need guides. They are rarely to be found in a confession box through the routine of confession and absolution even if priests had the time and were competent to delve into a person's background to learn where the person has been and the direction that person's life is taking. Furthermore, the diminishing number of priests points to the need for trained, lay spiritual guides, male and female. But airing our problems and failings with an intimate partner or in small faith communities may become the best way of growing spiritually.

Conscience, then, is an assortment of values acquired in the course of living, not all of which make sense for survival of individuals and the species. That is enough to account for all the variability we find. Occult explanations such as Original Sin confuse the issue and serve to point away from personal responsibility. We do not have control over our early formative years, but intelligent, adult behavior and its consequences requires a habit of reflection. Even a habit of reflection is not enough if our thinking is guided primarily by the idea of saving our souls. If we are going to use the term *conscience*, let it be a guide using the principle of promoting the life and well-being of everyone including ourselves. This is still a difficult and sometimes impossible goal but only giving it our best effort makes sense.

Thus the idea of acting according to one's conscience according to the church's concept is inadequate. We must also choose what kind of conscience we will have through an understanding of what kind of creatures we are. Standard Catholic teaching fails to teach what the options are and the process by which a proper conscience is formed. Instead the structure of a proper conscience is laid out in an absolute, undeviating form that we may not question. Many elements in what the church offers are questionable because they are either unreasonable or perceived to be. Imagine being a Catholic before mid-19th century who helped several slaves escape. One would be guilty of a mortal sin of having deprived someone of a significant amount of property. Or imagine having to confess the mortal sin of having sex with one's wife while she had a period. Yet we are told to simply accept without questions what authorities call a proper conscience. This is not how to persuade educated church members to act from conviction. An important reason for reclaiming religion from the church is its denial of experience in giving shape to morality. According to the church what was wrong centuries ago is wrong now and will be wrong forever. The same faulty logic would make what was morally proper then continue to be morally proper now and forever. We do not sacrifice animals; we do not own slaves; and usury is no longer sinful. Multiple wives, concubines and temple prostitutes are considered wrong in Christian cultures. In the matter of sex, consider St. Ambrose's statement: "Married people ought to be ashamed of the state in which they live" (Edokimov 1995:18). Jesus pointed the way to progressive moral evolution as our examination of the Ten Commandments in chapter six we will show. What societies declare immoral often depends on cultural biases, in effect what they have learned is socially proper up to the present. More to the point, church officials apparently thought they acted properly by killing and persecuting Jews, heretics and so-called witches. We must all keep in mind that we are learning animals.

For many of us the language of social psychology is well suited for speaking of morality, even religious morality, for three reasons: 1) The heart of Jesus' message is humanistic and even people who care nothing for Jesus are likely to be interested in the strategies for establishing and maintaining viable personal relationships plus social organization on a global scale. 2) Social psychology enables us to make explicit what is for most people tacit knowledge, i.e., the rules they use for relating to one another, making the language of that science highly appropriate to the subject. 3) It can reveal the elements of good interpersonal relationships and why many relationships fail. Learning only from personal experience to create viable interpersonal relationships is not cost effective if we weigh the effects of divorce on current and future generations, not to mention intra-family abuse, alcoholism and other residual effects. That is why we should reflect on the wisdom of others, past and present, including what religion offers while keeping in mind that we are all still learning.

By contrast, religious language regarding morality can be problematic for those who learn from experience and think for themselves. The ban on contraception could only be reasonable if, 1) it harmed one or more individuals, or 2) it had a destructive effect on community, A strong case can be made for the opposite of both these reasons. The ban on contraception is further evidence of hierarchical fallibility. Despite the ambiguity we often encounter in making moral decisions when they are tested against our own convictions we encounter less difficulty in deciding what must be done, and none at all in the matter of who is responsible. Best of all there will be no thought of having to defer to a transcendental mind, to which it is doubtful that anyone has access, or to alleged agents of a transcendental mind, who like us are human and fallible. The proper role of religious authority should be to engage in a dialogue that will aid us in arriving at a conviction of the rules we should follow for connecting or remaining connected, or the principles for determining such rules. If church officials are convinced, for example, that non-marital sex is wrong, let them lay out the reasons why in language that we can understand. Church authorities teach only one reason for the sin of non-marital sex--God says so. Such thinking puts rape and fornication in the same category. Either will earn a person hell. Consider an unmarried couple about to have sex: If the man uses a condom to keep from putting the woman at risk of pregnancy, is this a double sin?

Until recently the Catholic church managed to control the thinking of the faithful by convincing them that the moral code that they promote and that existed out there rather than within should be the basis for determining our behavior under the threat of going to hell or the hope of going to heaven. Behavior has consequences and we have to decide if the consequences are good for ourselves and the human family in the long run. By contrast, thinking of behavioral consequences in terms of heaven or hell can only distract us. Our own long-term good is closely tied to the good of everyone. We may still make mistakes with this kind of moral strategy, but we usually have communal experience as a corrective if we remain open to learning. With the church's morality the idea is to accept it and act accordingly whether we understand or not, making docility one of the church's chief virtues. Consequently those of us who grew up Catholic in the first half of the 20th century and depended on the magisterium were never equipped by church teaching to think for ourselves and arrive at a personal conviction of the rightness or wrongness of a particular behavior. It would be difficult to invent a more muddled system for promoting survival of the human family.

Furthermore, the church teaches the commandments as restrictive rather than liberating. This encourages us to think of how close we can come without breaking a rule, especially in matters of sex. Good moral decisions may be difficult if not impossible when we postpone thinking through to some kind of conviction of why certain behaviors are wrong until the time a decision needs to be made. By not presenting us with reasons other than that God, the Bible or the church says so, the church does not teach how to act out of conviction which can only arise from experience or unequivocal trust in our teacher. Lack of conviction added to the doctrine of our "fallen natures" provides a loophole making sin inevitable. Such thinking allows us to say, "I know it's wrong but I do it anyway." The way the church teaches not only permits, it actually promotes such arrant nonsense.

Our attention should be directed toward people instead of particular items of behavior. We should spend a great deal of time reviewing our history in a critical manner to discern whether we derive personal satisfaction from connecting with other humans through the way we

have acted with, for and toward them. This is how conscience formation takes place when we do it for ourselves. It does not come naturally and automatically for everyone as suggested by what Pius XII
and William May have said (1991:53). The ideas and judgments we
get from others, including the hierarchy, directly or through inference, is part of the process of discernment whereby we make decisions, but only we can make them. When we regard our knowledge
as tentative and are open to learning we are more likely to operate out
of conviction and accept responsibility for our behavior and its consequences. We will not blame what we have done on our "fallen natures."

Understanding our failure in interpersonal relationships cannot
come from what others say. If I am open to the person with whom I
am trying to be intimate I will detect my failure in that person's
response to me or the lesson will come later in subsequent relationship. Three elements are required for me to discover how ignorant I
have been in the matter of interpersonal relationships: 1) I must be
convinced that I am necessarily social and I must connect to others in
ways that are only partially genetically specified in order to survive;
2) I must have a solid conviction of my own worth; and 3) I must
have an adequate fund of experience on which to reflect. All this
must be learned just as I learn math, music or any subject. People
can be trained to conform to specific behavior patterns with a program
of rewards and punishments. This works with any animal; it is called
conditioning. This is a long way from induction into the creative
morality that is required in the ever changing circumstances of our
era, and especially for the moral refinement that Jesus taught. We
can infer from what Jesus said about caring for one another, especially the least fortunate among us, that this is the best approach to species survival.

Surviving socially can produce a false sense of self-sufficiency that
comes from developing competence in surviving apart from our
family and other intimates. Prior to our highly interconnected civilization survival was more difficult, but it was possible for families to
survive without the elaborate support system now available because
everyone within the family unit did most of what was necessary to
survive. Specialization has made us more dependent on others outside
of the family. The fact that those on whom we depend are anonymous and interchangeable does not negate the fact of dependence, and
even if we could survive completely alone, most of us are sexual
beings and would find complete independence unsatisfying. A necessary sociality demands of us that we work through the implications of
this requirement. Can we as humans promote the life and well-being

of some, such as those we care about and not others? What are the consequences of limiting our connections to some and not connecting to or of disconnecting from others? In other words is a tribal morality viable? Can we answer the question: "Am I my brother's and sister's keeper?" affirmatively with reservations, or is it an all-or-nothing issue?

If we answer negatively or affirmatively with reservations, then others are simply more or less useful to us and we should be completely rational in all our decisions, like the business person whose goal of making money is unaffected by sentiments concerning what happens to workers when they are not on the job. The problem with any decision, and a fact that we will have to take into account, is that any act that affects at least one other person is a moral decision, which leads us logically to the idea that when others make moral decisions we are also affected for good or ill. We have some control over what we do and practically none over what others do. Therefore if our behavior is such that we are creating a world in which we can disregard the effect of our behavior on others, it becomes a world wherein everyone acting similarly creates a world in which all are at risk. Even if we affirm kinship with all of our sisters and brothers we will have just begun the long process of discovering what such decisions mean due to our massive ignorance and the slow pace of progressive moral evolution.

A not so obvious way in which we are dependent is that to learn how others should be treated we have to inquire of them, also debate and negotiate with them. Interpersonal relationships do not evolve automatically. They require a process involving skills, notably communication skills. We cannot depend on the general moral rules we find in place in society, e.g., the Ten Commandments and what is socially acceptable. A profound respect and reverence for other persons, which is the ideal, begins with the recognition that other persons are essentially mysteries to us as we are to them. We share so much common life in many respects--language, customs, culture and so on--that we think we can read what a person is from what a person does or says. Ordinarily this is the case only in very limited circumstances that are of least importance to us, as say in determining if someone is a good auto mechanic or grocery clerk.

If we place the various aspects of life on a continuum from the least to the most significant, what we have in common with others would be on the least significant end--we eat the same foods, dance to the same music, and on and on. But we only have to look at our language to see that in matters of significance we are all unique. Our specialness may be opaque even to ourselves so that recognition and acceptance of this fact is usually a matter of faith, and with or without this faith we will in our dealings with others operate on the assumption that they are essentially just like ourselves. Only a sense of our own specialness provides a basis for treating others as the special persons they are.

We must first define morality humanistically before we can then begin to ask ourselves what is a "proper" morality because morality is not just for people who believe in God. The terms *moral* and *immoral* force us to conclude that human behavior in relation to others is always either one or the other because these concepts define the realm of morality dichotomously, i.e., as closed and static. Whereas, *proper morality* is an open, dynamic term since we do not start with the knowledge of what it is or should be. Wherever we happen to be located morally is not so important as the fact that we have taken the direction of growing and learning and being one with our brothers and sisters. The implication in this for our relationship with others is that we are called to be extraordinarily compassionate toward others because we neither know where they are on their journey nor where they are headed. We each face many difficulties in our spiritual journey, and dealing with our own is tough enough without trying to do someone else's job. If we give others time and space to be and do what they must, and we at the same time set an example, to the best of our ability, of how to act, we have found a good place to start in a relationship with anyone.

The position of the Vatican is that morality does not evolve, much less progressively, and that we have an absolute moral code because it has been given to us by God, and since God does not change, neither does his moral code. The idea that morality does not evolve is so contradictory to the facts that it is difficult to imagine the basis for such a conclusion except that it has been the tradition for centuries. The idea that God does not change came from Plato for whom perfection meant unchanging. To say that God does not change on the basis of a philosophical concept is idolatry as is the attribution of any human concepts to God. We just do not know, and we are better off admitting our ignorance.

The immutability attributed to God is actually a characteristic the church tries to maintain for itself as illustrated by a series of events that began in 1984 when certain bishops in the United States requested that Rome rule on whether girls may serve at the altar, just as boys always have. Rome, meaning the cardinals and the pope, took eight years to decide and then waited two more years to announce their decision. The sticking point was apparently the fear that girls might see that role as a step toward the priesthood.

I see in this pattern a connection with an incident that took place in my classroom some years ago. We got into a discussion of racial justice and one lad who took a negative view asked me, "How would you like it if a nigger moved in next to you?" "I don't have any trouble with the idea, just your language," I replied, "People are free to move where they want to." He then became more hypothetical. "Suppose they started throwing trash over your fence. What would you do?" "I'd ask them to stop." "And suppose," he continued "their teenager asked your daughter for a date?" "My daughter is free to go out with whomever she wishes." Totally frustrated with this dialogue, the young man exclaimed, "That's the trouble with you. You can't face reality--what could happen!"

And that is how Rome faces reality--"What could happen!" And to make absolutely certain there would be no misunderstanding immediately after the long-delayed decision on altar girls John Paul II reaffirmed his position on women priest--No! Never! It is not even a subject for discussion. Later Cardinal Ratzinger announced, presumably with the blessing of John Paul II, that a male only hierarchy is an infallible teaching. Rome is like the coach who would not let his quarterback throw a pass because there were four possible outcomes and three of them were bad and two of the three were incredibly bad.

If our ability to express certain ideas is problematic, and our ability to know what others mean in matters of importance also presents problems, then the certainty of our knowledge about anyone is questionable, and the further removed people are from us, i.e., beyond family, friends, and so on, the more questionable is our knowledge. This condition, along with the fact that our technology has compressed the size of the world through rapid transportation and instantaneous communication, means that in searching for an intelligent morality (i.e., one that promotes the survival and well-being of individuals and the species) we must think in global terms. Otherwise the petty conflicts that arise because we do not understand each other will grow into armed conflict, as they have in the past.

When what others "know" contradicts what we "know", we have good reasons to question our "knowledge". Others may in fact be dishonest or mistaken, but we should not automatically assume that. Even mistaken people see their knowledge as whole and consistent and every experience is an opportunity to learn. We will simultaneously bear witness to the value of really listening to what others say. Different systems of knowledge result from filtering perceptions through our different value systems. Rather than contradictory, these other systems may complement ours, i.e, they may, if we learn them, make up deficiencies in our own knowledge. As we proceed from things, to abstract ideas, to people, the categories we use for organizing knowledge become increasingly variable and complex. Negotiating meanings becomes our best option for communicating.

Knowing this we have to question oversimplified views of life that encourage thinking of humans as stereotypes. Labels such as criminal, lazy, fat, wimp, wino, homosexual, sinner, and so on, do not encompass the reality of humans. Anyone who has been rejected or dismissed as a type should have learned this from experience, but humans, being what they are may simply learn to dismiss or reject others in like manner, as when homosexuals are racist, or blacks are homophobic or anti-semitic. In the world of things, categories can simplify life for us, but when it comes to our ideas about people, simplifying categories generate anti-survival currents with which we must ultimately contend. "Saved" and "damned" are two of these simplifying categories.

Fundamentalist religions supply organizing and simplifying categories for their members that negatively affect the survival of individuals and the species in addition to the ones cited above. Fundamentalist Christians believe that the Bible is historically correct and literally true down to the last dot and comma. Such a belief produces a tribalist mentality with a vengeance because anyone who disagrees is their enemy, and not just their enemy but also an enemy of God. If in the Bible Jesus said, "Love your enemies," that can only mean for fundamentalists of every stripe what is popularly known as "tough love," that is, withholding demonstrations of love until the enemy sees the light and repents. As one Christian lady wrote to me, "I won't tell you where you are going but there are no unbelievers in hell." By "unbelievers" she meant people who did not believe what she believed.

Catholic fundamentalists are a different breed. Church officials at least no longer believe in the Bible as completely factual historically, and since Vatican II they admit that there are good Christians who are not Catholic. More recently John Paul II even admitted that evolution is a viable explanation of human genesis. Still, the church has a collection of writings from a group known as the church Fathers that have to a great degree given shape to the organization we know as Catholicism. And while the shape is different from evangelical fundamentalism it is nearly as inflexible. For a Catholic who grew up with a Catholic education, atheists were not just people who did not believe in God. They were enemies of God and of all good Catholics especially in their incarnation as Communists. We were not allowed to read what they wrote for fear of becoming contaminated by their insidious thinking. We were never told that there might be some validity to their thinking or how we could love an enemy we had to assiduously avoid. Christians of other denominations were not called enemies, just wrong-headed and people to be avoided also. A Catholic boy could dance with a Protestant girl but not attend her church services, and a dispensation was required to marry her.

In short religious leaders have drawn lines indicating who is in and who is out, a program of divisiveness that has somewhat moderated in the past half century but is still in effect to a great extent, primarily due to the intransigence of the Vatican. One of the objections Pius XII had to freedom of conscience was that it might allow a Catholic to convert to another religion. The culture and language of religion took a step into the modern world with Vatican Council II, but since that time the movement has slowed to the point of being regressive. John Paul II and the curia seem intent on recreating the Tridentine Church in which the faithful are sheep and the clergy are the shepherds. The behavior of Vatican officials has resulted in further alienation of the faithful that became something of a mass movement with the publication of *Humanae Vitae* (Kaufman 1995:90).

Women are in the forefront of change as we might expect given the patriarchal structure of religion as well as politics, business and every other kind of institution. The Vatican refuses to dialogue on matters of concern to women. They regard what they know as the absolute, unchangeable truth, such as the recent announcement that their teaching that women may not become priests is an infallible teaching. Transmission occurs in only one direction. They cannot conceive of learning from the People. Of course they will eventually learn but only after long, painful period of discovery that their medieval and patriarchal policies become increasingly less viable.

There is an advantage to their reactionary policies. The more aggressively they pursue them, the sooner they will arrive at the inevitable dead end toward which they are heading. At that time the laity will have to take up in earnest the task of evangelizing, only by then we may call it saving humanity and the planet instead of evangelizing. If nothing else the downward spiral in male vocations to the priesthood and the rapid expansion of earth's population will mean that conversions could never occur fast enough to make everyone Catholic. However, making everyone Catholic or even Christian is not what Jesus taught. It is, rather, putting an end to divisiveness, seeing everyone as a member of the human family, thus promoting humanity's survival by valuing everyone as family. And the language of the laity is better suited than religious jargon for persuading people to accept the survival strategies which are synonymous with that message.

The certainty we have concerning our knowledge cannot derive from the knowledge itself. We like to think that what we know has been tested against reality, and therefore confirmed by experience. We are not conscious of how much of our knowledge is simple faith that often contradicts experience. We experience a flat, motionless earth, but we are told and we believe that earth has at least five motions. This is the case with much of our knowledge, even for scientists (Polanyi 1962:375; Midgley 1985:107). When the knowledge we have is about people, or is in the realm of pure abstraction such as good and evil, the empirical referents we point to as evidence serve only to reveal the underlying value systems through which our perceptions are filtered. The absolute, transcendental values taught to Roman Catholics and other Christians cannot be tested against reality. These values have to be accepted on faith in the churches that teach them. Here again we have a language problem in the debate between modern moralists who claim there are no absolute values and the various churches that claim we do. When modern moralists (or moral relativists as the churches prefer to think of them) say that the prohibition against killing cannot be an absolute value they are not saying that murder is not wrong. The expression *murder* pre-defines a certain behavior as unacceptable within the human family, as is taking a poor person's means of livelihood.

The root of our communication problems with the church grow out of epistemological problems, i.e., the preconceptions on which knowledge is based. Humans have wrestled with these problems in a formal way for twenty-five centuries; many still do. The Vatican's epistemology partly depends on what they consider revelation but mainly on St. Thomas Aquinas' revision of Aristotle. If what they call revelation were God's own words such an epistemology might have some validity. What would count as God's word is not so clear. The church's view is an interpretation and only one way of viewing revelation. In chapter three we examined different perspectives on revelation from which we may judge a more realistic view.

The diversity of ideas concerning what constitutes intelligent (survival) behavior points to the need for establishing criteria that respects diversity while not putting us in conflict with those whose ideas differ. The most intelligent ideas keep our options open so that we can continue to learn and grow. The idea that we directly apprehend reality, or can know absolute truth, puts us at odds with persons who disagree. If we think we have a direct knowledge of reality, people who do not see our reality may be regarded as stupid, ignorant or as having bad faith. Kant's speculation concerning our perception of reality and confirmed by Adelbert Ames' experiments (Bateson

1980:35-40) makes the differences in perceptions of reality understandable, acceptable, and to be expected. With this open attitude our chances for survival increases. Ignorance can only be resolved at the risk of believing that knowledge must always remain tentative, otherwise we limit our ability to learn. Under such conditions women would be still dying of sepsis because doctors would not have learned to wash their hands.

Our concern here is with the problems of communication, especially with language, but it is impossible to discuss the problems of language without referring to related problems; "in discussing language philosophically we are in fact discussing *what counts as belonging to the world*" (Winch 1963:15). Language does not cover all of what belongs to our world otherwise we would have no myths only philosophy. The mind is not a "mirror of nature" (Rorty 1979). "The heart of the educational process consists of providing aids and dialogues for translating experience into more powerful systems of notation and ordering," and we can only do this by becoming conscious of our existing system of "notation in terms of which we have encoded experience" (Bruner 1968:20-21).

The encoding of religious ideas that the church looks upon as absolute and final occurred at times in history that make many of them irrelevant to our own times. As McSweeny pointed out in the quotation that opens this chapter, language then was thought to be unproblematic and unbiased (1980:250). For example, the language of modern anthropology, sociology and psychology did not exist for formulating thoughts concerning human behavior when early church leaders defined sin. They depended on what was acceptable according to the culture of the time. That meant explaining the world, including the Bible, according to Plato, Aristotle, and the Stoics among others, plus the ideas carried over from Jewish scripture. The analyses provided by Origen, Basil, Augustine and the other "Fathers" became as canonical as the Bible. And later when Aquinas wrote and summed up everything from the beginning, Greek science and philosophy became frozen in the medieval categories then available. The scholastic philosophy of Aquinas is still the official philosophy of the church despite its scientific errors and the limitations of Greek philosophical categories. Well into the 20th century Pius XII wrote and spoke as though Adam and Eve were real persons (*Humani Generis*) and drew logical conclusions from the allegory known as Genesis.

A much better source for drawing logical conclusions is what Jesus taught. *Good* is loving everyone, including our enemies, which simply means not excluding them in our efforts to survive. If promoing the life and well-being of others is good, its opposite, harming others in any way is bad, or in theological language, sinful. This is straightforward language anyone can understand as offending or pleasing God does not. Also, when the laity begin to carry Jesus' message into the world, as eventually they must, they stand a better chance of being listened to by those who do not share their faith if they speak in simple, non-theological language. Communication of any significance should be a joint, creative effort, a dialectic. Since this relates directly to survival behavior, we are talking about the "social construction of moral reality," to point out one aspect of Berger's and Luckmann's thesis (1967). Religious jargon might be listened to politely but if it is becoming meaningless to Catholics and other Christians we cannot expect nonChristians to comprehend.

We are also confronted with the problem of transmitting what we believe to our children. We can expect them to eventually apply what they learn from experience and to test the reasonableness of what we say. That God says so or the church says so will not stand the test of reasonableness, a test that if applied to the basic message of Jesus in the context of humanity's survival will be found reasonable. Our children are coming of age in a sexual environment where sexual taboos will appear quaint. They are not growing up in neighborhoods and ethnic enclaves where virtually everyone accepted that sex outside of marriage could incur eternal damnation if one died without confessing, or where girls and women risked ostracism and labels such as "fallen women." The time is past when parents, teachers and other authorities could frighten children into conforming behavior. We must educate our children to make responsible choices. They can only do this if their intelligence is respected and we demonstrate for them standards of behavior of which they can be convinced.

Religion and religious education is not entirely at fault, but they helped plant the seeds that have blossomed into a culture of winners and losers. Quoting Keith Thomas, McSweeny writes:

> But until the end of the seventeenth century, and in many cases long afterwards, the overwhelming majority of clerical writers and pious laymen sincerely believed that there was a link between man's moral behaviour and his fortune in this world. . . . It was impossible to reiterate the view that sin was the most probable cause of misfortune without conveying the implication that godliness was somehow linked with prosperity. Of course the preachers would have explained that it was only spiritual prosperity. . . . But their flocks only too often took a cruder view" (1980:10-11)

This view of the relationship between moral behavior and fortune neither started nor ended with the 17th century. It is the most common form of idolatry, an issue addressed as far back as Job. It still prevails in its secularized form. This is part of the reason behind the sometimes bitter feelings against people on welfare. They are perceived as somehow having merited their problems and it is therefore immoral to support them.

As a corollary to this view of the connection between fortune and morality, in our school systems, public and private, learning is artificial, both in subject matter and the way it is taught. The way that children learn naturally is not ordinarily taken into account (Holt 1972; Gatto 1992; Bateson 1988; Bruner 1968), probably because schools do not teach the value of learning for oneself, i.e., the enhancement of being. Conformity is rewarded instead of creativity (Moustakas 1967; Getzel and Jackson 1963). Our schools operate under the hidden assumption that they are separating the sheep from the goats, i.e., winners and losers. Instead of a commitment to a lifelong process of transcending one's knowledge, the primary purpose of schools seems to be success in a career, and even that must be qualified. Unless we are to become teachers of grammar we will never find use for diagraming sentences. We learn to write by reading and writing, just as we learn to speak by listening and attempting to speak. Students who play the school game successfully learn to become winners. Nothing will change unless we see reasons for changing and such reasons are not easy to come by. We usually wait for crises to force change on us, and the change will not be positive without the disposition to learn. Since we all start life by learning, some of us must reach a point where we cross a line and learn to become *homo stultus*, bearers of Ignorance II.

Although we are all victims of various forces to some extent, our interest in finding or inventing strategies to escape or limit the effects of such forces not in placing blame. Language is one such force. We learn a language before we understand what it means to learn a language. The language we learn shapes our thinking and feeling in ways that we cannot imagine until we learn the complex ways in which language and culture are intertwined. We get insights into this phenomenon when we study foreign cultures because the differences are obvious. But like a diamond merchant studying diamonds, we can only gradually learn to make finer distinctions, so that eventually we may see that every individual uses language that varies in significant ways from the language of others, even among people who are most intimate. For many social scientists humans have no freedom at all. They reduce human internal complexity, and the complexity of the relationships between humans and their environment to oversimplified exchange relationships. Homans, for example, would have us believe that all of human behavior can be explained by the seeking of rewards and the avoidance of punishment; he states this in the form of a proposition that holds for all relations between persons: "the more rewarding (valuable) to one man [sic] is the action of the other, the more often will the first perform the action that gets him the reward" (1967:15). This view bears a striking resemblance to the pre-Vatican II foundation for Catholic morality as an exchange between humans and God.

The problem of meanings cannot always be resolved by saying, "This is what I mean when I use a particular word." Words are isolated bits of information which have meaning in context. The context which determines meaning may be other words or the circumstances within which the words are used, or a context embedded in a larger context. Our conventional semantics and syntax makes us think that the property of a thing is "immanent in one end of a binary relationship," as when we say this table is hard, instead of its being a property of the relationship itself, i.e., between the table and ourselves (Bateson 1988:157). In addition many words have emotional and intellectual associations of which we are unaware, and the more important the words and their meanings, the more likely are they to have such associations.

Good and *evil* carry an occult connotation for people who believe that human nature is corrupt. Bad human behavior, however, for such people means the same as it does for those who believe that human nature is inherently good and who believe that human problems stem from the environment, notably corrupt institutions. However, the locus of the problem for each group is different. For those who believe human nature is corrupt, evil forces within and without drive us. This contrasts with the second view, first attributed to Socrates, but promulgated in a formal way by Jean Jacques Rousseau, that when we are "bad" we are acting in ignorance. We can see how problems may emerge when two people holding such divergent views attempt to have a discussion concerning a proper morality, one that is valid for everyone. *Good* and *evil* are burdened with a number of implicit assumptions that make common understanding difficult if not impossible except through creative dialogues.

Consider, for example, the relationship between language and thinking. There is a sense of unity in thought that disappears as soon as we try to express it in words, or even to think in words. A thought in words, expressed or not, is made of pieces spread out in time. A person listening to us or reading what we write in an attempt to understand our thought must assemble the pieces to recreate the original thought. The recreated thought may be radically different, because as recreated in the mind of the auditor or reader it is still made up of parts that can only suggest some sort of whole, whereas, in the mind of the originator it is a seamless entity that may have unverbalized abstract or emotional connections that must be known for a complete understanding by the other person but which have not been made explicit. Our ideas often cannot be made to fit within a given set of words. In going from whole to parts and back again there are inevitable losses. Seen this way we should appreciate language as an aid to communication, not the sole means.

From the foregoing we can only conclude that there is no such thing as a common language in matters of importance, a universe of discourse as the sociologists call it, and no way to fully express the truth in words. Except in relatively trivial matters we must engage in a dialectic, a process that allows meaning to be negotiated rather than imposed by one party on the other. This dialectic is not only necessary between individuals, it must also be the form that learning takes between religious institutions and their members. A consciousness of our fundamental differences should lead us to make the effort required to learn what others mean, the way mothers try to understand children who are just learning to express themselves. Mother-child communication exemplifies ideal communication. When it works, the attitude or disposition of the mother overcomes the deficiencies in the child's expression by careful attention to all the cues, audible, visual, contextual, and so on. In the terms of this book, the mother is said to have an open mind with regard to her child, the prototype of what I describe later as a Primary Disposition. She does not have fixed assumptions about what the child means. She simply considers possible meanings until she succeeds. Compare this with the way religion operates. One-way communication is an oxymoron. Nothing is more difficult and complex than communication about moral reality. Authoritative reductionism cannot resolve those difficulties for us.

CHAPTER VI
THE COMMANDMENTS: Rules for Survival

You must not think that I have come to abolish the Law or the Prophets; I did not come to abolish, but to fulfill (Mat. 5:17-19).

The church's promulgation of the commandments illustrates as well
as anything why religion needs to be reclaimed from the church.
Besides the flawed notion of sin taught by the church its method of
teaching does not call its members to the challenge of the high ideals
Jesus presented to us. For the church the Ten Commandments are
rules to keep, not something to think about. The ideals that round out
the meaning of the commandments are considered impractical--turning
the other cheek, walking the extra mile, giving away one's possessions. These are considered too impractical, too difficult for humanity's fallen nature and so they are largely ignored. They are not even
taught as goals toward which we should aspire, to remind us of how
we fall short of the ideal.

I hope to demonstrate that the Commandments are points of departure for the great adventure to which Jesus calls us and not a place at
which we are stalled because of our fallen nature. By reflecting on
them we can arrive at an understanding of what Jesus meant by fulfilling them instead of just keeping them. The Catholic magisterium, the
teaching arm of the institution, presents them as divinely revealed to
humans and unchangeable. I see no harm in calling them divinely
revealed if we understand them according to the fifth model of revelation as described by Avery Dulles. Those who subscribe to this
model see revelation as "a breakthrough to a higher level of con-

sciousness as humanity is drawn into a fuller participation in the divine creativity" (1992:115). Taking them as actually given to Moses by God on Mount Sinai does nothing to make them more credible in view of what we know from history. If they are unchangeable, their immutability occurred sometime after the creation of the institution we call the Catholic church. They are not, as we shall see, the same commandments presumably given to Moses.

The Ten Commandments occupy a central place in Christian morality, and they should, but not as conceived by the various Christian denominations. When Jesus arrived the Commandments already existed. He did not come to repeat them or make them more stringent and harder to keep as some theologians teach. My understanding is that he came to liberate humanity by what he says of the commandments. It is an important part of the "Good News" he brought. Properly understood, what he had to say about the Ten Commandments is liberating, but as the churches interpret them they appear to be a tightening of the restrictions on human behavior in contrast to the Jewish code. We do not know exactly what Jesus said. Most of Greek manuscripts we have date from approximately 300 years after the events in the New Testament were supposed to have occurred. But clearly his lessons have to do with how we should live and survive together. When he started teaching, the Law and the Ten Commandments had been around for about 18 centuries. Yet they remain important within the context of his teaching. The key to understanding what is new in what he said about the commandments is the word *fulfill*, sometimes translated, *complete*. His whole program is in fact implicit in the meaning of *fulfill*.

The quotation cited at the beginning of this chapter occurs in the Sermon on the Mount. A little further on he says,

> You have heard that it was said to the people in the old days, 'You shall not commit murder', and anyone who does so must stand trial. But I say to you that anyone who is angry with [a brother or sister] must stand trial. . . So that if, while you are offering your gift at the altar, you should remember that [a brother or sister] has something against you, you must leave your gift there before the altar and go away. Make your peace with your [brother or sister] first, then come and offer your gift (Mat. 5:21-24).

Those who point to this passage as evidence of increased rigor describe it this way: Before we couldn't kill; now we can't even get angry. If keeping the Law had been what Jesus had in mind, the requirements would indeed be more stringent, but fulfillment of the Law calls for a new kind of consciousness that makes keeping the Law simpler rather than more difficult. Keeping the law becomes a by-product of fulfilling the Law. Notice that in his revised view of the Law human-human relationships take priority over a human-divine relationship. We cannot connect with God at the same time we disregard a failed relationship with a brother or sister.

Anger is a step toward violence. Jesus is telling us that awareness of this says, "Don't take the first step." That in itself has the sound of restraint. Not, however, if we think of this as just a first step in consciousness-raising. Jesus reportedly said of the men that crucified him that they did not understand what they were doing. Most of us have read or heard these words, but if we understood and accepted them as the basis for our morality, we would undergo the most radical transformation that could occur to humans. As noted before we are learning animals and much of what we know is flawed and incomplete. Our culture, for example, currently dictates that we should not allow anyone to get away with anything. Our responses to personal offenses cover a range of possibilities from stony silence to verbal abuse, from character assassination to murder. There are no easy solutions to this very human difficulty. We need to find reasons for compassion. More often then not, when people hurt they express their hurt feelings by hurting others. We must learn to see such behavior as a cry for compassion. If our attention is focussed on promoting the life and well-being of others we are moving away from the possibility of killing anyone or stealing from anyone. This is one way of completing the Commandments. The new, stiffer requirement of the Law is only apparent. When we contemplate the Ten Commandments from the positive perspective Jesus taught we get a radically different view of what being good means.

When I was in high school religion classes my peers wanted to know how far they could go with a girl without committing a mortal sin, i.e., offending God as we were taught then. No one, including me, asked how far one could go before offending the girl. Their question in plain English was, "What can I get away with?" This attitude was so pervasive among adults as well as young persons that no one apparently had been taught the positive and creative aspects of the Law.

There is only one death but no limit to the ways we can promote the life and well-being of others. Not killing is not the opposite of killing; *promoting the life and well-being of others is*. Feeding the hungry and clothing the naked completes the prohibition against killing as does everything that promotes the life and well-being of others.

This is not to blame religion teachers of that time for failing to teaches us about fulfilling the Commandments. They were only passing on what they had been taught. Religious teaching emphasized the negative, that we were inclined to evil because of Original Sin, that we could not avoid sin no matter how hard we tried. There is an implicit permission to sin in this perspective, especially when one considers that the church had in place the machinery for reconciliation with God, thus making the faithful dependent on the hierarchy, and generating a perpetual round of sin and repentance.

This is not what Jesus taught. This is what religious officials have devised, although not with malicious intent. They have not accepted as fact that the ideas of God and morality have evolved over time in the direction of the ideals that Jesus taught. In particular, they have not accepted the attempt by Jesus to humanize religion. They have recreated a simpler form of the Judaic Law with this difference: that outsiders could more readily become tribal members. They have missed the part where Jesus tells us to erase tribal boundaries, that we are all members of one family. Jesus said that the whole Law could be reduced to two, love God and love your neighbor. These two can further collapsed into one because elsewhere he tells us that we love God by loving our neighbor, an idea that St. Paul reiterates (Gal. 5:14). The requirements are further simplified for us by how neighbor is defined: Anyone toward whom we act neighborly. We needn't concern ourselves with the question of whether the person we are with is a neighbor and therefore deserves our love. That question has been clearly answered for all time.

Using any concept of God we must know that God does not need us. We need each other. We can learn this even from Jewish scriptures. When a prophet, speaking for God says, "I desire compassion not sacrifice" (Hos. 6:6), he is telling us that we should be concerned with what persons need, not God. The idea of sacrifice to God was a holdover from the times when humans sacrificed to idols, when they thought of a god as wanting something from them to express their allegiance in some concrete form, or as a form of appeasement. What could the God of Judaism and Christianity possibly need from us? The negative perspective on the Law implies a self-sacrifice in terms of human freedom. My generation grew up thinking of the commandments as an abridgement of human freedom. Whereas if we are all treating each other as family, we discover a new, broader kind of freedom.

Much of what we learn from Jewish scriptures is best understood as transitional stage between the human invention of gods and the realization that God is beyond the possibility of human invention, that anything we can say about God is limiting, and if we become fixated on what we say we are idolaters. Reinhold Niebuhr gives as an example the idea that we could not have imagined anything beyond mutual love, i.e., love that expects love in return for loving (Ramsey 1962:146). Who could have thought that we would be called to love our enemies, and not just those that love us? There is another reason for attending to the positive direction our thoughts should take when thinking of the Commandments. By thinking in terms of fulfillment we can discern accretions to the Law that are not properly part of the moral code. The concept of what is wrong is often culture specific. A good example of this is the belief by early missionaries that the European dress code was moral and the South Sea islanders lack of clothing was immoral. To this and other so-called immoral behaviors we need only apply the criterion: Who is harmed? What is the harm?

If the whole Law is fulfilled by simply demonstrating concern for the life and well-being of our neighbors (who incidentally, we are not required to like; liking just makes it easier), then sin has two levels or degrees: 1) the failure to be concerned; and 2) a positive demonstration of our unconcern such as actually harming or killing someone. This is radically different from what most of the churches are teaching, including the church of Rome. In a book approved by Cardinal Hickey of Washington, D.C., Dr. William E. May, a lay theologian writes, "The Scriptures understand sin to be essentially an offense against God" (1991:114). This is a view of sin adopted from Jewish scriptures where we are given numerous examples of divine wrath allegedly being visited on offending individuals--Adam and Eve, Cain, Miriam, and Onan among the more prominent ones. If we understand scripture as a record of evolution in human consciousness we will realize that this is a case of the church putting new wine in old wineskins, a common human failing that Jesus warned us about.

Speaking of God being offended is a way of acknowledging God's unconditional love for humans. If as Jesus tells us we love God by loving our neighbor, loving God is a humanistic, earthside problem. Sin is an offense against our neighbor, a violation of the relationship, actual or potential. To speak of God as being offended is just a poetic way of expressing that reality. On this view the idea of sin is not some act with a negative effect in a transcendental realm. The mystery is not in sin; we can be conscious of harming someone deliberately. The mystery is our sinfulness. We could never be totally aware of all the ways we can harm others. Saying that a person who harms someone (sins) will be dispatched to hell for that behavior is a simpler and more powerful way of saying to ignorant peasants that doing evil is not in one's best long-term interest. If our problem is ignorance, it is something we are capable of dealing with if we can escape the mindset of a transcendental morality laid on us by the church. Fulfillment of the Law is then understood to be the complete acceptance by humans of their responsibility as a member of the human family and the work of bringing about the Reign of God (earthside peace and justice), not keeping the commandments to save our "immortal souls." The Ten Commandments are not rules abridging our freedom as they seem to be by the way they have been taught. They are, as we shall see when we examine them individually, the way to optimum freedom for all persons. On an increasingly crowded globe they must be seen as the ultimate means of survival and not a means of cementing a relationship with God unless we think of a relationship with God as immanent, i.e., God's indwelling in persons.

The common perspective on the commandments is that they limit our choices. In a survey of college students I asked the question: "Do you consider the Commandments restrictive or liberating?" Without exception they answered, "Restrictive." The alternative to the apparent limits of the Commandments appears to be frustration. We should not be surprised that people violate the commandments with this dichotomous view as the extent of their possible choices. For example, on this view "Keep holy the sabbath," offers us the choice of keeping it holy or not. With the idea of fulfillment in mind we come to realize that the commandment calls for minimum behavior. Meditating on the meaning of fulfilling the commandment we are led to ask: What of the other six days? Are we to keep them unholy? Hardly. Reflection on the meaning of the commandment should lead us to conclude that all days are to be kept holy and that one is set aside especially to provoke thought, as it were, concerning the other six days. There is also the implied question: What does it mean to keep a day holy? According to Jewish custom the most sacred time of an ordinary week is from sundown on Friday to sundown on Saturday, and the family meal is a particularly sacred time within that twenty-four hours, an expression of kinship, a time for affirming family bonds. This aspect of the commandment assumes special importance within the context of what Jesus taught. If we are to love God by loving our neighbors that loving must begin with those close to us. If we cannot love our immediate families, how are we to love strangers? By making personal salvation, hence personal attendance at Mass the most important part of keeping Sunday holy the church has taken the focus away from the family where it properly belongs. The obligation to attend mass does not entail doing it with one's family. Many families do attend together; nevertheless, it remains a private obligation, one of many reasons for reclaiming religion from the church.

Why does the commandment not prescribe that everyday be holy if that is what it is about? I submit that requiring every day to be holy would have made the commandment less provocative and too burdensome to initiate an evolution in moral consciousness. Learning occurs in stages. Also one day out of seven makes it a rhythmic occurrence that is more consistent with human nature. Then too what we do all the time becomes habit, and the commandments as Jesus teaches us should lead to a higher consciousness rather than habit. If we tend to think of the commandments as a prescription for salvation as many of the faithful do, it is because our religious leaders have either taught this or allowed people to believe it as relatively harmless superstition. Officially the church denies that keeping the commandments is a formula for salvation, but how else are we to interpret John Paul II's words in *Veritas Splendor*: "Jesus himself definitively confirms [the commandments] and proposes them to us as the way and condition of salvation" (1993:21). Catholic church officials see the great mass of faithful as too unsophisticated theologically for them to explain the difference. Thus a more detailed prescription within the commandment of what we should do would leave us even more convinced that it is restrictive rather than liberating. There would seem to be nothing to reflect on, only to obey. This in fact is the position taken by John-Paul II in *Veritas Splendor*.

Thus we must meditate on the Law. Rather than a complete expression of what we need to know and do it becomes the means by which we discover the meaning of creative relationships. I understand Jesus as suggesting that the Law should function as a stimulus to creativity. This is not standard church teaching. When at a meeting between high school seniors and an archbishop a senior ask why do we have to go to Mass on Sunday the senior was told that if he did not go to Sunday Mass he committed a mortal sin and would go to hell if he died. Perhaps the archbishop was afraid that the young man might next ask, "Why couldn't a bunch of us go to the park on Sunday and pray under the trees?" This has actually happened, and those high school students who did it were worshiping creatively, something Jesus could appreciate. Mandatory Sunday worship can become a deadly habit for both priest and faithful, which it was to a much greater extent prior to liturgical renewal following Vatican II. Better the kinship feelings generated by a trip to the park than the deadly dull sermons and appeals for more money preached to a captive audience. If we were taught to fulfill rather than keep the commandments, making failure to assist at Mass on Sundays and holy days a mortal sin would be at best pointless and at worst an insult to human intelligence, negating the potential the church has for bringing people together.

The whole idea of common worship in our time must be tied to the call for us to create a global community mirroring the role it played in promoting Jewish tribal identity. A global community in our time can only be a network of smaller communities bonded together by reasons other than that we have to do such and so at such and such a place at such and such a time to keep from going to hell. Rewriting the commandment in New Testament terms we get, "Keep one day a week especially holy by affirming the bonds we have with others, but look to ways of making every day holy through a greater involvement with the human family." When we look at the sacrament of love in chapter eight, this aspect of the commandment will assume a special significance.

Whatever form religion ultimately takes it needs to be something in which everyone participates. A world of insiders and outsiders may be as bad or worse than a world of winners and losers. Both kinds of worlds make a global community impossible. Non-believers won't ordinarily be able to make sense of the first three commandments since they are concerned with worship and reverence due to God. This problem yields to a simple change in perspective. None of us has direct access to a transcendent God. It is significant that St. John asked, "How can you love God whom you can't see when you don't love your neighbor whom you can see?" (1John 4:20) Nothing is clearer in the Gospel than that we love God by loving our neighbor. If we claim to love God while not loving our neighbor we are loving some self-created image of God making us idolaters. Loving neighbors is something atheists do thereby affirming kinship with us, so in this sense it is a commandment anyone can fulfill though atheists may prefer not to think in those terms.

A more serious problem and not just for atheists is how can we love some people when we cannot even like them. The word love has many connotation for us. Generally we associate it with a certain kinds of feelings and a certain level of attractiveness in persons, and some persons not only do not attract us, they may actually repel us. There is hope for us who feel this way in the statement by Jesus that, "Those who are not against you may be counted as for you" (Mark 9:40). A minimal love, then, requires that we do nothing against anyone including those who in anyway repel us. Are the relatives of murder victims who testify in court hoping that the judge will sentence the convicted murderer to death violating this commandment? We cannot look into the heart of anyone and make that judgment. We must look to ourselves. How would we respond in this situation?

And what of people who pass laws and rules that allow people to discriminate against anyone--Jews, blacks, same sex lovers? Do they pass the test of minimal love? That is between themselves and God. We are not capable of making such judgments. I raise these questions as examples of what we must reflect on and apply to ourselves, particularly those who aspire to be among the Christian elite. That is, "Anyone who would be greatest in the kingdom of heaven must be the servant of all" (Mat. 23:11).

If the transcendent God is inaccessible to us, the God immanent in our neighbor is readily accessible. This means that a total commitment to God can take the form of a total commitment of service to our neighbors. This is an ideal we may never reach but at least it is a goal we can comprehend. Sometimes the best we can do is express our commitment minimally by not being against our neighbor. Even this minimal behavior can require of certain persons great acts of courage. We all have different talents and charisms and there is no objective standards against which we can measure anyone. If God judges anyone it will probably be against the talents and resources available to that person, as the parable of the talents seems to say. Even the atheist, Karl Popper, tells us that persons who are "intellectually, morally and educationally superior" have "special moral responsibilities" (1971:49). Thus "total commitment" has different meanings for different persons, and even for the same person at different stages of life.

All of us are called to a higher consciousness. For the ancient Hebrews this call was made explicit in the second commandment which bid them to take special care with regard to the name of God. This meant not saying Yahweh's name. "Whenever the name occurred in text, the reader pronounced it *Adonai*, `Lord'" (Huesman 1968:57). Our ignorance of other humans, even among those committed to intimacy, is overwhelming. How much more is everyone, even believers, ignorant of God. When we overhear someone making assertions about God such as "God wants. . . ." "God feels. . .," "God likes. . ., this or that pleases God" we have to wonder where they acquired their information. Such thinking illustrates in part why idolatry may be our most common fault. The purpose of each law under the new dispensation is to rouse us to a greater awareness. Believers who cannot be conscious when speaking of God are indeed unconscious.

Belief in God was the foundation for creating a tribe as family extended through space and time. It was a magnificent first step and set the pattern for a global family that we must now create. Very likely we will always have tribes and certain aspects of tribalism tend to be divisive, a characteristic we must be on guard against. As for aggressive tribal loyalties they can be channeled into relatively harmless competition such as sporting events. The first three commandments when interpreted according to the New Testament are still about what we do with, for and toward one another and so they apply to everyone.

The Roman Catholic church has made Sunday worship a formal requirement. It tells us we sin grievously if we do not do it the way prescribed by the institution, but canon law is not God's law. The call to worship is best left to the imagination of the People of God, which is more inclusive than church membership. Atheists who serve the poor in soup kitchens, attending to God as immanent, qualify as God's people even though they do not believe in God. Although it may not please an atheist to be thought of this way Christians, especially church officials, must accept some responsibility for that.

The time for putting money into multi-million dollar edifices as places for worship seems past. Wouldn't this money be better spent on shelters for the homeless, battered women and children and other places that serve our needy brothers and sisters? This was the message of Dorothy Day and those who continue her work. Obviously God does not need elaborate houses of worship. This is a human thing. We should perhaps restore the Jewish custom of keeping a special day holy within the family. We read that Jesus told the Samaritan woman at Jacob's well that place was not primary in worship (John 4:23) True worship takes place within a person. The church already says that the law of charity is prior to the requirement of attending Mass. As long as worship is mandatory the definition should be broadened to include any service to the poor, the sick, prisoners and so on. Any time should be appropriate, leaving it to the faithful to be responsible for worshiping where, when and how they could. This new freedom would be a call for everyone to begin worshiping creatively, especially in pairs and small groups.

Small community gatherings for worship or even just family gatherings in the homes of the faithful could serve as a substitute for the Sunday Mass requirement, but that is not likely to be approved by the Vatican anytime soon. Once again as in other possible reforms, these gatherings would be beyond the control of Rome. There is nothing in what Jesus said that decreed the current structure. However, if families or the people of a neighborhood gathered in each others homes their breaking of bread can be as sacred as any gathering in a large building. "Where two or more are gathered in my name, there I am with them" (Mat. 18:20). If the Vatican thinks ordination is important, let them ordain ordinary people to a lesser kind of priesthood, including women, to facilitate such gatherings. Religious institutions do not control the movements of God's spirit, although the Pope and the curia may act as if they do. Common worship can be a form of tribal identity that can connect rather than divide.

With the fourth commandment in the Catholic canon we begin defining more specifically what is proper among humans. At one time honoring one's father and mother must have meant, among other things, taking care of parents in their old age. With social security and pension plans that aspect of caring for parents is no longer necessary for many people. As with all the commandments, fulfilling this one requires reflection. We are called to love all humans, but to honor is to love in a special way. This may create serious problems for some of us. How are persons to keep, let alone fulfill, this commandment when the parent who must be honored also happens to be a brutal monster or sexual molester of ourselves or our children? This situation may call for more creativity than we feel we can muster, but a molester is certainly one of the enemies Jesus told us to love. There are no generic solutions. We must find our own way in the dark, perhaps aided by the knowledge that God is immanent in child molesters.

Of one thing we can be certain. Admonishing children to obey the law does not constitute fulfillment of the 4th commandment. It is a commandment for adults. Children are not capable of appreciating the gift of life that parents give. It would seem to be the responsibility of parents to act in such a way that appreciation for the gift of life is a natural response of children as they grow in wisdom and knowledge. I was taught as a child that the honor required by this commandment extended to all adults and authorities. The purpose of the commandment seemed to me and my peers to be control, especially considering that the penalty for noncompliance was believed to be hell. However, a little reflection should reveal the futility of threatening a youngster with eternal damnation for failing to obey parents, teachers and others if for the youngster such obedience equates with loss of identity, which is just another name for hell. Let adults honor their parents, even the abusers and sexual molesters, by being good parents, thereby demonstrating to their children what honoring parents means. If the task proves to be too much it can furnish material for humility. When we are identified as the child of our parents, let that identification be the honor we owe them. We are the personification of the love with which we ought to have been conceived.

Another point that calls for serious reflection has to do with parents as the source of life. Anyone who contributes to our life and well-being, especially our spiritual development, is also a source of life, as also anyone with whom we engage in creative relationships. Seen in this context the command to honor our parents becomes a special case of honoring everyone. As with Sunday observance it is a place to begin.

"The prohibition against killing" is one that virtually everyone can accept." Given the need to create community inherent in the first commandment, and the need we all have to survive, this is a law we can all understand. It is significant that this law does not proscribe murder, although that is how most people think of it. Killing someone ends, absolutely, the possibility of a relationship with that person. For this reason it is regarded by many as the most serious breach of the Law because there is no possibility of healing. Anger and anything between it and murder are proscribed because these are movements away from promoting human life and well-being. Fulfillment of this law calls for us to transcend the minimum requirements and promote the life and well-being of all family members. This commandment offers the greatest possible scope for human imagination, especially for those who feel called to be one of Jesus' elite. Few of those burdened by traditional church teaching would regard teaching a small child to read as fulfillment of this commandment, but since such behavior promotes the life and well being of the child, that is exactly what it is. After people are fed, clothed and housed there should be opportunities for development of their potential. As with other commandments we are led to a greater involvement in life by pursuing fulfillment through reflection. If we hate our own life, we are not likely to rejoice in the life of others, much less promote life and personal development for them. Thus habits of anger and violence are clues that we are less than completely oriented to life, that we are facing in the wrong direction. Awareness of this fault is an opportunity to practice humility and for us to correct it. The fullest realization of this law will lead to a greater personal growth through our efforts to aid and abet others. I have noted above that the commandment proscribes killing not murder. The Jews interpreted this narrowly to mean do not kill another Jew, a rule which they themselves violated if they stoned anyone to death for a breach of a commandment.

The proscription of adultery tells us not to have sex with someone else's committed partner. The original wording of this commandment is too narrow for our own time. But as in the case of anger which is movement toward a breach in a relationship, we have to reflect on what is movement toward destroying what is potentially the most intimate of all bonds. I would therefore express the commandment in this way: "Do not intrude on the relationship of a pair-bonding couple." Also, I do not consider that the commandment applies only to sexually bonded couples. All intimate relationships should command our respect, especially those with children.

I am inclined to think that certain violations of this law are possibly the most serious harm anyone can do. The effects of encroaching on a pair who are engaged in the difficult process of bonding may reverberate through several generations when we consider the possible effect on children in addition to the couple themselves. The legal and canonical definitions of adultery as they stand today are both too broad and too narrow. They are too broad because the church has gathered the idea of every possible sexual behavior within the scope of this commandment, including masturbation which is not sex at all. Fornication is commonly thought to be proscribed by this law, but there is no way to determine from the usual interpretations whether the breach is different from adultery in degree or kind. We can presumably go to hell for either. Then there is the fact that the sacrament of matrimony is mutually self-administered, making it difficult to determine from outside of a relationship whether anyone has been harmed or if a couple has made an unconditional commitment without having been married according canon law. The proscription as defined by the magisterium is too narrow because it fails to focus on the seriousness of the harm that can be done with or without sex, viz., the possible destruction of what can an important foundation for a global community, the relationship of the pair-bonding couple.

One problem we have with sex is that it can give the appearance of unity without the reality. No one considers the connection achieved by rape as human bonding. But all sex acts can be placed on a continuum ranging from rape to the bonding that occurs with mutual, unconditional love. The failure to bond through rape is only a degree removed from the sex that occurs as the result of deception, as in a promise to marry or pair-bond that a person cannot or will not keep. Closer to the real thing but still some distance from unconditional pair-bonding is the sincere but ignorant couplings of the young who are not likely to be capable of deliberating and choosing responsibly in matters of sex. They may be more inclined to perceive it as just recreation, a reaction for which the various Christian denominations bears some responsibility because of the way sexuality has been viewed for the better part of two millennia. Equating fornication with adultery has not had the effect of making fornication more significant. Rather, it has made adultery seem less important. If a person can go to hell for masturbating we are witness to a further trivialization of what may be the most significant proscription of all.

As with the other commandments the first requirement for fulfilling it is to reflect, keeping in mind that the goal is a greater awareness of our common humanity and the need to form a global community. Reflection implies an awareness of our ignorance and the assumption that the depth of our ignorance is beyond our own comprehension. In other words our main problem is not sin. It is, rather, sinfulness, the fact that we can harm others without being aware. We do not know the ultimate consequences of our behavior. If someone throws a bottle on a beach that gets broken, another person could get seriously cut which could have further harmful consequences. Ignorance may make us less accountable for an act but that by itself does nothing to increase our awareness or decrease the harm.

The magisterium tells us that one of the characteristics that determines if an act is a serious sin is sufficient reflection, but their idea of serious reflection is simply a knowledge of the rule as it was taught, then remembering it and the so-called consequences, viz., hell, when we are tempted. Under these circumstances the rule may not have been internalized as a matter of conviction and conviction requires that the rule be reasonable, the way that "Do not kill" is seen by everyone to be reasonable (especially when equated with murder) because of the ease with which we can achieve consensus concerning its validity. If a Catholic couple are entangled in the back seat of an automobile, they may both think: The church says what we are thinking of doing is a mortal sin. If we go through with it we will have sinned mortally. The reference they use is out there and is not a matter of conviction, otherwise they would not be thinking: "The church says. . ." Reflection of the kind called for by the commandments cannot occur under the pressure of hormones as in this situation. The magisterium has not taught the need for prior reflection and conviction, just a bare knowledge of the rule and the consequences of violating it. The hierarchy thinks it has done its job when it has proclaimed the law and the sanctions, both temporal and transcendental. They fail to realize that for a rule to carry conviction depends on its being perceived as a reasonable way for humans to act. The problem with being reasonable in matters of sex is that the circumstances for each person will vary to some degree. Rather than deal in subtleties the church just bans everything outside of marriage. What happens when there is no priest to perform a canonical ceremony? The reasons given by the church for proscribing sex outside of marriage are totally irrational: God says so, or we say so, or that persons who die without confessing will lose their "immortal souls". This carries very little conviction on the back seat of an automobile or anywhere for that matter. Death is a very remote possibility for young people. The proof is in the actuarial tables, but the hormones are very present. Also, *soul* is religious jargon copied from Greek philosophy for which it is difficult to imagine any reality. How can we lose what is not perceived as real? There is also the fact that for a ban to be reasonable it would have to be reasonable for all humans, not just Catholics, just as in the case of stealing or killing.

If we look at the chief criteria for sin proposed in this study--Who is harmed? What is the harm? We cannot look in the window of said automobile, check ring fingers, and make a determination. Everything depends on the disposition of each person. They may by having sex seal a commitment they have made to unconditional love of each other. Or, they may be just having fun while taking care not to put the woman at risk of pregnancy. One or both could be acting irresponsibly toward each other because of lying, extortion, and so on. The sex itself is not the sin. It can be the means of harming someone, depending on the disposition of the persons involved, and that disposition would be better informed if church officials had a well-thought-out theology of sex and intimacy and knew what they were doing when they taught the morality of sex.

Our attitude toward developing a sexual awareness in children seems to follow the church's lead. It appears that we must save them at all cost from sexual play, or even from any awareness of the existence of sex. If we had deliberately set out to encourage consciousness of sex and sexual experimentation, we could hardly have had greater success. We tend to make an attractive mystery out of an easily satisfied childish curiosity. We do not want our children to have genital sex, but to act as though we walked in on a Wagnerian tragedy if we catch them playing, "You show me yours. . .," will only stimulate a greater curiosity because they may not be able to understand what all the fuss is about. They need to know enough not to be vulnerable to strangers. They need to know, when they become capable of understanding it, the risks of physical intimacy, psychological as well as physical. There is much they need to know concerning sex but there are no blanket prescriptions, and to terrify sensitive children into thinking that they will go to hell if they masturbate can do great harm.

In the sexual climate of the sixties and since then many people were somewhat conscious of the criteria I propose for determining if some behavior is wrong, but if they could conceive of no wrong in having sex then they felt free to act. Not recognizing the harm is not the same as there being none. It is the old problem of sinfulness again. Many girls and women, because of the way they have been brought up are vulnerable to very aggressive men and may submit to sexual demands without full assent thus complicating their lives with guilt they may have no way of resolving, or a pregnancy that requires some complicated resolution.

For those who have been burdened by the magisterium with the idea that *body;* and *soul* are real entities rather than abstractions the problems of sex may be compounded. Sexual desire is felt with our whole being, not our body as distinct from our soul. We quite naturally intuit the oneness of our nature, so restraint without reasonable cause appears frustrating and destructive; yielding appears fulfilling and integrative. Without a habit of restraint based on the questioning of our knowledge and motives, in other words the need for reflection, we cannot honestly say that we are not harming someone. The purpose and basis for restraint is poorly taught if it is taught at all. Two motives for restraint can be found in church teaching: The fear of hell which at least in the past may have worked with uneducated peasants who live on the edge, and for whom death is never far away. But for young educated persons who live in American suburbs, and for whom the actuarial tables say they will live into their middle seventies and beyond, hell is not a factor. The second reason for restraint looms large in church history. It is achieving self-mastery by not giving in to sexual impulses. The early church adopted this from the Stoic who considered it heroic behavior. Many people, mostly men, went to the desert to do battle with their sexual fantasies. Asceticism was seen as a way to attain heavenly glory. One had to overcome the body, which even when it was not thought bad as did the Manicheism or some forms of Gnosticism, was still the source of evil because of the obvious difficulty people, especially men, experienced in controlling it. The only modification Christians made was that one controlled for God instead of just for one's ego. The Stoic influence lives in our own day in the required celibacy of the Roman clergy, and in the attitude toward sex with which the church has burdened the laity. It also is why celibate clergy and religious up to Vatican II were considered superior to lay persons. They were the Christian elite. Contrast this with Jesus' description, that the greatest person is the one who is the servant of all. Unfortunately *servant* can be interpreted in different ways. John Paul II and Cardinal Ratzinger see themselves as servants of God by their self-appointed task of keeping us in line, but Jesus' concern was with serving his People not a transcendent God to whom we do not have access.

Moral behavior is that which affects at least one other person, either negatively or positively. In theological language, negatively affecting one or more persons is sin. Thought of this way the consequences of what we do can often be immediate and knowable. This is not what the magisterium is teaching. Sin they tell us may have consequences in the here and now but its most important consequence is in the transcendental realm; or, as they put it, it is an offense against God. If our thinking is confused by the possibility of offending God whom we cannot see, we will lose sight of the possible harm we may be doing another human whom we can see. Hell cannot be a felt consequence despite well-meaning but uninformed teachers who try to associate guilt feelings, a product of neural conditioning, with the incipient torments of hell. This misconception is further confused by the explanation that habitual sinners lose their sensitivity to guilt and develop hardened consciences. After the first "sin," the second, third and twentieth happen more readily. Actually what is lost is simply neural conditioning. If this were not so we would have the awkward task of explaining good people who were never conditioned to feel guilt, who experience guilt as an intellectual awareness instead of a feeling.

According to the magisterium's sexual morality, any voluntary assent to venereal pleasure among the unmarried is a serious breach of the law as is any deliberate wasting of seed (semen). Putting these two ideas together, St. Augustine concluded that there might be sin in the case of intercourse between husband and wife when they definitely knew that conception was not possible, as during pregnancy. Some of the Fathers were more explicit saying that such behavior is definitely a sin. The thinking of Augustine and the Fathers indicates how one can have flawless logic and still derive a wrong answer because the original assumptions are questionable. It would appear that for the church pleasure without unwanted consequences is a problem. We have been asked to measure ourselves against a Greek ideal, not the Gospel.

In considering the morality of venereal pleasure according to the magisterium the question arises: is the degree of sin proportionate to the pleasure as we might infer from their teaching? What if there is contact or even penetration without pleasure? Is there no sin? Perhaps by extension, painful sex, of which women are the most likely to complain, is virtuous. Obviously harming a person has nothing to do with the kind or amount of pleasure involved. The real issue is the nature of a proper human relationship. There is a possibility that two unmarried persons can have sex in which neither is harmed, but because of our massive ignorance of what goes on inside of another person and the intensity of the emotions involved, certainty in such matters will be elusive, and so it would be difficult to act with certainty when disregarding the rules. Females are not the only ones vulnerable. Young men may believe they are loved when a woman gives sex. To learn otherwise can be devastating.

There are other risks of which we should be aware. While fornication is technically less serious in the eyes of the church, according to the criteria established here it may be more serious, for example, when adults seduce young persons, or when persons in positions of power use their office to have sex with someone as in the case of therapists, doctors, priests and teachers. The seriousness of the harm that might be done involves many factors. Chief among these is our responsibility for developing convictions about what might be good or bad prior to the time we must make decisions. This has not been the way morality, especially sexual morality, has been taught.

There is a serious danger to the evolving morality of children in becoming sexually involved before they are able to distinguish between the illusion and the reality of intimacy. They may grow up thinking that sex *is* intimacy if real intimacy with the adults who care for them has not been a part of their lives before experiencing sex. We may perhaps understand this better if we put sex on a continuum from rape to an ideal sexual intimacy. Such an intimacy requires an active involvement of minds that is entirely missing in rape but can be present without sex. Women I know who have been raped report that their rapists insisted that their victims tell them how much they wanted to have sex or how much they liked it. They have been known to ask their victims to beg for it. So even for rapists, sex is not just a mindless involvement. Yet rape is only some degrees removed from sex accomplished through of any kind of coercion. The problem with sexual coercion is that it is coercion, not that it is sexual. Then there is deception, as in a promise of love made only for the purpose of obtaining sex, or the coupling of youngsters who do not know the meaning of intimacy. But awareness of what constitutes an ideal intimacy cannot be imposed on young persons through suggesting the terrors of possible sanctions which has been the strategy of most Christian churches. Awareness must grow naturally. We can promote this growth in awareness of what intimacy is really like by having an intimate relationship with our children. We can only connect with them as with other humans through communication which is always *with* never *to*, and once connected they will learn that the joys of intimacy will make any kind of hedonism pale in comparison.

There are several implications in the foregoing. We must clearly understand our own values, i.e., make choices from conviction, and the lines of communication must be kept open from an age when children can still trust us. Once children lose faith in their ability to communicate with us only a radical effort can restore it. Becoming imperious and forcing conformity by imposing restraints and limits on their lives to prevent behaviors we do not like is far from the ideal of acting from conviction which should be their goal as well as ours because it is the ideal for humans. There is a clue in this as to what and how we should teach children. They need to know the value of reflection, hence of postponing certain decisions of importance. This is perhaps done by reflecting together; i.e., that is discussing what is important in relationships. They need to have some idea of how to arrive at a conviction of what is in their best long-term interests, by which I do not mean going to heaven or avoiding hell. But perhaps most of all they need to see how false is the culture that would divide humans into winners and losers, especially when the winners count sex partners as scores, usually in the past, a male preoccupation.

Few of us will question the value to children of a permanent relationship between parents. When a crisis of temperament occurs within a committed relationship, a prior disposition to maintain the relationship can lead to considering ways of resolving the conflict instead of dissolving the partnership. A committed, intimate relationship should be made up of three parts, the commitment each partner makes to the other and the commitment each makes to the relationship. If they only commit to each other, when troubles arises the relationship may be broken, but a prior commitment to the relationship leaves them still connected, and if they resolve their difficulties the result should be a greater intimacy.

If we are ever to have a global community, committed relationships will provide the major portion of the foundation upon which such a community will be built if for no other reason than that the next generation will emerge from those relationships. Few of us are likely to be committed to all of humanity. Most of us must find the satisfaction we need in a committed intimacy with one person and lesser intimacies with a few others. For most persons who are unable to find that satisfaction by engaging in a creative intimacy with one person the resulting frustration and anger may be visited on the world in some measure, hence wars, terrorism, crime, and assorted lesser reprisals for failing to get what is perceived as one's due, although through a mostly unconscious process.

The institutional church by concentrating on the prohibition of certain kinds of sexual relationships and failing to promote fulfillment of the commandment through proper intimacies is largely responsible for the kind of world we have today. Oneness is the law of our nature. The fact of our being necessarily social is even more significant in the realm of intimate interpersonal relationships. It is what we are born for. If the only alternative to oneness is frustration, no one should be surprised that many will opt for the oneness of just sex if they are not aware of other possibilities. The hierarchy does not promote or even teach as a matter of course the nature of true intimacy. Intimacy is not just about sex otherwise we could not be intimate with our children, but the close association of intimacy with sex has been enough to keep the magisterium from wanting to deal with it.

Our clergy might be better positioned to handle the problem of guiding people in matters of intimacy if they experienced it in their own lives with or without sex. The Vatican will never allow a married clergy as long as they think the supernatural world is more important than this one. The so-called sexual revolution should be called the sexual rebellion. It is a direct result of the confusion caused by the negative attitude of the church toward sex for over seventeen hundred years. The bishops during Vatican II finally admitted that sex had a value for humans beyond the possibility of procreation, but they have yet to figure out what it can mean for the creation of a global family which is what Jesus' message is all about. Rome is still acting as though we might be getting away with something if we can have sex without the chance of making a baby, evidence that they do not yet see the big picture. They insist that we act according to a biological ideal in having sex. Making contraception a sin is equivalent to insisting that we act the way other animals do by not being concerned with the problems brought on by uncontrolled procreation. Our attention should be focussed on a more intimate connection with our partner, not whether we will or will not make a baby unless that is what we want. Making a new life out of two could be the most intimate of acts, but not everyone can see it that way.

The concept of stealing generates an image of taking some thing that belongs to another person. In our contemporary world that view is too narrow. The new commandments are about community and life. We can discern the relative value of the law if we consider the difference between our culture (USA 2002) and a culture of scarcity (Chiapas, Mexico) where lives can depend on what is owned. If I am a peasant and someone steals the sack of corn I have saved for planting, this is radically different from the case of someone stealing my VCR if I belong to a middle-class family in the United States. In the case of the peasant's corn the theft actually violates the fifth commandment against killing, evidence that in fulfilling or violating one we fulfill or violate all of them. Fulfillment of the Law directs us to promote the life and well being of other humans and in any culture we have failed this imperative if we steal.

If we believe in God, we have to believe that the bounty of the earth somehow belongs to everyone, at least to the point of being able to survive. The purpose of this law is not to protect our VCRs from crooks. Jesus tells us that the ideal, hence the challenge is to give everything away. By doing this we liberate ourselves from even the fear of losing our possessions which can also be an obstacle to connecting with others. Faith in earth's bounty is the ultimate fulfillment of this commandment. If we cling in fear to what we own when we have plenty as though we can assure ourselves that we will not be without on the morrow, we may not have a tomorrow. Tomorrow is for the living. Excessive attachment to things is an aspect of security that is wasteful for contingent creatures. Being overly attached to things means that if we are separated from our property our lives can be diminished in proportion to our attachment. Those who are most attached make the identification so complete that the loss of property is death. They may throw themselves from a tall building to demonstrate what has already occurred.

If we place any value on an evolved consciousness we have to concern ourselves with the magnitude of violations of this commandment from the economic structures of the world which permits millions to starve to death and millions more to suffer the lifelong consequences of malnutrition for children. Unless we make some effort at resolving the inequitable distribution of the world's resources we cannot count ourselves as fulfilling this commandment. All of us can begin by simplifying our lives. We should perhaps make a commitment to simplicity to help us reflect continuously on how we might fulfill this commandment.

"Do not tell lies about anyone, including yourself." Since all laws are fulfilled within a person, and there is only one integrity, then every law is a different ways of looking at the same reality. Lying disconnects us. This commandment is concerned with the reality of other persons as mysteries. As with the other laws this one describes minimal behavior for an authentic human being, and as with the other laws any attempt to maintain a minimum observance will eventually result in a violation. The Law as Jesus taught it is to initiate a process, not to end one.

If we are open to the possibility we can begin to experience the reality of another person. This openness is characterized by the effort of reaching out with understanding toward what is essential in the person we confront, even if that person is obnoxious. Those of us who have loved know that the experience of another person is unspeakable. If we say anything it must be qualified by explaining that no matter what we say we will not have begun to disclose the beauty and reality of the person we are coming to know. Now, if as every lover knows we cannot speak the truth about a person toward whom we are well disposed, what of all the statements by which we classify people without first loving them? Is not every statement, especially the negative ones, about other persons an expression of limits which we have no way of knowing actually exist? Is not, then, every judgment false? Does not fulfillment of this law require that we never say anything about a person without qualifying, as the lover does, that we in fact do not know what we are talking about? This again is more often a matter of sinfulness rather than sin. Meditating on the sinfulness this law points to is one way of avoiding sin. It may help to think of God as immanent, the real source of the mystery of persons.

As with every law, an explicit statement of what we could do would place arbitrary limits on our behavior by creating the impression that there is nothing more to do than what was specified. Ultimately, if we love our neighbor we must go beyond admitting that the neighbor is unspeakably better and more beautiful than we can know. To admit that is not the limit of what we can do. We can make a positive declaration, like a lover extolling to the world the charm and beauty of the beloved. In doing this we cannot but realize the truth that we ourselves are beautiful beyond what anyone can know. Unlike a recognizable achievement to which we can point to with pride, this is the ultimate secret. When we recognize that we cannot completely disclose ourselves to anyone because our identity is basically incomprehensible even to ourselves, then we have gone beyond any difficulty in keeping the law. It is fulfilled in us.

"Do not withdraw from the world into sexual fantasies" is a commandment implied in the sixth insofar as fantasy is a stage in the development of a destructive physical intimacy. Still, a separate statement of limits is needed because there are persons who may not go beyond fantasy in the matter of sex. Fantasy for such persons can be a complete experience. The proscription against masturbation makes sense when it is used in connection with these closed fantasies, not as the church has taught, that is, because seed is wasted. The sex drive is one way our nature impels us to connect with other humans. If the drive is short circuited by masturbation fantasies we may be abdicating our responsibility to build community because we do not attempt to make connections that we should make. Masturbation may also be wrong, for example, if a committed couple have an argument and instead of making the desire for sex an occasion for reconciling, one or the other gets release by masturbating instead.

Within the framework of the sixth commandment fantasy may need to be restrained because it can lead to an inappropriate realization of the fantasy. Technically, then, pure fantasy, or fantasy plus masturbation is not a violation of the sixth, but in some respects may be worse. Fantasists do not encounter the limitations inherent in the attempt to actualize a relationship. Having no real persons with whom they must communicate and to whom they must adjust, they can enjoy the illusion of unlimited power over people. They can possess anyone they want, anytime, anyway. For fantasists an encounter with real persons only adds the possibility of rebuff. Reality may subtract instead of adding dimensions to their existence. All they want they can create; books, movies, or simply observing real people provide all the material their imaginations need. These persons have one advantage over those not plagued with this problem. If they ever have the courage to face life they will have a well-exercised imagination working for them. Not much of what has been said applies to juvenile masturbation. There is little danger that for most of them it will be part of a closed fantasy.

"Do not seek fulfillment in fantasies about the acquisition and use of property." This law is not just a corollary to the prohibition of stealing, although fantasies may lead to actualization. It is also closely related to the limitation defined in the ninth commandment, i.e., the avoidance of a confrontation with life. Fulfillment requires more than that we should accept life as it comes. We must go out and find it or create it. If we daydream about what we would do with the power of wealth, we do not even have the advantage of persons who have wealth and fear losing it. They can have peace of mind and their wealth by becoming detached. But there is rarely a compelling reason to detach ourselves from fantasy wealth because there seems to be no way to lose it and it seems so harmless. Engaging in such fantasies does not enhance our humanity because such fantasies connect us with no one, hence are disintegrating. I have known men who fantasized making a big win by gambling and instead lost rent and food money for their families. As with all negative behavior there are degrees of harm one can perpetrate. As always we need to reflect on the possible consequences of what we do. This need for reflection applies strongly to politicians who promote lotteries for raising money instead of a fair system of taxation.

The Commandments as the magisterium teaches them, tell us what we must do and not do to be saved. They establish the boundaries of reality in one direction but they do not tell us what reality is. We discover the reality Jesus pointed to when we stop being concerned with the few things we cannot do. Wanting to do what is forbidden is like trying to enter a small forbidden circle when the space outside runs indefinitely in all directions. The challenge posed by the limits of the Law is not in breaking them. It is in working within them. As we apply our imagination to what we can do, we find instead of boundaries, an ever-expanding power to become fully human. We become like a poet working within the apparent limits of the sonnet, capturing a boundless idea in fourteen, iambic pentameter lines. In a series of such poems a poet can put ideas so vast that in a lifetime of searching we could not come to the end of them.

Recognizing our limits instead of a cause for sorrow is a cause for rejoicing. Because we could not fly like birds we learned to fly like humans and have surpassed the birds in some respects. The impulse to create and achieve grows out of our frustration with boundaries, but not where easy solutions are available, on account of our disposition toward closure as we learned from Genesis. In a society that has lost the challenge of wresting a living from the world, we find ourselves increasingly forced to meet the challenge within. Some elementary thinkers propose going back to a less sophisticated level of existence to find the ready-made challenge of fighting the weather, the soil and what-all. That kind of challenge may have been adequate for the discovery of one's identity in another time. In our present circumstances a more conscious search within is required. Avoidance is not creative, and only with a creative effort can we learn the extent of the power possible to us, which has no foreseeable limit. Only then may we glimpse what is meant by being the gods we are called to be. This I believe is how Jesus taught the Ten Commandments.

CHAPTER VII
WHAT IS SIN?

[I]f, while you are offering your gift at the altar, you should remember that [a brother or sister] has something against you, you must leave your gift there before the altar and go away. Make your peace with your [brother or sister] first, then come and offer your gift (Mat. 5:21-24).

No thinking person should have to be persuaded that humanity's survival is threatened by destruction of the biosphere and modern weapons that can kill millions instantly. We humans have a serious problem. Genesis tells us what that problem is--"Man [sic] was evil from the beginning." Unfortunately, the language it uses to tells us seems to make it a transcendental problem and that is how the church, at least since Augustine, has taught it. If we read the statement thus: "Humans did not know how to act in their own best interest from the beginning," It becomes clear that the problem is one of ignorance that humans are born with. We are born radically dependent on other humans to survive. As a consequence we are necessarily social, i.e., we must survive together. It is from the necessity of surviving together that all evil (sin) flows. There are some who try to survive alone and against others. These are sociopaths. Most humans are members of tribes; they group together for survival and sometime survive at the expense of individuals and other tribes, generally under the assumption that resources are scarce. The third group are those who believe that if we share there is enough for all. Even this third group will generate evil (human suffering) through ignorance. This is

186

probably what Biblical writers probably mean by proclaiming that no one is free from sin which is the harm we do to one or more persons.

The Catholic magisterium will agree that sin (evil) is precisely not acting in our own best interest. Their reasons, however have to do with eternal salvation, i.e., how behavior affects our relationship with God, whereas from the quotation above we learn that our primary problem concerns our relationship with other humans. There is an analogy between the sin that affects one or more persons and a disease in the body. A tribe is not a tightly structured organism but the goal should be organization rather than simply order, i.e., a community, wherein each member contributes to the health of the whole according to the member's talents and abilities.

The church correctly teaches that the problem is intractable because God has laid a curse on us making it a transcendental problem. A simpler explanation, one that fits the empirical facts, is that every human is born massively ignorant of how to relate to other humans and consequently how to survive. The humans who teach us generally recognize the social requirement of surviving together, but only recently have many of us begun to recognize that togetherness must transcend tribal limits. This is of course what Jesus taught. Our problems are with each other, not God.

The expression *sin*, despite how the non-religious may feel about it, provides a good, short name for the problems humans have with each other. I have previously defined sin as the harm a person does to one or more persons. Even according to orthodox teaching God must remain unaffected by what we do. If our most fundamental tasks in life are to "survive" and "together" we must have a common language to accomplish this task. We cannot communicate with non-believers using the church's definition of sin.

There can be no more important reason for reclaiming religion from the church than the need to reconceptualize sin. Sin, the harm we do to others cannot be a problem just for church members. The negative effects of sin fall on everyone. It is what adversely affects the survival of all humans including the sinner. What the church teaches about sin has virtually no effect outside of the church and is increasingly less effective for its own members. I have contended throughout this essay that a major problem regarding morality for most people is the lack of conviction resulting from the way it is taught by the church which regards sin as a transcendental problem whereas for those outside the church it must be recognized as a human problem or it will not be accepted. We must first agree on a definition of morality itself so that we could identify the topic of discussion we must all engage in. I offered a definition generic enough for atheists as well as Christians, that is, the rules each of us has or the principle for deriving such rules for acting with, for or toward other humans. Our personal rules may be conscious or unconscious, but we need to ask: Is our morality such that at a minimum it does not negatively affect the survival of anyone, including ourselves? Is it a proper morality, that is, can we make sense of it in a personal way as we can e.g., with the prohibition against killing? The criteria used for judging has to be the positive or negative effect such rules have on the survival of individuals and the species in a way that can be tested in interpersonal relationships and communal experience. There can, of course be no complete knowledge in this respect. We frequently do harm without being aware, a condition referred to as sinfulness which calls for constant reflection and learning.

In his encyclical *Veritas Splendor* Pope John Paul II writes, "The rational ordering of the human act to the good in its truth and the voluntary pursuit of that good, known by reason, constitute morality" (1993:110). Admittedly the Pope's audience is the bishops and this represents a translation from Latin, but why should the explanation be different and less muddled for anyone else? Even allowing that the statement might be meaningful for Christians it is difficult to imagine that it would be for non-Christians. That in itself becomes a major problem in the task of building a global community for which we must devise a proper morality for the sake of survival, one that most people can understand. The pope's definition of *morality* suggests that it is the opposite of *immorality*. Given the absolute morality that the church teaches immediately puts the church at odds with those whose morality is different. This is no way to begin a conversation in the hope of achieving a global community enlightened by a morality proper for all of us. I feel that I clearly demonstrated in the chapter on revelation that a proper morality will emerge from an evolving process that has been going on from the very beginning; we are not there yet. Actually it is a process that will not come to an end. To grow in learning is not to descend into relativism. When what we know today about how to live together supersedes what we knew yesterday the church calls it relativism with a negative connotation. It is more appropriately called a stage in the development of our knowledge the way that Newton supersedes Kepler and is in turn superseded by Einstein. In the moral realm it is how we came to believe that slavery is wrong. It is why we have teachers and schools. Humans are learning animals.

Most Christians will agree to the proposition that sinful behavior is not in the best interest of oneself and the community but rarely will anyone understand why this is so. The church provides answers in religious jargon with little or no useful information. For example, "Sin causes us to lose sanctifying grace." Or, "We will go to hell if we die and we are not in a state of grace." There are persons who have faith that these assertions mean something. But there are those of us who want reasons that we can understand, without which there can be no conviction. Calling sin an offense against God undoubtedly meant something to people at one time, but try imagining God, then try imagining what happens when God is offended. The church's way of teaching morality is clearly designed to teach masses of uneducated peasants, who hope for justice in the next world.

There are persons who subscribe to the descriptions of God in Jewish scriptures where emotions such as anger are attributed to God, and they may imagine an angry person, but any educated person will recognize this as an anthropomorphism, the correct name for which is idolatry. Now people who are concerned about sinning do not want to commit idolatry, but it is difficult if not impossible to avoid being idolatrous. A significant amount of that idolatry occurs through thinking which the church does not and perhaps cannot clarify, viz., that humans can create an effect in a transcendental realm. Any image of God will be idolatrous because it will inevitably be a projection of some human quality. Whatever we say of God can only serve to manifest our second order ignorance, i.e., faulty knowing rather than simply not knowing. By teaching that sin is an offense against God the churches have unknowingly perpetuated this kind of ignorance, the way they once taught that slavery was an element in a hierarchy created by God. We cannot imagine an offense that is not against a person or the community. But for those whose consciousness has been "formed by the twentieth century, *person* means . . . a center of consciousness" (Dewart 1966:147), and consciousness may be the most significant human characteristic we know. But for believers to attribute consciousness (a human characteristic) to God is once again an anthropomorphism, hence idolatrous.

The Catholic Encyclopedia tells us that in the Old Testament, "The words used for sin have generally to do with human relations. . . In sin the goal is a person, and hence it is a failing toward someone, a violation of the bond uniting persons to one another" p. 236c). This definition in the context of morality as defined in this study says in effect that the person who harms another has a defective morality, that such a persons has a set of rules for acting with, for or toward someone that needs revision. Saying that it is an offense against God is a manner of speaking because it is believed that "sin reaches God insofar as it hurts a [person] whom God loves" (p. 236d).

If we examine the problem of what sin could be from the other direction we may be able to clarify just what the concept sin could mean to modern persons. Here we are on firmer ground because we have explicit descriptions in the New Testament of what being good means which we can presume is the opposite of sin. Being good means feeding the hungry, clothing the naked, attending to the sick, visiting prisoners, and in general promoting the life and well-being of everyone, especially the poor and outcasts of this world, even one's enemies. By promoting the life and well-being of everyone, we are included, as Bonhoeffer noted. Thus, neglecting the poor and the outcasts may be sinful, but directly harming them surely *must* be sinful. To speak of God being offended is a poetic expression for that reality. The effects we have to be concerned with are in this world not in a realm about which we can have no knowledge, and these effects must have a meaning that virtually everyone can understand--Christians, Buddhist, atheist or whatever--because in the end we are a family and we must begin to act like one regardless of our beliefs about God. You were reminded in chapter one that if faith is a gift as every Christian is taught, then no faith is likewise a gift. Thus we see that transcendental morality cannot be the basis for a global community. Morality has to do with the rules governing human relationships, and as we have seen in the chapter on the Commandments, these are the rules for survival of the individual and the species. We have also noted that survival generally requires a cooperative effort, and on a global level cooperation becomes increasingly urgent because of our tendency toward tribalism and the destructive power that tribes now possess.

Communication is necessary for establishing and maintaining cooperative relationships, and as we saw in chapter five it is a two-way process. If we could communicate with God there would have to be a response that humans could recognize as meaningful. When people pray with words the assumption is that they are talking to God not with God, unless as in common worship they are conscious of God as immanent in each other. The magisterium tells us that God responds to prayers. The catch is that whatever happens is the response. If we are praying for some favor and we get what we ask for or our request is rejected that is God's answer to our prayers. This is hardly a meaningful dialogue. The institution we call the Catholic church, recognizing that God does not respond in a way that we can ordinarily understand, claims to be the divinely appointed mediator between ourselves and God, that is, church officials are God's voice in this alleged communication with us (See Wm. May). But does God speak to the pope, the cardinals and the rest of the clergy? Even they do not claim that. They do lay claim to special guidance by the Holy

Spirit. Such a claim is based on inferences from scripture and inferences from those inferences which they call tradition. But if God
speaks to the Catholic hierarchy in their official capacity (or guides
them) then was it God who told them to burn heretics and witches?
And what about sending armies to the Holy Land to slay Jews,
Muslims and assorted infidels? This is hardly promoting the life and
well-being of everyone as Jesus taught and it lays a big question mark
on their claim to speak for God. All the evidence points to the church
being a very human institution and all that entails.

The question of how we communicate with a transcendental God is
a non-problem for which the hierarchy calls itself the solution. Jesus
made it clear that our concern must be with God as immanent, God
dwelling in people. St. John tells us that we cannot love God whom
we cannot see if we do not love our brothers and sister whom we can
see (1John 4:20-21). Jesus did not simply say to love God by loving
our neighbor, he demonstrated it through his whole ministry. If in
fact Jesus called himself "The Way," this may be what he meant.
Since God is immanent, as even the church teaches, we already have
a built-in relationship with God, and according to Jesus this relationship is fostered through our connections with people in whom God is
also immanent. Given that, what then is the proper function of an
institutional church? The answer of course is that they could adopt
the task of teaching people how to relate to one another as well as the
God within and of reconciling with one another when relationships
breakdown or falter, i.e., when sin is committed. Their most notable
failure in this respect has been in not developing a theology of intimacy. If they did this we could understand them because they would
have to speak in human terms. There would be fewer problems,
however, since we are perfectly capable of speaking to each other.
That is, we could solve many of our own moral problems without
mediation which is what we ordinarily do when the problems are not
thought to be transcendental. Jesus taught us to deal directly with the
problems between ourselves (Mat. 5:23-24).

The magisterium warns us that we could not manage to deal with
moral problems without divine assistance, i.e., grace. This is also a
non-problem, unless we can think of God playing games by giving
and withholding grace at various times. If God is immanent we are
perpetually immersed in grace, all of us down to the last anti-theist
who presumably rank below atheists. Church officials have confused
the issue by teaching us that we have two sets of problems, one with
humans and another with God and only they can solve our problems
with God. But if we relate to God by properly relating to humans the
second kind of problem does not exist and the self-appointed interloc-

utors we call the clergy need a different job description.

The substance and method of church teaching would have the effect of putting our moral well-being in their hands. Conviction about what is wrong might be easier to come by if instead of being told, for example, that adultery is an offense against God we were helped to understand how destructive it is to all the individuals involved and that ultimately it is a threat to survival of the species of which we are a member. A developed theology of intimacy would include these cautions as well as pointing people in the right direction. The magisterium must learn how people may be persuaded without the expectation of heaven or the fear of hell. Expressing the problem in terms of eternal rewards paints a black and white picture that does not portray reality to many of our contemporaries. People will not be motivated by what is not perceived as real.

An opportunistic lie or theft manifests a lack of conviction about the rightness of always being truthful or honest, but if a person is untruthful or dishonest with some and not with others, that person's morality is tribal, his or her tribe being those with whom the person is perhaps truthful and honest. This is the moral code of most people. It is not generally one that is thought through and accepted on conviction which is why I added the "perhaps". Instead, for one reason or another, people fall into these patterns of behavior through imitating those around them or by acting on impulse which may then become habit.

While it is not literally the case, the hierarchy seems to have a stake in producing muddled moral thinking if we judge by the results. Instead of helping us to develop a consciousness of the proper way to act with, for and toward one another by rules that we can understand and accept as reasonable they teach as though the really real is supernatural, that when we act we produce an effect in another realm from which there is no feedback, at least that ordinary mortals can expect. Thus, we need the clergy to tell us if we are producing good or bad effects. They suggest that we can know for ourselves by comparing our behavior to the rules they teach, as in the little pamphlets used for an examination of conscience. This is in fact their own method for determining whether we have been good or bad, although in a more nuanced way, since they must allow for mitigating circumstances, a pastoral practice that goes by the name of casuistry. We cannot really know if what they say is actually the case. We can only have faith that they know what they are doing. We have been told that the rules the church teaches are God's rules and they exist outside of us unless we reflect on the rules and become convinced that they are right and reasonable and make them our own. Therein lies the hitch. The magisterium puts little effort into demonstrating that the rules they promulgate are reasonable. They have not yet learned that they are not dealing with medieval peasants for whom, "God says so," or "We say so," might be a compelling argument.

But we do not have to operate in the dark this way with second-hand knowledge and inferences. Jesus did not teach the negative approach to morality used by the church. He taught explicitly that what we do for our brothers and sisters we do for him (Mat. 25:40). Even atheists understand that their care and concern for others makes for a better world in which the threats to survival of the species is diminished.

In all my years of Catholic education, and in all the years of hearing sermons, I never once heard a priest, brother or nun speak of fulfilling or completing the commandments, the meaning of which I demonstrated in the previous chapter. It was always *keep* the commandments. There is a vast difference between keeping and fulfilling them. By taking a creative approach to morality we move away from harming others to promoting their life and well-being. This approach to the rules relieves us of the concern with whether we are sinning. We may discover retrospectively that we have harmed someone at an earlier time as we grow in moral refinement, but with the consciousness of which I speak it would never be deliberate. Furthermore, this approach can provide direct knowledge of the effect we are producing when we act loving or unloving. With this feedback we can adjust and adapt our behavior appropriately if we are convinced that such adjustment and adaptation is in the best interest of ourselves and others.

Question: How do we know what is in our best interests, short or long term? Until the middle years of the twentieth century most Catholics believed that it meant acting so that we would achieve personal salvation, sometimes referred to as going to heaven, or avoiding hell and eternal damnation. Heaven and hell seemed real enough for me and most of those in my generation as a consequence of living with a ghetto mentality, another instance of Ignorance II. Truth is communal. If everyone we know believes something to be true, chances are we will too. We were happily all in the same predicament together. We could make jokes about confession and the kind of penances the easy priests gave. Then came Vatican II, closely followed by *Humanae Vitae*.

There are two main reasons why the supernatural morality the Catholic church teaches has become less convincing and has generally not been effective. According to this supernatural morality the most important effects of our behavior cannot be directly known because presumably God is affected and God is not telling. The church tries to convince us that the guilt feelings we are supposed to experience is God's way of telling us, and if we do not experience guilt it is because our hearts have become hardened so that we no longer hear the voice of God. But fear and guilt are feelings produced by conditioning as any Psych 101 student knows. Attributing these feelings to God is an attempt to control people, especially youngsters, when they are beyond the range of parents or other authority. It is also a form of idolatry, as is any attribution to God of a human quality.

Another reason for the ineffectiveness of religious morality as it is commonly taught is that the reward or punishment for "keeping" or not "keeping" the commandments is too unreal and too remote, that is, postponed until we are dead. The church seems to offer a more immediate reward, a kind of inner peace available to us if we become totally submissive to the hierarchy, but it is the peace of slaves who have become reconciled to their state of life. Such slaves enjoy the freedom of never having to think of what they must do. Their lives are completely directed by authority. This is a life for sheep not humans. This way of living may provide a sort of freedom *from* anxiety but it does not offer freedom *for* anything.

Those who resist becoming sheep but have retained some faith in church officials, sometimes break the rules, sometimes they keep them, just as predicted. When they break them they go to the clergy for interior reorganization, and start the cycle of sin and repentance over again. There is no clear direction to such lives. They do not even enjoy the pseudo-integrity of religious slaves. These two ways of being are not the only alternatives however. There is the way that Jesus taught, viz., the free, creative life of those who fulfill the commandments rather than just keeping them. This requires a different kind of consciousness than that which is produced by absorbing the culture of church religion and being docile to the hierarchy. The gospel as I understand it requires a deep commitment to learning how we ought to relate to the world and everything in it, especially people. Such learners actually seem to be keeping many of the commandments the church thinks are so important but not for the reasons given by the church. They keep the rules incidentally in acting to fulfill them.

We saw in the last chapter that if we are promoting the life and well-being of everyone we are a long way from killing anyone or even being angry with anyone. We simply move in the opposite direction. By promoting minimal behavior, that is, just trying to keep the commandments, the church underestimates the creative potential of humans. When people have the mind-set that considers how close they can come to breaking the commandments they will break them, as with the teenagers who want to know what they can get away with sexually without crossing the line. People who fail to develop a conscious morality based on conviction that the rules are reasonable and that keeping them is in their best, long-term interest will act sociopathically at times. A woman I know who regularly steals from stores, just as regularly excuses herself with, "They overcharge for everything anyway." "They," of course, are anonymous others. There was a time when anything stolen belonged to a person. Now with corporate ownership of businesses the owners are the stockholders and their reality as persons may not be readily perceived.

Persons who act this way at times are not true sociopaths. They are simply muddled in their thinking. For a complete sociopath no relationship is sacred. We say, for example, of certain drug addicts that they would sell their mother for a fix, or that there is no honor among thieves, meaning that they will steal from one another. Pure sociopaths are probably rare. In a species that is necessarily social it would be difficult to achieve anything close to the satisfaction humans seem to require if a person were crass enough to only take and never give.

The third kind of moral code exists more as an ideal than as a reality. We can, however, put in this category those who regard every human as a family member and act according to the best of their ability to work within the context of that ideal. The reason such a code can never be fully realized has to do with the impossibility of knowing what is in the best interest of everyone all the time, in the long run, including ourselves, and whether our behavior at any given moment is appropriate to that ideal. Frequently we cannot know until after we have acted, perhaps months or years later, that what we did was flawed in some way. There is also the difficulty of feeling brotherly or sisterly to those who hurt us and the ones we love, and those who seriously violate what we believe in, for example, the way abortionists present a serious problem for many pro-lifers. A very large part of the problem in realizing the ideal is that whatever we do that affects another person has a moral quality. We cannot begin to imagine all the effects of everything we do. Do we, for example, concern ourselves with the amount of resources we use when so many of our brothers and sisters have none? We would have to be concerned in order to claim membership in a group concerned with global family morality. Although simple living can be variously defined (it would be radically different for millionaires and poor persons) no one who is not committed to simple living can claim membership in this category. As with most human behavior we cannot judge simple living from the outside. We can only reflect on and question our own behavior.

St. Thomas tells us that we do not choose evil. Rather, we choose what we perceive to be good. Correctly understood what St. Thomas tells us about not choosing evil means that our problem is not so much sin as it is sinfulness. Sinfulness has to do with the harm we can do, mostly in little ways, without being conscious of it until we reflect on how we have acted. Such reflection may never occur given our massive ignorance. I gave an example earlier of realizing I had been wrong to yell at a student. I was reacting to what up to that time had been one of my pet peeves. After giving an assignment, a student would ask a series of question that if I allowed them, the result would be me doing the assignment. This kind of behavior is easily recognized and easily deflected without being unkind. In this instance I let my negative feelings (probably from an entirely different source) determine my behavior. After the incident I also realized that I had reacted similarly in the past without being conscious of having done anything wrong, hence without having apologized. It was a moment of evolving consciousness, referred to by some as an epiphany. As noted earlier, the agnostic doctor also presented me with an opportunity to pursue moral refinement, one I did not make use of at the time.

In nontechnical language the three kinds of morality can be described as: sociopathic--me against them, tribal--us against them, and global family morality--all of us for everyone and against no one including people we do not like. We may not like someone's moral code. We may not understand someone's moral code, but that is irrelevant to the fact that the person has a moral code. Whether it is a proper moral code or even a conscious moral code is an entirely different issue, one that requires dialogue and experience to resolve. We can determine a proper morality by its consequences for survival of individuals and the species insofar as we can discern those consequences, both short and long-term, an assertion that only hints at the complexity of the problem. At the very minimum a proper morality would be nondivisive, or as Jesus put it, "If they are not against you they are for you" (Mark 9:40). If we are clear-headed about what morality is and what it is for, we stand a better chance of understanding the consequences and of choosing wisely and from conviction, or perhaps of choosing or not choosing at all. I suspect that people generally do not choose, properly speaking because of the way our behavior becomes conditioned. Also when we operate from conviction there is no question of where responsibility lies and to whom the consequences belong.

We should not have to think hard to learn which of the three kinds of moral codes we subscribe to. We just have to check the persons with whose survival we are concerned. With tribal morality we draw a line somewhere and say in effect these are my people. The line is not absolute because we can join with some over one issue and not others. The attitude of different people toward the Vietnam War was a good illustration of this kind of division. One of the chief problems with tribal morality is the in-group, out-group mentality that it fosters and the fact that it is generally not fully thought out with respect to its consequences. Furthermore, if someone steals an item from a store, no one can tell from the act itself if the person's code is sociopathic or tribal. A person who lives by a tribal code may actually be sociopathic at times making that person at least mildly schizophrenic.

A transcendental morality that supposedly connected humans to God was an innovation in the domain of tribal morality among the Jews. It reinforced and gave support to family morality at a time when no human could have spoken with enough authority to persuade anyone that it was to their personal advantage to act like family with all family members no matter how remote in space or time. Some of the early Christians lived communally, but promoting a greater community was perhaps not their primary interest; they may have thought the second coming and the end of the world was near. We know that at least eventually, personal salvation became and has remained to this day the focus of attention in most Christian denominations. A concern with personal salvation has the effect of turning our attention away from the human family to the state of one's alleged "soul," i.e., to how we can connect with God instead of humans. Christian doctrine is specific in regard to this relationship: God connects with us; we do not connect with God. For us it is a matter of recognizing an existing connection, i.e., God as immanent, and responding to that connection. Also Christian doctrine teaches that there will be a resurrection, a process over which we obviously have no control. Saving one's soul, like so much else in Christian thinking is a manner of speaking. Some Bibles translate *soul*, in certain places, as life. In view of the idea of resurrection it might make more sense to speak of saving our lives instead of our souls if we could save anything at all. The idea of body plus soul derives from Greek philosophy. The illusion that there is some reality we call soul, that can exist disembodied is fostered by the fact that in our encounter with dead bodies it is easy to think that some animating substance called a soul is what is missing. The Catholic church does little or nothing to change this unsophisticated view of reality. In fact the 1993 *Catechism* speaks explicitly of the soul separating from the body at death. At the other end of life they speak of God immediately creating a soul for each human conceived, giving the impression of soul added to a body. But if the doctrine of resurrection means anything, in death there is only a dead body, which is no different from what every atheist sees.

We are necessarily social and must connect with others in some way and our choices seem to be limited to the patterns for connecting we see around us or creating patterns of our own. In the context of the massive ignorance with which we are born the only clue we usually have to go by is simply the need to connect itself and the available patterns for connecting. The patterns of one's family or a reaction of some sort to those patterns are the most likely to be adopted and maintained. When these patterns fail, as they frequently do, we have to find or create others. With most of the patterns available, how to connect is problematic even between persons for whom this is supremely important--lovers, parents and children, and so on. There are many factors to our difficulty in connecting. Three stand out: 1) The lack of a theology of intimacy, probably as a result of its possible connection with sexual intimacy. 2) The early conditioning many of us receive of giving priority to connecting with God over human connections, and 3) the lack of conviction based on reason. Transcendental aspirations are a source of many problems because there is not and cannot be any way of directly knowing whether our efforts are successful, at least for ordinary mortals. Given the way we learn, i.e., by trial-and-error and subsequent reflection on what we have done and the consequences, we can safely assume that we need not concern ourselves with occult events, as Bishop Robinson refers to them (1963:107).

A transcendental morality that prescribes how we should act with, for and toward one another is virtually useless for interpersonal relationships. Such a morality is flawed in three respects: 1) The reference exists outside of us and does not necessarily have the force of personal conviction; we have to ask ourselves, "Is this what God wants me to do?" with no response from God to rely on. 2) The code is too general. If a man were to say, "I don't commit adultery, not even in my heart; I don't beat my wife, and I don't lie to her; therefore we have a good relationship," we could immediately see how ridiculous is his claim. 3) Along with transcendental morality the church, prior to Vatican II, and still to some extent promotes roles for married partners, the husband/father role and the wife/mother role. Marriage is potentially the most intimate kind of relationship. But confronting each other as role types does not foster the greatest kind of intimacy because along with roles there are role expectations (standard scripts) on the part of each partner. The resulting lack of creative response to each other diminishes the potential for a growing intimacy. I will have more to say on this subject when we examine the meaning of intimacy in chapters eight and nine.

None of the churches teach about the moral refinement as it is understood here. When the Catholic church still taught that priests and religious lived in a higher state than lay persons there was talk about being "perfect as our heavenly Father is perfect" apparently through ascetic practices, notably poverty, chastity and obedience. The text that summons us to "being perfect" follows a passage in Matthew telling us to love our enemies and pray for those that harms us. The corresponding passage in Luke substitutes "compassion" for "perfect." Jesus is telling how to act with, for and toward others when our feelings run the other way. He reminds us that we don't generally have a problem loving friends and family, that moral refinement (being perfect) means being compassionate toward all. In the context of compassion we will not insist on executing murderers, and if we are compassionate toward murderers everyone else will be safe from us. Pope John Paul II spent nearly all of *Veritas Splendor* addressing the bishops on persuading people to keep the commandments, which for ordinary folk, as the church sees it seems task enough. He underestimates human potential. When we examined the meaning of fulfill the commandments we learned that by adding this creative dimension the commandments were being kept incidentally in a higher pursuit.

Rules for moral refinement cannot be generic. They have to be relative to the requirements of the persons involved particularly in interpersonal relationships. Except in the most general way I cannot know in any nuanced way how I should treat you unless I learn from you while you are learning from me how I should be treated by means of self-disclosure. None of us start with the knowledge of how anyone should be treated under every possible circumstance. These particulars can only be learned as we move through life and come upon the need. Relating to other humans according to roles is to intimacy as paint-by-number is to art. The rules as taught by the church carry no inherent conviction and work poorly as basis for deciding whether we have sinned. Perhaps the church thinks that no persuasion is necessary since the standards are objective and absolute and given by God and "written on our hearts," giving us an infallible tool for measuring our moral quotient.

The magisterium's criteria against which we are to measure our behavior are: serious matter, sufficient reflection and full consent of the will. Such criteria are useless in trying to determine if we have sinned, and worse than useless for establishing and maintaining relationships with others which should be the purpose of our morality. Serious matter is what the church says is serious matter without generating conviction. Sufficient reflection means we know that we have been told that certain behaviors are wrong but not necessarily with reasons we can accept. And full consent of the will means that we choose to do it despite the knowledge that the church says it is wrong. What could full consent of the will mean for people who have been conditioned to act in various ways, and who violate rules that are out there, hence lack conviction? But the most serious fault with this system of morality that has been around for centuries is that its focus on the negative aspects of morality does not lead people to even consider the creative possibilities of moral refinement. It is a me-centered morality. Grit your teeth and keep the rules as the church teaches and you will go to heaven.

Philosophers with an anti-religious bias have claimed that moral propositions are meaningless, and that may be because of the way moral propositions have been taught, that is, as absolute, unchangeable and given to us by God. If we begin to look at morality from a humanistic perspective we may find that although moral propositions cannot be tested the way that scientific propositions are tested, they are subject to testing. Moral propositions prescribe or proscribe certain behaviors between humans and these behaviors have empirical consequences, then just as with any scientific lab procedure we are justified in drawing conclusion concerning the anticipated consequences, hence of deciding if those consequences are good and the ones we want. We may decide incorrectly but if we reflect and are open to learning our thinking and behavior is subject to correction. This makes shared experience and important component in developing our morality. We can subsequently decide if our original theory has been borne out by the results. This is the kind of thinking contemporary humans can feel comfortable with. We may then legitimately say that if you do this or do not do that this may be the result based on experience. Therefore, we can make rational choices on the bases of probable outcomes. This cannot be the case with transcendental morality. I know of no way that we could have knowledge of how what we do either connects or disconnects us from God. That is why labeling a behavior as right or wrong because God says so is irrational. With the practical kind of testing based on experiences we won't recognize opportunities to learn if the important results are in another world as the church teaches. Pope John Paul II insists that good intentions and good consequences are not enough to determine if an action is good. But the divine economy which we are taught is the only appropriate basis for making moral judgments remains absolutely beyond our comprehension.

If the consequences of our behavior are in the transcendental realm; i.e., if our relationship with God is affected negatively or positively we have no way of knowing. Church officials tell us they can provide certainty because of their power to "loose" or "bind" Yet everyone knows that different priests give different answers to moral questions and different penalties for making ourselves right with God. These divine mediators manifest an astounding unevenness in capability, reintroducing uncertainty into a system that is supposed to give us a sense of security. Can we get what we need from them under those circumstances?

When we are confronted simultaneously with a personal problem and a social problem we naturally give priority to the personal problem because we cannot walk away from it the way we can with persons. This is especially the case when the personal problem derives from our transcendental morality which it surely will if we are living according to a transcendental code. If we believe what we have been taught, we accept the fact that we have incurred guilt and must act to make ourselves right with God. Putting concern with a human person ahead of God would only seem to compound our problems if the goal is to connect with God. This dilemma is entirely artificial, and as the scientific philosophers say, "meaningless."

All Christian denominations have the words attributed to Jesus but they have yet to learn what they mean. Misunderstanding has become traditional. Since we can do nothing directly to attain everlasting life, the task toward which we should direct our efforts is connecting with one another with the goal of establishing a global community; in Biblical language we are to help bring about the reign of God. Such effort is within the scope of our talents and skills. Our attention is misdirected by focussing on eternal salvation. Jesus' teaching revealed the means for bringing together the whole of humanity. He directed the bulk of what he said and did to this end. Perhaps our efforts toward this end will incidentally result in salvation, whatever that means, which according some scripture seems to be a communal thing. We just do not know. Humans find it difficult to work for a goal that is beyond their imagination, one of the main reasons for the ineffectiveness of traditional, Christian morality. We can work at creating community, and that produces satisfying results that people can experience here and now, not potentially decades in the future.

There is absolutely no doubt that Jesus tried to humanize morality, saying in effect that whatever transcendental requirements there may be are completely fulfilled by a proper humanistic morality, the limits of which are expressed by, "Love your enemies; do good to those who hate you" (Luke 6:27) and "Greater love than this no one has, that he lay down his life for his friend" (John 16:13) We cannot all attain these ideals but we can hold them before us as what we should aspire to. Meanwhile we are certainly capable of feeding the hungry, clothing the naked and healing the sick. With these kinds of behavior the quality of our behavior is evident. We do not need anyone to tell us we are doing right. We are also engaging in the process of moral refinement without having to think about it.

Luther and Calvin, among others recognized the difficulties inherent in a transcendental morality directed toward saving our souls. Their solutions were no solutions because despite their belief in the impossibility of making a transcendental connection with God they still maintained the importance of personal salvation within their innovative religious systems. That is, their main focus was still on the problem of eternal life instead of community formation. We have only to test anyone's ideal of behavior against a statement by Jesus speaking of God: "I desire compassion [of one human to another] not sacrifice [to God]." Many who come to a realization that some goal is impossible give up. This is frequent response to an impossible transcendental moral code.

The philosophers of the Enlightenment did not think of social problems as caused by transcendental morality. To them that was just the means of controlling people by autocratic, institutional churches. In other words they perceived the churches as causing a political problem not a religious one on account of the connection between the church and state. If the political power of the pope and the hierarchy in support of the monarchy and the aristocracy were the problem, liberty, equality, and fraternity were the solutions. By throwing out all prior rules and trying to create the rules for social organization *ex nihilo* their dependence on the theory of innate human goodness proved to be a serious flaw. There is some truth to the theory but it is totally overshadowed by a massive innate human ignorance, a state of being which results in behavior harmful to others because people do not understand what kind of creatures they are. The result of the enlightenment experiment is history. The chaos of the French Revolution begged for a strong leader to tell people what to do. Enter Napoleon as a replacement for the church.

The Bible is used to support the idea of transcendental morality, but properly read it provides even better support for a humanistic morality. Example: "The Sabbath was made for humans not humans for the Sabbath" (Mark 2:27). There is no question but that Jesus was a humanist who presented us with clear ideas of how we should treat everyone as family. The idea of God sanctioning morality among masses of unlettered humans who have not been entirely weaned from their tribal gods and are just emerging from barbarism perhaps made some sense with the early Jews and again with the mass of Christians under the feudal system of the Middle Ages. Physical appetites such as those for food, sex and owning things can readily dominate the thinking of people so impoverished they have little else to think about. Also we can see how the burden of a relatively constant anxiety brought on by day-to-day contingencies could lead people to see one solution as appropriating the resources of others unless restrained by, say the fear of eternal damnation or the hope of eternal compensation. Without sanctions from some all powerful source there would seem to be nothing to constrain the wildest kind of behavior under these circumstances. Unfortunately, when humanity became more civilized and had other psychological resources, the churches did not respond accordingly. Instead church leaders have continued to preach hellfire as though they were confronting wild beasts with a whip and a chair instead of people with more education than most of the clergy had through most of history. They apparently believe with St. Augustine

> Take away the barriers created by laws, and men's brazen capacity to do harm, their urge to self-indulgence, would rage to the full. No king in his kingdom, no general with his troops, no husband with his wife, no father with his son, could attempt to put a stop, by any threats or punishments, to the freedom and sheer, sweet taste of sinning (Johnson 1976:117).

Not many educated contemporary persons will identify with Augustine's description which without the theological language could have been written by Konrad Lorenz or Sigmund Freud. However, even in Augustine's time educated men were infected by stoicism which defined Christian perfection in terms of perfect control of one's appetites. Judging from reports of men who went to the desert to do battle with their temptations to sins of the flesh, those men had a problem with their sexuality (Peter Brown 1988). This problem no doubt played a significant part in the overdefined sexual morality of the church which encroaches upon private commitments with prescriptions for how couples should treat one another. If there is any certainty to be had about the quality of moral behavior it is more easily discovered in actual interpersonal relationships than from philosophical or theological theories because if I treat someone well or ill I do not need to refer to some external code for confirmation. What I do results in existential knowledge. I need to be convinced that treating all others well is in my best long-term interests, that among other factors, as Bonhoeffer wrote, "The world is so ordered that a basic respect for ultimate laws and human life is also the best means of self-preservation" (1972:11). This is what the church should teach. The theories of heaven and hell do not provide that conviction.

If I have a partner and we are committed to maintaining and promoting a relationship, we can communicate our feelings and negotiate whatever changes are required. A third party can have some value in teaching us how to communicate and negotiate because these are acquired skills, or perhaps to mediate when communication breaks down. But passing judgment on the rightness or wrongness of what happens within a relationship by a third party is inappropriate. This is an issue that must be settled between the two people involved in a dialectical process. Also, by working out the moral requirements for two, experiential knowledge is gained for dealing with others outside of the relationship, a task that would make sense for humans even if there were no God, an important factor in the relationships of non-believers. There is another factor. Two people engaged in working toward moral refinement as described here will enjoy what is for humans possibly the greatest satisfaction that humans can experience and they will not be carrying anger and frustrations into other relationships.

When the churches say that some acts are by their very nature wrong, or that such acts are objectively wrong they leave no room for working toward an ideal, the way my mother taught me. The process involves learning from experience the way we learn language. The church in effect insists on what they presume to be ideal behavior before a person is convinced of its value. For example, we may engage in a certain behavior because we cannot understand why it is considered wrong by the churches. "Because God said so," or "Because we say so and we speak for God," are totally inadequate reasons unless we had faith in the hierarchy. We cannot know God, but a God who would ask us to behave in a way that goes against our nature and experiences is beyond belief.

The Bible provides many instances that remind us of our inability to have a direct relationship with God in the manner of humans. We cannot, for example, interpret what happens to us as either approval or disapproval on the part of God because "The rain falls on the just and the unjust" (Mat. 5:45) and from Job, "Who has given to Me that I should repay *him*?/*Whatever* is under the whole heaven is Mine" (41:11).

In contrast with transcendental morality a humanistic morality simplifies life immensely. When we treat another person well or poorly we usually get immediate feedback with the possibility of adjusting our behavior accordingly. Unfortunately in our culture such behavior is not standard. It can only be found in subcultural pockets, small communities, families and interpersonal relationships. Of the three kinds of human moralities, sociopathic, tribal, and global family, our culture tends to condition us to a tribal morality--us against them--from which it seems so easy to slip into me against them, or in the case of interpersonal relationships, me against her or him. When lines of exclusion are drawn in tribal morality the advantages are presumably for the individuals of the included group. At anytime any member may become excluded and any member may decide to exclude anyone else. We need a flexible morality not an arbitrary morality. Everyone's survival is at risk with a morality that allows for exclusion. The institutional churches that presumably exists to unite humanity are themselves examples of tribal morality with their lines of inclusion and exclusion. There is little doubt that present secular tribal morality is a direct descendant of religious morality.

Tribal morality is too narrow for long-range survival of the human species in the context of the common idolatry which equates success and prosperity with divine approbation. Such thinking accounts for most of the current technological onslaught on people and resources and the ever present possibility of seeing terrorism and war as a way to solve tribal problems. If we do not concern ourselves with the survival of everyone, i.e., answer yes to the question, "Am I my brother's [and sister's] keeper?" everyone is at risk. That is why acting intelligently requires that we look for values appropriate to the survival of everyone. The values we actually live by are learned through experience in a cultural milieu that is basically tribal in its perspective. The morality of us against them was not a threat to the human family when tribes were small, widely spaced, and the means of killing limited. With tribes as large as nations and the ability to kill millions with a single bomb, we are past the time when we can live by such narrow codes.

A complicating factor in our time is that large national tribes tend to be made up of many smaller tribes with conflicting agendas. Strange tribes are not just people who live in faraway places speaking incomprehensible languages that we might accidentally encounter in the forest and who may be hostile. A tribe can be any group with enough common interests to make them act in concert in relation to other tribes. Fundamentalist religious groups of whatever stripe are well-defined tribes. Arms dealers of the world are a transnational tribe that will act together to prevent or eliminate restrictions on the sale of arms. Their ideal is to sell arms to both sides in any conflict. Isolated tribes, totally unaware of a larger world probably no longer exist, but we still have technically isolated tribes such as the arms dealers that threaten the existence of other tribes. With the complex human interconnections we now have, the threat to the world is not just to the immediate tribe that another tribe would like to subdue, destroy or simply exploit.

Case in point: Not all Palestinian factions are bent on destroying Israel although some are. These are in effect tribes within tribes. As the Israelis perceive the situation they cannot limit their defensive posture just to the factions (tribes) who would destroy them because the nonthreatening tribes are closely related to the hostile ones and virtually indistinguishable in appearance. There is no practical way to tell the hostile from the nonhostile until after the fact of some aggressive move. This puts Israel in the position of having to maintain a police state, contradicting the most fundamental reason for its foundation. This also reinforces the belief of the hostile tribes of the necessity for Israel's destruction. The problems generated by such conflict are not limited to the warring tribes and those caught in the middle. There are tribes in other states with sympathies for one side or the other who could become involved if one side or the other makes a threatening move toward a state not directly involved in the conflict. For example the political and military tribes of the U.S. regard Israel as a strategic military outpost in the Mideast. They would not allow Israel to be destroyed, but for the U.S. to enter a conflict overtly on the side of the Israelis would draw into the conflict those tribes sympathetic to the other side, and so on. A similar scenario could be written for the Bosnian Muslims and Serbs, the Indians and Pakistanis, the North and South Koreans, and the various Cambodian factions.

I mentioned above the tribe of arms dealers and the political and military tribes of the U.S. all three of which are in conflict with environmentalists and assorted pacifists. Obviously tribal membership is a complex issue. Politicians might join with others to face one problem, say Israel and the Palestinians, yet be on opposite sides as it concerns the environment, abortion rights, or whatever. What defines a tribe then is a tribal perspective. In matters that concern all of us a tribal perspective is inherently divisive, i.e., holds to non- or antisurvival characteristics, hence is unintelligent. We often hold such perspectives in ignorance of their long-term consequences to ourselves. This happens because we absorb tribal myths (a set of sacred values) uncritically from the tribe into which we are born and the tribes into which we later move, wherein myths are not regarded as myths, rather, the way the world is and which provides the rules for how one lives in the world. To act intelligently we need to adopt a critical stance with respect to our values. To do this we must turn our myths into philosophy to the extent that we can. That is, we need to make our rules or principles for deriving rules explicit. This may provide some help in reflecting on the long-term consequences of acting according to our rules allowing us to adopt or create explicitly humanistic rules that are more likely to promote everyone's survival. When we follow tribal rules without being fully aware of the consequences we are living within the context of a tribal myth convinced that we are merely responding to reality--an ontological fallacy. If we are actually aware of the consequences of our tribal code, and many of us are, we are assenting to the belief that in this world there must be winners and losers in the battle between good and evil and we have faith in the goodness of our side thus making conflict inevitable.

There is no one way to peace and harmony for everyone, but one characteristic that has to be common to all ways is a healthy respect for pluralism. If my belief, philosophy or whatever, puts me in an adversarial relationship with others because of their beliefs then my beliefs are in some ways inadequate or defective. My brothers and sisters are family, not adversaries. I am not for arms dealers selling arms, but arms dealers are my brothers (and sisters?) and I must act accordingly. One way of dealing with the problem is to join with others in creating a world in which no one will feel they need the products of arms dealers, similarly with abortion providers. Perhaps some of the reasons used to abort fetuses are relatively trivial, but many of the women who resort to abortion feel trapped and are desperate. They perceive themselves as acting in self-defense. More importantly abortionists and people who believe in abortion as a right are also our brothers and sisters. If we are against abortion we cannot simultaneously be against people who believe that abortion is not wrong. The task of anti-abortionists must be to create the circumstances in which no one would want an abortion, for example, by giving young people an honest sex education and providing examples of how to relate to other humans in a responsible manner. We must also stop telling them they are offending God by having sex before marriage. There are many good reasons why they should not engage in sex outside of a committed relationship. Offending God is not one of them. The focus needs to be on a person's responsibility toward another human. In a sexual act a person may get hurt, but not God. If our main problem is sinfulness rather than sin, that is the harm we can do without necessarily being aware of it, then sex offers the prime situation for doing harm unawares, particularly among the young, and particularly to females by males. Sex in itself is not inherently wrong; lying, manipulation, extortion, the use of force and otherwise acting irresponsibly is, in other words our lack of consciousness about what is harmful.

In the meantime we must love and respect others who are not actually destructive to the community or its members. Whatever else they are, fetuses are not yet perceived as members of the community by those who have abortions. When abortion opponents get highly emotional and start calling their brothers and sisters "murderers," they have to accept some of the responsibility for breaking community bonds, not just their opponents who may be acting in good faith. I am not sure what anyone could do to change the mean-spiritedness and intransigence of certain anti-abortionists who feel they are doing God's work mainly because they live by a transcendental code. Under our system of government we have only the possibility of persuasion to work for change and we are not going to persuade a person of anything if we start by calling that person a murderer. The church bemoans the fact that it cannot get a constitutional amendment outlawing abortion. They could interpret this state of affairs as a divinely inspired call to learn that there are better ways of saving fetuses and embryos than they now envision.

I mentioned moral refinement earlier in connection with trying to establish the idea of what I call a proper morality, given the fact that we each have a morality. I pointed out the inappropriateness of transcendental morality because we get no feedback from God and our relationship with other humans is secondary according to the terms of transcendental morality. If our inability to relate to divinity creates problems for our ordinary relationships with other humans, there is no way to describe how serious are its effects on our interpersonal relationships. We need to engage in dialectical relationships with our partners and not with God, although we may legitimately think of relating to God as immanent in our partner and relate that way. This in fact is the basis for the sacrament of love in chapter eight as we shall see. Moral refinement can best be achieved through a dialectical relationship between two persons acting with the humility and respect proper to the recognition of the God immanent in the other.

A certain kind of morality is required before we begin moral refinement. This morality need not be a set of explicit rules. It can be a disposition to act in a certain way with, for or toward other persons that is not divisive, although I see advantages in having explicit rules for relating to those who are not intimates. With intimates we can begin with a commitment to love unconditionally and what that calls for should be obvious if the commitment is reciprocal. If it is not and we happen to be in love with someone with boundaries of one kind or another we have to learn where the boundaries are and respect them. Occasionally we will cross a boundary inadvertently. The location of boundaries are not always evident even to the person who has them.

When this happens we need good communication skills. Developing communication skills is important for everyone; for intimate relationships it is a top priority. The need for such communication skills are critically important with those whom we are intimate because the consequences of not being able to communicate are more serious for everyone.

The morality we must have before we begin moral refinement is the basic, generic morality of nonviolence, honesty, truthfulness and so on, the kind of morality that enables us to connect with people, or at least not disconnect. Given this foundation we are prepared to move to the next stage. Obviously not killing or hurting people is not enough. We notice this immediately if we reflect on the way we treat someone with whom we are intimate. We not only do not kill or hurt that person, we promote his or her life and well-being in a special way. We cannot be as good to everyone as we are to intimates but moral refinement calls for movement in that direction. Intimate, interpersonal relationships offer our best chance of working toward the ideal of a global family morality. Unconditional love, the ideal for everyone is best begun with one person. And what we learn with the one person we can begin to practice with others to include as much of the rest of the world as possible.

Until Vatican II, the state of being ordained and celibate was considered superior to being married, as though getting married was giving in to a weakness. This may in part explain why the Vatican's commitment to not changing its sexual morality is more firmly entrenched than any other aspect of religious morality. The Stoics, from whom the church primarily derived its attitude toward sex, by way of St. Augustine and other church Fathers, found the sex drive that men experience a particular embarrassment because their ideal in life was total self-control and the sex drive for most men remains rather constant until diminished by age. The monks who went to the desert prayed for the time when they no longer had to resist their sexual impulses. There is an obvious connection in all this with the Vatican's insistence on celibacy for priests, but we find even more compelling reasons for celibacy, as previously noted, in the Vatican's governing structure adopted almost point-for-point from Plato's *Republic* (Popper 1966:46).

In our own day surveys of married partners show that a large percentage of men are satisfied with marriage, while a smaller percentage of women express satisfaction. This is understandable if men are seeing sex itself as a means of bonding and women expect something more. In other words men are apparently projecting their sense of satisfaction onto women, hence fail to be concerned with the needs of women, sexual and otherwise of which they are usually not even aware unless a crisis awakens them. The evidence is anecdotal, but in an informal survey several men were asked if their wives had orgasms. *They did not know.* Most women have difficulty imagining the sex drive of males which inclines males, even among the most committed celibates, to see women as sex objects. That women are a problem for men may be inferred from the rush to desert hermitages by St. Anthony others in his time. Also by Aquinas who said that the only value of women for men is for procreation. For any other purpose a man would be better served by other men. We should not wonder why some women consider the patriarchal system of the Catholic church an abomination.

Sex outside of marriage is considered by the church to be inherently sinful. If sin is offending God and God has revealed that sex outside of marriage is offensive then the answer is yes. But has God revealed this? We would be hard put to find evidence of such a revelation. Jewish scriptures proscribed sex with another Jew's wife. Beyond that, wrong hinged on other matters such as hospitality and compassion. The issue of inherent sin is entirely an inference derived from the negative attitudes toward sex in the early church. If sin is harming another person, then there are many ways of harming someone involving the use of sex, with child molestation and rape at the top of the list. But it is not difficult to imagine situations in which persons could engage in sex outside of marriage in which there is little or no harm. Under humanistic moral standards the harm in most cases is acting irresponsibly toward a partner--transmitting a disease or getting the female pregnant in an uncommitted relationship, or not acting responsibly afterward. If a woman is not capable of getting pregnant, say a post-menopausal woman, that leaves only the responsibility the two persons have toward each other. I do not see the institutional church buying this view of sex anytime soon. In fact I think this may be the main unstated reason behind *Humanae Vitae*. The magisterium cannot point to any harm inherent in deliberate, nonprocreative sex. By separating sex from procreation and leaving only the lesser responsibility of two adults to each other the door will have apparently been opened to recreational sex to those who were infertile or could positively prevent pregnancy. There are other more subtle reason why people should perhaps refrain from sex, but the church has no tradition of subtlety in such matters, nor does it have a reputation for being a quick study.

In religious talk one sometimes hears the expression "a sense of sin." As in the case of "evil" the phrase has a penumbra of otherworldly connotations. Such ideas belong to a time when humans felt a need to relate to some being in the sky or just out there beyond the world of sense. In purely humanistic terms this "sense" if one has it, should refer to one of two possibilities: 1) an ex-post-facto sense of having damaged, broken or failed to maintain a connection with another person, as for example, a spouse or family member; or, 2) of having missed an opportunity to connect. This "sense" should not be some vague, unformed feeling or sense of guilt. Rather, it should result from the belief that we are necessarily social, and that we sometimes exhibit a tendency to act uncharitably or unjustly (anti-social) without being fully aware at the time. This awareness may come about by being called down by someone, or it can come from a recognition by ourselves in special moments of sensitivity of having unconsciously disconnected or of having failed to make a connection we should have made. With such discoveries we are on the path of moral refinement, the ideal for which we should all aim. If we can fail while aiming for the ideal, we can be sure that with no effort failure is guaranteed.

Only when our morality has gone beyond an avoidance of rule breaking to a positive pursuit of humanistic morality, or as Jesus teaches, fulfilling the Law instead of keeping it, are we positioned to develop a sense of sin in relation to moral refinement. A crude "sense of sin" is derived from having offended someone then having become reconciled, but a morally refined "sense of sin" comes from a realization of having violated charity or justice without having intended it at some time in the past.

If we translate Eugene Kennedy's "sense of sin" (1976) into "a sense of moral ignorance" the idea he is trying to communicate may make more sense to contemporary humans. We have problems with the poetry of earlier ages. To be "born in sin," for example, connotes some kind of mysterious trap from which escape is improbable because we cannot know what it is that exercises such a hold on us. However, to say that we are born in ignorance of what is in our best interest immediately identifies the problem. Like "sinfulness" it is a problem from which there is no absolute escape, but we know how to engage in the process of resolving it. After a period of learning (resolving ignorance) we begin to understand that the more we learn the more we realize how little we know, so that an expansion of knowledge brings with it an expanding awareness (sense) of ignorance that promotes humility rather than guilt and despair over an ever receding horizon as in the case of a "sense of sin." This is a third kind of ignorance, a higher ignorance, the kind claimed by Socrates, whereby persons become aware of how little they know in the context of all possible knowledge. The word *sin* as in the case of *evil* as explained earlier has been burdened with connotations of otherworldly meanings. Another way of describing sinfulness in purely humanistic and in nonsexist language, is "Humans are born without the knowledge of how to act properly with, for and toward others, and in the process of learning they frequently make mistakes."

Probably because he feels the need to connect "sin" and responsibility Kennedy describes a sinner as someone who is as knowledgeable as someone capable of loving. This is contradictory. We may legitimately wonder how much a person knows who would deliberately choose what Kennedy describes as self-destructive. This conceptualization points up the difficulty of being logical with metaphors and analogies in religion. What we have here is one of two kinds of ignorance--the one we are born with or the acquired one, viz. Ignorance II, knowing falsely.

CHAPTER VIII
THE SACRAMENT OF LOVE

Where two or three have gathered in my name, there I am in their midst....(Mat. 18:20).

In church parlance communion is something one receives. In this study it refers to the creation of a bond between persons through the activity of those persons. One only has to present oneself to receive communion. No personal involvement or connection with another person is required to receive communion. The recipient does not need to know the priest or minister administering communion nor any other person participating in the ritual. This is what the shared meal of early Christians has evolved into. Those shared meals resembled that part of the Jewish family's celebration of the Sabbath except without the tribal boundaries. The meal was supposed to be open to the human family. Overcoming tribal boundaries, as I see it, was to be a first step in the evolution of a global community which could not have been envisioned at the time. Many steps later most of which appear to be digressions, we have arrived at a point where the need to see ourselves as a global community has become quite obvious if humanity is to survive.

If we are to become a global community, women can no longer be excluded from positions of influence. The idea of forming a global community is somewhat misleading because we cannot operate at that level as anyone knows who has given thought to changing any kind of entrenched institution such as the Federal government or the church.

Some wise person I am unable to cite said that if we want to change the world we must begin with ourselves. That remains the case and such change is more readily accomplished in pairs and small groups.

It is precisely through pairs and small groups that religion will be reclaimed from the church. I'm inclined to think that pairs and networks of pairs is the natural way to proceed in this quest. Luther's reform was an attempt to restore some of the more primitive aspects of the church. He did not go back far enough. The people in the primitive church were not members of a denomination; they were not anonymous to each other. They thought of themselves as the People of God. They were in fact a Church as defined by the bishops at Vatican II.

For a brief time after the death of Jesus women were not simply adjuncts to the lives of men, when in fact the church and the Church were indistinguishable. As the church became increasingly institutionalized patriarchy reasserted itself and women were pushed aside. Resistance to the development of women by the patriarchal church has resulted in much of women's evolution as persons taking place outside of the church which could not exactly guide a process it was resisting. The independence of today's women comes with one very special advantage: Women can now connect with men in a partnership of equals. Unfortunately, when the liberation of women occurred outside of the institutional church it also sometimes took place outside of the Church, that is, the People of God. Now men and women connect with or without marriage and disconnect through divorce not having any better reason for staying together than the church's mantras, "God says so," or "We say so, as God's agents."

I've been told that the institution of divorce by the Jews was a significant advance for women, that prior to that a man would simply kill the woman he did not want. Jesus taught that women couldn't be cast aside even through divorce, a ruling aimed at men if the response of the disciples is any indication (Mat. 19:10). This was also progress in the liberation of women although in a time when women can initiate divorce it may seem restrictive.

The sacrament of love has certain elements in common with what the church calls marriage but like the definitions of *church* and *Church* noted earlier, they are not identical. Both marriage and the sacrament I will attempt to describe may involve physical bonding or mating by mutual consent with the prospect of living together permanently, and more often than not, of creating and raising a family, but not necessarily, because the sacrament of love is available to all people at all times, in or out of religion and does not necessarily involve sex or a priest. The love relationship that is sacramental and involves mating is a special aspect of the sacrament and should be built on earlier manifestations of the sacrament. If it were, the frequent failures (approx. 50%) that church officials finds so scandalous but which they seem helpless to change is a problem for which they are largely responsible.

The mating relationship has been formally defined in canon law and is called marriage. But one of the great open secrets in Roman Catholicism is that priests do not marry anyone. The sacrament is self-administered by the couple themselves. The priest simply satisfies the legal requirements of the state and the canon law of the church. That is why a marriage is not considered complete by the hierarchy until it has been consummated. Consummation entered into the concept of marriage because at one time there had been a disagreement among theologians as to what constituted the sacrament. One group thought that marriage depended upon mutual consent while others thought that the sacrament required consummation. A compromise was effected by which consent made the marriage valid but consummation made it indissoluble (Martos 1981:426). In the light of what is happening to marriage in our time such technical discussions are like deciding what we will have for breakfast after the Titanic hit the iceberg. The evolution in morality that has occurred since Trent has caused consternation the among hierarchy but not an examination of conscience.

Actually only the couple can know when a mutual commitment to an intimate relationship has taken place and such a commitment should be the most important element in a marriage. Obviously a ceremony and consummation can have taken place without such a commitment, just as surely as such a commitment can have taken place without the ceremony or the consummation. If this is the case then why are some priests insisting that couples who live together separate before a ceremony can be performed? This is a one-size-fits-all application of a rule in a situation where the priest should be asking question about the sincerity of the commitment and background questions to gauge the viability of the relationship.

"There was no obligatory Church ceremony until the eleventh century" (Bokenkotter 1986:249). Even then the requirement only called for the marriage to be blessed by a priest after a civil ceremony or whatever form of public or private commitment people happened to be using at the time. Only gradually did the church take complete control. The Council of Trent reiterated Augustine's theology of marriage as a sacrament in opposition to both Luther and Calvin who had denied its sacramentality. Eventually the faithful began to think of the priest as actually marrying the couple, though as noted above the sacrament of marriage is administered by the couple themselves. Abuses in the matter of secret marriages (private consent and consummation) was a factor in leading church officials to assume control of marriages, hence the requirement that the priest officiate. There was also the matter of secret marriages by priests themselves at a time when officials were trying to enforce celibacy.

In the beginning, before leadership became formalized and centralized, there seemed to be a recognition among the faithful that they were the People of God, and while there was no formal declaration, i.e., the sacrament of love did not become canonical, the faithful clearly practiced it. With the development of a centralized authority which eventually established the canon of sacraments, the failure to recognize and promote the sacrament of love is understandable. Besides being beyond the control of church officials it perhaps seemed redundant in view of the love feast that the Eucharist had been in the early Church. Promoting love as a way of bringing the world together does not seem as neat as having a set of black and white rules that proscribe and prescribe, against which the faithful can measure their behavior and which are enforced by authority.

As the church evolved into a large and all encompassing institution it got into a condemnatory mode through fighting heresy that it only began to escape with Vatican II. In that mode the interest in condemning evil took priority over promoting love. Morality had to evolve progressively a few centuries before it could occur to anyone that this is *the* sacrament and the others are merely various ways of administering the one. When Jesus said, "Where two or three are gathered in my name, I am there with them," he described the ultimate sacrament. There is no clearer statement anywhere concerning the "real presence." There can be no greater grace than the presence of Jesus himself. The institution of some other sacraments cannot so readily be demonstrated, for example, ordination (Martos 1991:399). Baptism and all the sacraments derive their sacramental nature from this simultaneous encounter between two or more humans and Jesus. Like the marriage commitment, which is perhaps its most important form, the sacrament of love is mutually self-administered. A priest may be present but not necessary. The advantage of seeing the sacrament of love as proposed here is that as in the case of any expression of morality it has no necessary connection with religion. Atheist may not care for the term sacrament in which case I refer them to Gregory Bateson, an atheist, who was not put off by the term. "Sacrament" is just another name for the connections between humans that are ultimately necessary for humanity's survival and happiness.

The inability to control administration of this sacrament is reason enough for the church not to promote it and another reason for the People to reclaim their religion.

As an official ceremony marriage has a value as legal protection for children and both persons getting married. It provides a public recognition of what should be a mutual commitment to continuously administer the sacrament of love, but the church presents it as a one-time event. Marriage is a potential training ground for the spread of the sacrament's use throughout humanity by means of the couple and the children that could result from the sacrament. As a one-time, past event, marriage does not promote the consciousness of the sacrament of love as a continuous process nor its potential role in the cosmic scheme of things. Consequently marriage usually does not, as it should, lead to the development of principles that can be put into effect for establishing a global community. If community cannot be established between two persons who are supposed to have made a commitment to do just that, and who presumably start off with positive feelings for each other, they will have little to offer toward the creation of a global community.

As it now appears, the church is legitimating consensual sex for the purpose of making babies rather than the recognition of the couple's future as ministers to each other of the sacrament of love. It is just since Vatican II that interpersonal intimacy received some validation by the church as a good in itself. Prior to that sex carried a taint for the better part of two millennia from which humanity, even beyond the boundaries of Catholicism, has not yet cleansed itself. We who are pre-Vatican II adults can understand the effect of this kind of thinking by asking ourselves: Which would have been considered the worse sin, a young unmarried couple having consensual sex, or the young man punching the young woman in the face? Under such circumstances virginity became a commodity a woman traded for marriage; the sacrament of love was not an issue, evidence that the church lowered the bar of morality in the rules concerning marriage. What has been lost sight of under the church's current system is that the goal of marriage and other manifestations of the sacrament is Communion. In church language we "receive communion" rather than achieve Communion which is a bond of intimacy that grows to a great extent out of mutual self-disclosure for which sex is symbolic. In a Eucharistic service the wafer given to people may or may not be the body of Jesus as the church claims. The potential significance of "communion" as offered by the church is assembling large numbers of people, who if they are gathered in his name achieve communion with or without the wafer. This communion is more suggestive than real since most of the people involved hardly know each other.

Dissatisfied persons in a relationship that is supposed to provide them with possibly the highest degree of satisfaction in life will likely carry that dissatisfaction into the world with them with the negative consequences that tend to flow from bad feelings. People on opposite sides of the world can have serious disagreements and still trade, exchange students and diplomats, and even fight a common enemy while putting aside their differences. Couples living together generally have to confront their differences and resolve them, or if the differences are too great to be reconciled the attempt at community formation comes to an end, an event that occurs with such frequency that it has reached the crisis stage in the United States. Couples attempting to establish an intimate relationship might find making a three-way commitment helpful. In addition to the commitment to each other they should make one to the relationship. When the commitment to each other appears to be broken, if they remain conscious of it, they still have the third commitment to bind them. Instead of the one-time event marriage appears to be, this third commitment would receive considerable reinforcement if the hierarchy promoted it, along with the consciousness of a lifelong commitment to administering the sacrament of love to each other, their children and an expanding network of those with whom they experience some degree of intimacy. This can be problem for church officials because the sacrament of love would be beyond control of the clergy.

The church could remain involved if they were knowledgeable about intimacy and viewed themselves as primarily teachers rather than administers of sacraments. They could for example teach that being open to producing new life when having sex can be the ultimate sacrament of love with a potential third person gathering in his name, instead of telling people they will go to hell for practicing contraception. Conscious behavior will always be superior to unconscious behavior. Choosing to participate with each other in producing new life has to be a more attractive choice for humans than accepting pregnancies that just happen (Evdokimov 1995:178).

Church officials use the expression "real presence" in referring to the Eucharist, but if Jesus is where two or more or gathered in his name, they will have to admit that he is really present when families gather to baptize a child, when couples commit themselves to each other whether in a marriage ceremony or not, and all the ceremonial and ritual gatherings in or out of the church, e.g., birthday parties. With the current mindset, bringing up the presence of Jesus at a birthday party might make a person seem hyper-religious, hence odd. This is the unfortunate result of the church's need to be the mediator between God and the human family. If the words attributed to Jesus are true then his presence is not limited to the seven sacraments, church sponsored events or participation by the clergy, nor is Communion limited to the Eucharist. There are many ways for people to connect and all human connections are Communion although on various levels. Current church practice of controlling the sacraments has the effect of holding Jesus hostage to the institution's need to be in charge of the People's access to the divine presence. If my diagnosis of this sacramental situation is correct a great liberation awaits the People of God who are in fact *the* Church as recognized by the bishops of the world during Vatican II (Abbott 1966:24-37). Our consciousness has evolved to the point where it now makes sense to reclaim religion from the church.

When couples or families circle (hold hands) before sharing a meal in recognition of God's gift, they are administering the sacrament of love to each other thereby making the meal sacred and experiencing the "real presence" of Jesus as surely as if they were at Mass. They are symbolically united by the food they eat which will become their bodies. However, while consciousness of God and the gift of food may be superior to unconscious behavior, when hippies in a commune join hands before sharing their meal they recognize each other's sacredness, if not God's immanence, and it is also a sacramental moment.

I am not proposing the elimination of Mass in a church. Joining the larger community in this celebration is a worthy part of community formation at another level, but the time has passed for attending Mass as a formal obligation under the threat of sin. Families are central for worship by the Jews. The church has displaced the family from this position of primacy. We should reconsider the value of large church gatherings in his name. Mass as it has been often presented to us does not in itself lead to Communion between people and in the long run may have a negative effect. (See the anecdote about the archbishop and the senior class p. 168). We would be better off at home with loved ones and the "real presence."

If the Vatican wants us to have these sacred moments with a priest, they could ordain more priests so that we can have a large number of "house churches." For this they could dip into another pool of candidates for just this purpose: former priests, including those who are now married; married men and women; vowed religious; virtually anyone who felt called. There is a precedent for this kind of ordination. At one time the Vatican ordained priest solely for the purpose of saying mass continuously in order to collect stipends (Martos 1981:403). Priests for small faith communities would not be persons saddled with administration of a large parish. They would be solely for the sake of creating a greater consciousness of the small gatherings as sacred. We could still have the kind of priests we have now as resource persons, who could say church Masses, promote education of the faithful, and facilitate larger gatherings. However, we do not actually need a new kind of priest. When Jesus spoke of two or three gathered in his name he did not say, "With a priest." It would, however, be a way for Rome to stay connected with the People of God. With small faith communities participating in the sacrament of love, fulfilling formal obligations would become a non-issue. People will be gathering because they want to, as they did before the institutional church existed. The people would be more likely to become conscious of making every day holy thereby fulfilling the third commandment instead of completing an obligation. This is the ideal and the challenge taught by Jesus as pointed out in chapter six.

There are countless ways to create sacred moments and achieve Communion, or as some might call it, the real presence--conversation, play, sharing nature's beauty, sharing a beer with a friend, and of course, having sex. Unfortunately, friends do not often think to drink beer in the name of Jesus, and the church has done such a good job of desacralizing sex that couples are not likely to think of acting in Jesus' name, whether married or not. They are more likely to feel awkward thinking of Jesus while having sex, a sad commentary on the attitude toward sex that has come down to us. Sacred sex would not seem odd if the Vatican had developed a theology of intimacy, including sacred sex, to promote that kind of consciousness. Unmarried persons might then be inclined to ask themselves, "Can our sex be sacred? instead of wondering how far they could go before committing a mortal sin. Sex can be an important part of intimacy. We can achieve an intimate relationship with or without sex, but sex by itself will never get us there because the intent could never be Communion as understood here. Many persons find it difficult to transcend the idea that sex itself is Communion. They cannot imagine any closer connection with another human, although it takes no deep analysis to understand that a mutual assent to sex is hardly a profound mental connection in itself. During all the centuries that sex was not quite nice and couples acted according to the father/husband and the wife/mother roles intimacy was not an issue. Couples had community sanctions and brute economics to hold them together. In advanced industrial societies such as the United States, where couples from diverse background find each other and marry or commit without marriage, the need to work at developing an intimate relationship (Communion) becomes imperative. Role expectations and community sanctions no longer bind

Given the tendency people have to continue doing what they have always done they might feel reluctant to accept the idea of a sacrament of love that does not involve the institutional church. Thus it would be better if, for those persons, this new consciousness were broached by Rome. However, this is so important for the future of the People of God that we should not be put off by official reluctance. Obviously the People of God are in no way dependent on priests in this matter, just as they would not be dependent on the church for marriage if there were not a tradition of control that the faithful had come to accept during all these centuries.

With the liberation of conscience emerging from Vatican II, and the growing recognition by people that "We are the Church" rather than the pope and the hierarchy, we are on the verge of making the 21st century, the century of the laity. This is a great time for the sacrament of love to gain full recognition in the process of reclaiming religion from the church. While leadership at the institutional level can provide certain advantages to the faithful, progressive moral evolution has always occurred and will continue to occur with or without religious leadership. For Rome moral evolution tends to be equated with relativism, a greater permissiveness and a general loosening of moral standards. But as we saw in examining what Jesus taught about the Ten Commandments we are actually being called to higher standards than those the church offers. The greater rigor in observance of the commandments that John Paul II seems to be proposing is a dead end. What does one do after not having killed someone or stolen from someone, or after attending Mass? Rigor implies a more strenuous effort, something unpleasant whereas feeding a hungry person or teaching a child to read promotes their life and well-being and is satisfying in itself while fulfilling the commandment against killing.

The Roman Catholic church, in the person of John Paul II, has officially accepted the idea of humanity's biological evolution. The church, however, remains a long way from admitting humanity's progressive moral evolution despite the evidence of history, even its own history, and the Bible. In teaching about the Ten Commandments Jesus clearly pointed the way to the next stage in the evolution of human consciousness as I demonstrated in the chapter on the Decalogue and which was evident in the explanation of revelation. When the People realize that mediation of the clergy is not an absolute requirement to live with the presence of Jesus a more complete liberation for humanity will have been attained.

If the hierarchy, as they claim, exists to serve the People of God, then by clinging to the consciousness of an earlier, less enlightened age, they do not serve the People well. The metaphor of the end of humanity's childhood used by Bonhoeffer in the 1940's is apropos. If the People were made aware of the ease with which sacred moments can be created, that they did not need a church or a priest they might be less inclined to wait for Sundays and holy days or for the clergy to take the lead in their spiritual lives. We saw in looking at the Ten Commandments that keeping one day holy pointed to fulfillment of that commandment as keeping every day holy through the exercise of human imagination. Can the leadership be excused for not teaching this to us? Of course. Their consciousness could not have been much advanced over the People out of which they emerged, and it is only since Vatican II that the questioning of the leadership has reached numbers that can no longer be ignored. Everyone should be glad that the church is now mostly recognized as a human institution and not the perfect society it was once thought to be, although there has been some fudging on that. In a document that took eleven years to produce, *We Remember: A Reflection on the Shoah,* by John Paul II dealing with the institutional church and the Holocaust , Vatican officials express repentance for not having done as much as they could have to save the Jews. But

> To protect the church itself from blame, the statement invokes the subtle distinction, long recognized in scholastic theology, between the church as such, which is pure, and the sons and daughters of the church, who sometimes stray from the path of salvation (Dulles 1998).

If this pure "church as such" is not the hierarchy nor the People of God, what is it and where is it? As always the truth is liberating.

The concept of an evolving human consciousness probably would not have made sense even to the few persons who were highly educated at the time of the Council of Trent, from which Roman Catholicism took most of the form it maintained right up to Vatican II. At the time of Trent people generally believed in the literal truth of the Bible and the authority of the church to speak for God. The scholarly study of scripture has changed how we view the Bible and its origin, which is itself evidence of cognitive, moral evolution. Blaming popes and cardinals for holding on to a system that the people see as arbitrarily restrictive is an easy exercise. Officials of the Vatican are fighting for what they believe in with all the strategies at their command. Out of the tension between institution and the People, truth will emerge. Meanwhile the apparent lacunae in leadership is generating what seems to be the greatest crisis facing Roman Catholicism since the Reformation. The faithful are increasingly less likely to respond to a religious system meant to serve illiterate peasants of medieval times. The People of God have become better informed. They are beginning to realize that their church wants them to remain docile and accept ideas that can no longer be regarded as reasonable.

All reasoning is based on assumptions and if the assumptions on which the reasoning is based becomes discredited so does the reasoning. A blatant example of a discredited assumption is the belief that male sperm contained homunculi, little men. Thus "wasting seed," as the church expressed it, was a kind of murder. Yet this is one of the assumptions on which the original ban on contraception was based. Another assumption supporting the ban, this one recently discredited by the church itself, is the belief that the pleasure in sex is unavoidably sinful, hence by preventing birth people were enjoying the sin without cost. The People of God are beginning to consciously shape their morality for themselves, and they are voicing their dissidence in ever larger numbers. The Vatican bureaucrats have difficulty listening. They see their job as preventing change, and perhaps even going back a little in time, say to pre-Vatican II days. This intransigence may have a positive value in keeping some of the wilder ideas from taking hold but having a system of discernment that allowed change would keep the People and the hierarchy on the same side.

A few of the new breed of dissident Catholics are claiming that the church should be more democratic in a political sense, and while the church could survive local elections of pastors and bishops, we should not be voting on which rules we will follow. Changes in the rules have come slowly giving the People time to garner from experience what will work. The change in attitude toward slavery is a good example of how morality changes. In that case it took centuries for the idea of banning slavery to even occur on a scale to be effective. In our day, however, with rapid global communication such changes could happen more quickly. There is a teaching that goes by the Latin name of *sensus fidelium*, literally the sense of the faithful. The Holy Spirit does not operate only among ordained clergy. As they themselves teach, "The spirit blows where it will." My reading of *sensus fidelium* is that if the hierarchy believes a certain idea to be true, and all the faithful believe something contradicting that idea, the People have it right. The current crises in the church is a result of the faithful recognizing that the morality taught by the Catholic magisterium badly needs updating. When the bishops at Vatican II tacitly admitted that the church had made mistakes in some things they opened the door to reflection by the faithful and theologians on other errors that had not been admitted.

With the Platonic foundation of Catholic morality the hierarchy must maintain an absolute and unchanging morality. When Cardinal Ratzinger proclaimed that the greatest threat to the church is relativism, he failed to mention that there are different kinds of relativism. The good cardinal did not specify, but we may infer that he favors no change at all. John Paul II's policy of appointing conservative bishops is evidence that he is trying to undo some of the changes that have already occurred as a consequence of Vatican II. The changes in the last few centuries in regard to the morality of slavery which is related to the belief that one's status in life is divinely ordained reveals a relativism that few people will argue against. The church is also guilty of relativism in its teaching on the morality of war and capital punishment, and on sex in marriage. So when Cardinal Ratzinger rails against relativism he needs to speak with more precision. I suspect he is referring to some kind of absolute relativism, according to which nothing is true, or all truths have equal standing. Few people believe that. Before relativism there was and is the problem of idolatry, the false images of God we cling to, a much more pervasive and serious problem.

In Avery Dulles' arguments for certain kinds of acceptable change in church teaching (a proper kind of relativism) Without going far enough to draw condemnation he does go beyond what the magisterium considers prudent in advocating change. His argument is that within the historically conditioned hence relative theological concepts there is an absolute toward which we are groping. This absolute is what must remain through any changes. Dulles unfortunately uses an empirical example.

> When I say, therefore, "the table is square," I am simultaneously aware, at least in some vaguely implicit way, of the incomplete and approximate character of my concepts of"tableness" and "squareness." What I designate as table," from one point of view, another knower, from a different perspective, might grasp by means of other categories. The shape of the table is not exactly square, even in the Euclidean sense, and perhaps it could be better measured by some other geometry than Euclid's. While conceding all this, I am confident that whatever new concepts might be devised to speak about what I am referring to as the "squareness" of the "table," they cannot validly change what I really mean when I say, on the basis of the evidence before me, "the table is square." My realization of the circumscribed value of my

own assertion is precisely what protects it from being falsified by a subsequent, more refined statement (1985:194).

I have quoted this passage at length because the use of an empirical
example, "table," instead of a theological one such as "salvation,"
calls Dulles' argument into question. However it is expressed, the
dogma of the Immaculate Conception can neither be falsified nor
verified so the protection cited does not apply. Social scientists'
whose work more closely resembles theology than physics act similarly. Arthur Stinchcombe, for example, while trying to explain causal
laws in a book entitled *Constructing Social Theories* cites the sun's
effect on earth's temperature (1968:31). Both Dulles and Stinchcombe recognize the difficulty of citing examples in their respective
fields, Stinchcombe because so much of social reality is what people
believe that it is. The same holds true for religious reality to the
detriment of Dulles' theory which is why people can argue about the
existence or non-existence of God without coming to a conclusion.
This tells us that the church needs to find other grounds for persuading people other than "we say so," or "God says so."
There is still a role for the hierarchy to play in a Church identified
as the People of God. We should not expect an open break on the
scale of the Lutheran revolution. Many have left but the mass of
dissidents who seek reform want to stay and change the system from
within. Still we may find that the future of the Church will be in
small faith communities. The institutional structure now in place
could provide an exceptionally good way to begin teaching and
preaching the sacrament of love, especially between couples and in
small groups where the possibilities for making intimate connections
are greater than in large church gatherings.
The hierarchy is also admirably situated to set an example for the
whole world and not just the faithful because the media attends closely
to what the leadership says. If our goal is a global community,
having a leadership already in place would be extremely helpful,
especially in spreading the idea that intimate relationships, especially
those in the family, are the most likely foundation of this community,
and perhaps the best place to experience the "real presence." They
might begin by announcing that some of the absolute standards they
have clung to are actually ideals toward which persons should work.
I have already described in the chapter on commandments how the
absolute requirement to worship God could be changed to promote
creativity in worship that would probably result in an expansion of
divine worship, with the drive to worship coming from within instead
of an obligation from the outside under the penalty of sinning and

losing one's soul, whatever that means. Instead of an absolute ban on contraception the hierarchy could teach that deliberately choosing to participate in the creation of life as an ideal way of administering the sacrament of love. There has been a move in this direction, however backward it may seem, as indicated by the recent pastoral directive on this subject. With regard to birth control the Vatican has put in place a "don't-ask-don't-tell" policy in hearing confessions.

The Catholic magisterium has always taught the indissolubility of marriage. Unfortunately the reasons given do not serve well at this time, viz., that marriage is indissoluble because God or the church says so. This is especially the case because the magisterium has viewed marriage as a man and a woman filling husband and wife roles, with the husband in control. In addition to a theology of marriage the magisterium needs to develop programs to educate people in the nature of intimacy and the skills required for making marriages more stable. Resolving a difficulty offers more satisfaction to a person then walking away from it.

Dr. Beck ably demonstrates that love is never enough (1988). The bishops should hire professionals to teach communication and conflict resolution for couples planning to marry. The modern view of a coupleship emerging is a mutual commitment of two equal persons sharing the responsibility of decision making, and not necessarily a male and a female. With so many couples entering into the church's concept of commitment without adequate preparation, especially concerning the sacrament of love, no one should be surprised that marriages fail. When such failures occur, church policy unrealistically dictates that the couple remain celibate for the rest of their lives. To commit to intimacy again without annulment of the prior marriage means automatic excommunication according to the church. This results in a loss of membership for the church that church officials tend to deal with by reiterating the rules already in place. For the new, "We-are-Church" mentality, however, this does not mark the end of the relationship with the Church as the People of God. Many persons who remarry are recognizing that when they apply institutional standards to their previous relationship they can in conscience say that their marriage was not in fact valid. In some cases they may have been refused annulment or the annulment was successfully challenged. In other cases individuals do not even apply because it means dragging dirty laundry through the annulment process. A typical case would be a woman who married to escape physical, mental or sexual abuse by a parent. In their role as pastors some priest recognize the validity of such thinking, dubbed colloquially as "annulment in a box."

Still, even young couples with no such problems are not likely to view themselves as the foundation for a global community unless they have received preparation for such thinking early in their lives. Their view of themselves as a budding community does not ordinarily achieve this scope on its own. An enlightened leadership would be helpful in developing that kind of consciousness. We cannot, however, wait for the present leadership to initiate necessary changes. We, the People of God, have to take the lead and let them follow if and when they will.

The church currently uses the idea of natural law as a way of reinforcing the Ten Commandments and church law. The basis for this thinking is that rational human beings can figure out the natural law on their own. The law of love is considered too ephemeral as a basis for everyday morality. Witness the attack by a church approved theologian (Von Hildebrand 1966:130-154) on Fletcher's *Situation Ethics* (1967) which puts the law of love before everything else. If, as Dr. Beck tells us, love is never enough, even for committed couples, we should not wonder that the natural law, the Commandments, and Canon Law will not serve to bring about a global community. We need the cognitive revolution proposed by Julian Huxley, an atheist, who wrote that "our destiny is to learn what our role is in the evolution of our species in order to fill it more adequately" (1958:209).

The basis for natural law is certainly built in. It is "survive," and because we are necessarily social we can add to that law, "together." We are not born with genetic coding telling us how to survive, individually and collectively. We have to create ourselves out of the materials at hand, usually the culture of our family and the larger society. Our helplessness at birth forces us to accept that our survival requires other humans. From that basis we have to derive specific rules for how we can survive. That means that a certain amount of flexibility in deriving specifics is required. The Jewish scriptures, for example, reveal that in the early stages of Judaism the failure to procreate was a serious fault. How serious was demonstrated by the story of Lot's daughters who got their father drunk in order to get pregnant by him (Gen. 19:31-38). Further illustrations are to be found in the behavior of Rachel and Leah (Gen. 30:1-24), also Tamar who posed as a temple prostitute so that she could get pregnant by her father-in-law (Gen. 38:13-26), cases the church does not cite for the importance of procreation. We are no longer a small tribe surrounded by hostile heathens. Therefore, we can no longer derive from the law of survival a ban on contraception. For the same reasons the ban on same sex love, a holdover from those times, also does not have the same validity. Now that trade, transportation, communication and our burgeoning population are global in scope, survival is a global problem. A survival morality has to be part of everyone's repertoire, in and out of religion.

The church leadership talks about the oneness of body and soul, but they teach that disembodied souls can exist (*Catechism* 1994:93) as when they speak of saving souls, and praying for the souls in purgatory. Body and soul are Greek concepts and their use among the faithful calls into question the church's teaching on the unity of being. Perhaps the contradiction persists because the soul is supposed to be immortal, and a rational way to explain what happens at death has yet to be found. However, if the promise of resurrection is for real we do not need a disembodied soul to explain anything. If we are all dead when we die that should clarify for everyone the fact that we cannot save ourselves. Still, popular belief has it that there are formulas for salvation.

Christian love could not be primary within Greek Philosophy. Consider, for example, that Aristotle thought humility was a vice, and communing with another person through the sacrament of love requires a respect and reverence for that person based in part on humility. If Augustine had thought about war within the context of the Gospel with its emphasis on love, he could never have developed his particular theory of a just war, an idea held by the church until recently. It is as if they had said, "Yes, Jesus taught us to love our enemies, but we must be prudent and practical," a purely human perspective on the law of love.

Perhaps the worst effect of not having recognized the sacrament of love is the hierarchy's continual interference in its administration by couples committed to each other whether married or not, whether heterosexual or not. Vatican hangups about sex adopted from the Stoics, Gnostics and assorted sources, plus its traditional paternalism are directly responsible for a great deal of marital and other problems of intimacy. By neglecting the sacrament of love the church has made marriage appear to be a one-time event, whereas, properly speaking the sacrament of love, especially in its marital form, calls for continual administration, a fact that the hierarchy has failed to recognize if their silence on the subject is any indication.

The hierarchy currently makes an effort, prior to the church ceremony, to develop a consciousness of canon law requirements on what constitutes a good marriage, but their main concern after the ceremony has been the ban on contraception and the indissolubility of marriage once contracted. At least married sex is no longer thought of as necessarily sinful although John Paul II has recently revived the idea that a man can commit adultery with his wife by being too lustful in his pursuit of sex. Wives were at one time told that they could not refuse sex to their husbands under pain of mortal sin. According to a priest I questioned about this recently the church no longer teaches this; it has been dropped without fanfare. This had been a significant part of the "wife-role." My understanding of this rule for wives was that to refuse a husband sex would be to put him in danger of going outside of marriage to satisfy his "need" for sex.

Perhaps the hierarchy uses the expression "sacred sex." I have never heard them use it although I went through a preCana course twice before marrying. Yet it would be hard to imagine any activity by a couple more conducive to making a commitment stable than such an intimate gathering in Jesus' name. However, the priests and married professionals who conducted the preCana courses did not tell us to think of having sex in his name. I suspect that many of the clergy are still a long way from admitting that Jesus could be in bed with two lovers who were there in his name.

If, as I contend, sin means harming one or more persons, putting such persons at risk for harm, or neglecting one's responsibility to one or more persons, then good is the opposite, hence the negotiated reality of the committed couples, married or otherwise, especially their creative sex life is properly beyond church control as it is among the Eastern Orthodox. If a couple find delight in each other through a variety of sex acts, especially when they are conscious of mutually administering the sacrament of love to each other, the hierarchy will just have to concede that the couple are sharing their space with Jesus just as he said. With this analysis we can see the real significance of understanding the difference between social and empirical realty. The hierarchy still regards certain sexual practices as unnatural within the parameters of their Aristotelian biology and their Augustinian and Thomist philosophies, but we may legitimately ask, "What is natural for humans? Theologian Reinhold Niebuhr and the atheist Sartre agree that human nature has to include what humans can become (Ramsey 112-113; see also Max Otto, 1954:33; and Berger 1967:49).

If the church promoted consciousness of the sacrament of love instead of focussing on violations of their so-called natural law, the issue of marriage's indissolubility might rarely arise because many of the problems of committed couples among the faithful have been a result of the magisterium's negative attitude and teachings about sex for the better part of two millennia. The magisterium managed to convince many women that sex was tainted, thus indirectly inserting themselves into the conjugal bed. Church officials need to establish a program of positive, responsible sexuality. The importance of a female virginity at marriage had more to do with heirs and male ego than spiritual purity. But as with everything else about the church, we should not wait. We should begin to model administration of the sacrament of love for one another, especially our youngsters in their formative years.

Adolescents used to ask, "What's wrong with premarital sex?" Perhaps some of them still do. What we can be certain has not changed is the response of the Roman hierarchy: It is a violation of God's sixth commandment, a mortal sin, which if you die without repenting you will go to hell. This is all very abstract and theoretical for a teenager, meaning it carries little conviction. It is also bad logic if one considers that this behavior seems to have the same weight as adultery. God is remote and inaccessible, the alleged penalty seems unreasonable, and the immediacy of the hormonal pressure is very real, apparently signaling a need rather than mere desire, the way that hunger signals a need for food, or thirst a need for water. There are excellent reasons why young unmarried persons should not engage in sex, but the Roman hierarchy does not feel it can rely on teaching responsibility and the nature of true intimacy to keep youngsters from having sex, so they continue to preach fear of eternal damnation despite the fact that it is no longer effective, if it ever was. If they taught instead that every encounter between humans is an opportunity for Communion, to share the sacrament of love, young men and women would be more likely to have this kind of consciousness in their relationships. Then if they thought of having sex together they might ask themselves if sex at that time is compatible with sharing the sacrament of love, i.e, can it be sacred.

From about the second century onward the whole issue of sex and sin has been seriously distorted in Church teaching, particularly by associating sexual sins with the pleasure that humans experience and the one time conviction, only recently modified, that sex was only for making babies and any other use resulted in various degrees of sin even within marriage. Even if one had the intention of making a baby the behavior was still grossly sinful if any but the missionary position was used (Fagan 1979:99). In other words playfulness in sex was sinful. Some church leaders solemnly declared that they were unable to see how the taint of sin could be avoided in any sexual behavior on the assumption apparently that sex is inherently pleasurable.

According to church teaching if a young man accidentally brushes against a girl's breast, he would be required in his daily examination of conscience to ask himself if he experienced pleasure. If so he then had to ask himself if he willfully assented to the pleasure, making it a mortal sin, hence matter for confession. I noted in an earlier chapter why we cannot sin all by ourselves. Sin is social, always involving a relationship; specifically, some behavior results in a negative effect on a bond or potential bond between humans. If a young man deliberately touches a girl's breast and she does not want him to, he has violated her. The seriousness of the violation would depend on a number of factors such as the nature of their relationship, age disparity, where the violation occurred, whether force was involved and so on. The pleasure the boy experienced is *not* a factor in the degree of sinfulness. In any case it is highly unlikely that except for using threats or physical force that such an offense could be serious. One of the problems humans have with sexual pleasure is that it may lead one person to violate another or otherwise act irresponsibly to obtain the pleasure. The pleasure is not itself the problem. *It does not harm.*

One of the difficulties confronting the Roman bureaucracy is being able to come right out and say, "Our teaching on sexual morality needs to change; the church needs to spell out precisely why sex and sin are sometimes connected." Typically when a change takes place in Catholic morality Rome first becomes quiet and no longer brings up the subject then the issue quietly dies and over a long period of time gradually becomes a non-issue, e.g., usury and slavery, or the need to burn heretics and witches, or like the requirement noted above concerning the mandatory assent to sex by a wife. This, fortunately or unfortunately, depending on one's perspective, cannot happen with sexual morality. Church officials have made too big an issue of this for too long, so there is no way it can quietly die. What will happen is that people will figure out for themselves what is right and wrong and bypass church authorities as they have done in the matter of birth control. When Vatican II liberated the Catholic conscience the death knell rang for the presence of the hierarchy in the bedroom. By holding on to an absolutist morality, one which they themselves defined, and by misinterpreting the nature of sexual sin in the first place, church officials risk losing all credibility in teaching about sin. The official line on sexual sins has so distorted the thinking of the hierarchy and the faithful that sin and sex had become practically synonymous.

The original proscription against adultery was against having sex with another Jew's wife. Besides generating disharmony within the tribe such behavior was 1) a violation of a man's property rights; and 2) called into question the paternity of the children, an important factor since children were a man's immortality as well as heirs to his property. Having sex with a slave, a heathen woman or a man's own concubine was not forbidden by this commandment. The law was intended to prevent discord in the family, i.e., the Jewish tribe. The law said nothing about sex being bad. The implication, rather, was that it was good (Peter Brown 1988:95). What is wrong with adultery should have become clearer from what Jesus taught, viz. that the most important activity humans can engage in is community formation, which for Christians means promoting the eventual reign of God in the hearts and minds of all humans. The primary message of the Gospel concerns the realization of the worldwide kinship of humanity. The prohibition against having sex with someone else's mate, or any movement in that direction, should at present be recognized as incompatible with the sacrament of love not to mention global community formation. In the larger picture it also has to do with the fact that two people committed to each other are a community in the process of formation. The locus of wrong is not in the illicit sex, and it certainly is not the pleasure derived from the act. Rather, it is the fact that someone is intruding on or destroying from within this potential community of two which is the most likely basis for building a global community, especially if children are part of the relationship. Violating a relationship wherein the partners are supposed to be committed to creating sacred moments together obviously cannot itself be the sacrament of love, but who among us were told about creating sacred moments?

Sex in adultery is *the means* by which sin is committed; it is not itself the sin. If two people who are committed to each other cannot resolve their differences and work toward the ideal community of two, where else will we find a foundation for a global community? Committed pairs and networks of committed pairs plus the children they care for, by connecting in ever larger numbers will significantly move us toward a worldwide community. Perhaps it is the only way it can be achieved. Viewed from this perspective, anyone intruding in this potential community of two is contributing to the destruction of one root of a tree that is supposed to ultimately constitute our global family tree. This is serious indeed, perhaps the most serious sin there is because it strikes at the very foundation of everyone's survival.

Establishing and maintaining an interpersonal relationship is a difficult enterprise with many fragile moments. When these moments occur an outsider can appear as an attractive reason for giving up the difficult task of pair-bonding. This is not what the Roman hierarchy is teaching. They are telling us that this kind of sex is a grave sin because God said so, or they say so. We have already seen that the reason for something being wrong must be rational, i.e., it must make sense to us. That something is wrong because God says so is acceptable only if a person has faith that church authorities know what they are talking about, a possibility becoming increasingly less likely.

The distinction I am making concerning fornication and adultery, i.e., the sex itself is not the sin, may be too subtle to warrant thinking about from the perspective of the hierarchy. It appears after all to be the same physical behavior and it is still sin. The hierarchy seems unaware that if people really understood exactly what makes behavior wrong they just might be more respectful of committed couples, married or not, and of their own commitments because they are a community in the making. In any case the way the church teaches morality has hardly been effective. They claim that the sexual experiments of youngsters are just as serious as adultery. They could be right, but not for the reasons they give. Youngsters also manipulate, extort, coerce and otherwise act irresponsibly with varying degrees of consciousness. The hierarchy seems unaware that they have not offered good reasons for not having sex, and what priest has the time, even if he were competent, to talk about true intimacy Several theologians have spoken and written of the "new morality" (Curran 1968, Milhaven 1970, Maguire 1968, McCormick 1989) but the Vatican is not conceding anything. The theologians who get the *imprimaturs* and *nihil obstats* such as William May and Dietrich Von Hildebrand are telling us that nothing has changed in the church sexual policies and that it cannot.

Couples should be taught that creating a two person community is *the* most important activity in the world and probably the most satisfying. It is not hard to imagine the kind of world this would be if everyone could be persuaded to see it this way. It is not the sex, and it especially is not the pleasure of sex that is sinful. It is the fact that using sex in certain ways can harm persons and be destructive to our proper task--contributing in our small way toward establishing God's reign on earth by creating community. If a young man goes to confession and reports that he had sex with his girlfriend, that may be a serious matter independently of the sex act. He may have manipulated her, or extorted sex by making her feel guilty. He could have lied and professed a committed love, and so on. The sex is not evil in itself. The evil is in whatever physical or psychic harm is done to one or more humans. Compare such thinking to Trent's catechism which required that sins be confessed by kind and number, making it more important for the young man to say that he had sex twice than that he lied to obtain it.

Sufficient reflection, one of the supposed requirements for serious sin, may be radically impossible under the influence of hormones. If there is to be sufficient reflection it must occur a long time before the immediate interaction that leads to sex. In other words, it is not enough to know that there is some rule out there that says, "Sex outside of marriage is wrong." With only this idea to reflect on we should not be surprised that young people say, "Why not?" There must be an internal conviction of it's being wrong. This kind of conviction is extremely difficult to come by when the reasons given are irrational such as "God says so." There is no evidence to persuade anyone that God ever said that. But the main reason for the lack of conviction that prevails is that sex by the unmarried is not inherently wrong. The evidence points to God's revelation generally being the evolving consciousness of humans based on the accumulated wisdom of humanity as we saw in earlier chapters. If an idea does not eventually find acceptance in the larger community, the idea is not a good one or humans are not yet ready for it.

We have to ask, "Who is harmed by unmarried sex?" and "What precisely is the harm done?" We might also ask how serious is the harm before we can make a judgment, and of course we can only make the judgment for ourselves, never others. Making fornication equal to adultery as a mortal sin has the effect of decreasing the importance of adultery instead of increasing the importance of fornication. Trying to arouse conviction through fear of eternal punishment has not worked to prevent unmarried sex, and will not work with most educated persons. Unless church leadership becomes convinced itself that the real evil is the lying, manipulation, extortion and so on, and especially in the case of the young, the irresponsibility, they stand little chance of generating the kind of conviction people need to act responsibly toward others, whether in sex or any other interaction. When we are convinced of what is in our best interest we act or do not act according to our convictions. If the church has a role in helping people become convinced it will have to be other than preaching supernatural rewards or punishments. They should be teaching the communication skills required for developing intimacy between persons and promoting the high degree of satisfaction possible in the Communion that can be achieved.

The distortion of sex by the church Fathers obviously affected more than the Christian view of sex. It tended to draw attention away from more serious kinds of harm that people can perpetrate. The concept of a just killing is one overriding example. Hundreds of millions of people have died in the 20th century alone from that concept which allowed Catholic bishops to bless cannons for either side. The problems of unmarried sex could become much less of an issue if, as I suggested a few paragraphs earlier, the hierarchy promoted at an earlier age the sacrament of love in every encounter between humans, and especially in *all* interpersonal relationships.

The sacrament of love, if the Vatican thought of it at all, might be limited to matrimony. But even there it should not be thought of as being administered once and for all time. It is the ideal we should all have before us continuously regardless of our state in life. Marriages die because people do not understand what will keep them together. Same sex relationships also fail to achieve stability for the same reason. The Roman bureaucracy and other social forces can and probably will hold out for a long time, maybe forever, on legal and canonical recognition of same sex couples, but human rules are not God's rules.

The sacrament of love cannot be contained or constrained by anyone. It is God's special gift to humanity and is available to all including same sex partners, with or without the clergy's approval. Officials in various religions, including Roman Catholicism rarely understand the extent to which they are shaped by the culture in which they are immersed. Reading Jewish scriptures are instructive in this regard. When the Jewish religion started, they proscribed human sacrifice, but they did not thereby eliminate the idea of sacrifice. They merely substituted animals. People could not imagine God not requiring sacrifice. Obviously God does not need the sacrifice of humans, animals or anything else. Apparently it is still a need for people according to current thinking on capital punishment. Such thinking makes Caiaphas reasoning look noble. He "was the one who supposedly advised the Jews that it was expedient for one man to die on behalf of the people" (John 18:14). Also, the death of Jesus has been interpreted as a sacrifice to redeem sinful humanity and is reenacted as the sacrifice of the Mass, an event that badly needs reinterpreting if we are to escape the mindset that connects God and sacrifice.

Looking at the evolution of the idea of God and morality in the context of history and culture offers us a clue to clarifying our ideas of right and wrong. Examining these ideas in the context of cognitive evolution we can no longer say this or that is wrong because the Bible says so. Clearly, some of what has been considered right or wrong were simply cultural norms in place at the time a law was promulgated as we saw with the proscription against same sex lovers. If sin is the harm done to one or more persons by a particular behavior we must apply the questions cited above: Who is harmed? What is the harm? When same sex lovers commit to each other and create their own social reality many people are offended, presumably as God's surrogates. There is a large difference between taking offense and giving offense. Committed same sex couples are generally not trying to give offense. They mostly want to be left to themselves. Once again, as with heterosexual couples they, like everyone else, should be taught to administer the sacrament of love as children so that as adults they will form stable, loving commitments. They are not exempt from harming one another, but it is not love that harms. A more likely candidate is cultural patterns of abuse in interpersonal relationships for which religions must share much of the responsibility. We are all supposed to be connected by love, especially in pairs. By devaluing same sex love, links in the chain of love will be missing, thus delaying the reign of God. The prejudice against same sex love will take longer to die than racism or sexism, primarily because of the churches, especially the Roman church. There is hope however. I see movement toward acceptance by people who recognize themselves as *the* Church, i.e., the People of God.

Catholics everywhere are intuiting that something is wrong with the present system of sexual morality but they cannot imagine how to make it right. They sometimes take off on their own without guidance and experiment, and since they are operating in the dark they frequently err and their experiment fails. This is where a proper institutional church would be an advantage. A wise leadership would be in service to God's People. Instead of drawing lines that a person can't cross or presenting the world as black and white they could present ideals toward which people should work and by teaching people to learn from mistakes. They need to promote responsible loving and not just within their current, narrow guidelines. We should want everyone to be involved. It should not be limited to those of our denomination, or even just Christians. Walter Lippmann, Julian Huxley, and Gregory Bateson are a few notable atheists who have held life sacred. Many with no religion could be easily persuaded by a word or example that life is indeed sacred and would be willing to share such moments with us because it involves no complicated belief system. Imagining how we might administer the sacrament of love to each other could release the greatest era of creativity in the history of the world. We are all supposed to be connected by love, especially in pairs and small groups. We have to find a way to do it, even if it means not mentioning God or Jesus. If two persons are committed to serving humanity and one of them believes that Jesus is divine and the other believes that he was simply a superior human what can their differences in belief possibly matter to God?

Are there any limitations to administering the sacrament of love? Yes and no. I mentioned above that there were good reasons why youngsters should not engage in sex. It would be a rare pair of teenagers who could administer the sacrament in its committed or marital form. While not impossible, the sense of responsibility required to follow through if a pregnancy occurred is not likely at that age.

Creating a problem for a young woman that calls for solutions such as an abortion, a shotgun wedding, giving up a baby for adoption, or absorbing it into one or the other family can hardly be called administering the sacrament of love. This is also the case with uncommitted adults, although adults are usually better positioned to commit to each other in case of an accident, admittedly not the best of circumstances. We might note in passing that the church is not saying, "If you must have sex, prevent conception." Thomas Aquinas teaches that contraception is a worse sin than having sex with one's mother or father.

The gift of virginity of which so much was made at one time is not particularly important these days, especially considering that it was a rather one-sided gift in the days of the double standard. A commitment to each other and to the relationship is significant, however, and within a commitment, exclusive sex is a special gift. It is a closer kind of circling, potentially the administration of the sacrament of love in its highest form. By committing to each other and the relationship the couple, heterosexual or homosexual, are in effect saying that the administration of the sacrament, while not excluding others will in this special way (sexually) be offered only to each other for as long as they both shall live.

Under the old rubrics for commitment, sponsored by the hierarchy, heterosexual couples committed to each other and to the fulfillment of husband and wife roles rather than to a lifelong sharing of the sacrament of love. After the ceremony they might act with love toward each other on occasion, but not having started with an ideal of continually creating sacred moments, that is administering the sacrament of love, the ardor of the couple might gradually cool because marriage was something that happened in the past and gradually diminished in reality, as has been the experience of so many couples, especially when the husband was considered the head, and the woman's role was to submit. The church has the word of St. Paul, St. Ambrose, and other church Fathers. Such a design for a relationship fitted well within the larger scheme of patriarchy, of which the church was also one of the chief sponsors. In this scheme the pope, the bishops and the priests were the shepherds and the faithful were the sheep, who, like women in marriage, were not to challenge authority. The hierarchy alone had a pipeline to the transcendental realm, and who consequently knew all that was necessary to know about God and morality.

We cannot discuss the sacrament of love without considering the church's policy regarding the divorced and remarried. All educated Catholics know the requirements of a valid marriage according to canon law. But if a person's conscience is primary as we learned from Vatican II, then the church should accept a declaration by the persons involved that this or that condition obtained, that a marriage was not valid, especially in cases where to disclose the reason might sully the character of someone, alive or dead, who is not one of the pair that is splitting. In the 1950s priests did not ask anyone who intended to get married if either or both were escaping abuse or an unbearable home life. Perhaps they do now. Yet "escaping" has been a common reason, mostly for young women, to get married and it invalidates the marriage according to canon law. This is a problem area that needs a great deal of exploring. If it were explored, some tragic errors might be prevented. In any case it should be enough for a couple who are marrying or separating to be interviewed together and separately by one or two responsible persons, even a priest, who could help in the clarification of conscience. If the decision were to separate it would still be up to the couple who would then know that their decision is supported or not supported by a mature third party.

If the couple decide to split in good faith, whether their decision is supported or not it could still be a time for a ritual involving the sacrament of love, such as that proposed by Bishop Spong in his "Service for the Recognition of the End of a Marriage" (Hays 1996:371). The church could thus help prevent much of the bad feelings often associated with dissolving a relationship, especially when children are involved. They would also demonstrate that they were serious in teaching that love and the individual's conscience are paramount by having the couple share the sacrament of love at their parting. On the other hand if the magisterium had this attitude the couple might not be divorcing in the first place.

CHAPTER IX
PRIMARY RELATIONSHIPS
Sacrament of Encounter

The final judgment of the fitting way to [act in a relationship] will be based on an immediate intuition and on a sympathetic sense of what this concrete situation requires. . . . Maguire

Gregory Bateson, an atheist, was not afraid to use the words "sacrament" and "sacred." By "sacrament" I believe he meant something like communication between persons that approaches that which occurs between the DNA and a developing embryo. That is how I am using sacrament in this chapter rather than in the religious sense of the previous chapter. The result is still Communion between two people who pursue a growing intimacy. I will try to show in this chapter that this kind of Communion is a little known and little understood need we all have. Even those who actually experience this kind of Communion more often than not have no concepts for describing what they have experienced. If we see the ecstasy on the face of a mother and a infant who is being lovingly squeezed we have witnessed the Sacrament I am trying to describe. The parent or other adult knows that a need of the infant has been met but generally does not understand that this particular need remains when the infant's helplessness which communicated the need diminishes. In these circumstances the adult also experiences a sense of satisfaction which signals that a need has been met but generally does not think in terms of need because the whole process is unselfconscious. Bringing it to consciousness is liberating (Avis 1989:68). Having concepts help.

239

Having concepts help. Without concepts the adult and the growing child cannot ask for what they need in that respect. And since the adult may no longer recognize the need of the child as it grows out of its helpless stage the need may not be filled consciously or unconsciously. As a child grows, parents may become increasingly concerned with control and boundaries and withholding what a child needs may seem to be the least costly means for getting what the parent feels is necessary.

When a need, whether real or imagined, is satisfied we experience a sense of completeness, peace or well-being. This "sense" is proportional to how strongly the need is felt. Similarly when a need is not met the sense of dissatisfaction is proportionately great. If I were imprisoned my most compelling thought would be of freedom. If I am starving I could not imagine anything that would give me greater satisfaction than getting food because I could not imagine a greater need. Imprisonment is a nearly perfect analogy for the human condition. We are all imprisoned by ignorance at birth and like someone in prison the newborn is driven to escape. Gradually the child acquires some freedom through interaction with others such as learning to communicate needs with words and in other ways.

Increasingly, the child's need for bonding can be satisfied with knowledge of some sort. Adult and child can develop ways of connecting on the level of mind while still maintaining physical contact. The adult has to make the greater effort to achieve intimacy through self-disclosure and by showing respect for the growing powers of the child, allowing freedom in matters that do not put anyone at risk. Children are fascinated by what parents think and feel. Sharing stories of any kind replaces in part the loving squeeze that satisfied an infant. Sharing stories of growing up, how parents met, their first date and so on can help to maintain that close contact children need. In trying to explain how adults can have a Primary Relationship, that is, achieve Communion and the freedom that flows from it, I will use the patterns of parent-child relationships extensively. An adult has the same need as a child for close contact with at least one other human. In its absence an adult may take desperate measures.

In our culture freedom seems to lie in possessing money, power, or fame. It is certainly the case that possessing any of these, singly or in combination, offers more choices than we would have without them. One of the main attractions for possessing them however is in the possibilities they offer for connecting with other humans. With fame the adulation of the crowds says in effect, "I want you." The possibility of sharing power can be attractive. Or with it, people may be bent to one's will, making connection the choice of the power holder. As for money, when we see sixty-five year old millionaires marrying women in their twenties and thirties we might assume that money helps in the perception of the older person's good qualities by diminishing, if not eradicating, prejudices against age and other aspects of a person that might be considered negative. But if we need a certain kind of connection with others, then the long-range and uncertain process of acquiring money, power or fame in order to accomplish this goal seems wasteful in the extreme. Since we are all afflicted with the need for Communion why not approach others directly for precisely the purpose of connecting in a way that satisfies the needs of both? The reasons we do not are complex, requiring a degree of unraveling that can only be suggested in a single essay. Just getting someone to recognize the need is difficult. Understanding the need and making it as explicit as possible is the purpose of this essay.

Liam Hudson reminds us "that those aspects of our personal lives that are most real to us are precisely those that are the most difficult to pin down" (1975:1700). One of the more serious problems we face in arriving at an understanding (this is the case especially for some men but for women also because of men's problem), occurs at puberty when the onset of hormones complicates the need to connect with a desire to connect sexually, perhaps under the illusion that sex is Communion. Such feelings can be so strong that they override any sense of the need for Communion when there has been no prior experience of Communion that enables the person to distinguish between sex and sacrament. Children they are usually wholly dependent on parents to have this enlightening experience of Communion which can establish that the need is non-sexual. We cannot with sex by itself achieve Communion otherwise rape, which is as far as one can get from Communion, would be enough. Many persons especially Children are passionate learners and the passionate pursuit of learning, especially in the arts is a good model for what takes place in a relationship between two adults who are trying to establish a Primary Relationship. From an aesthetic perspective if we think for example of the passion exhibited by the poetry of Keats, the painting of VanGogh, and the music of Beethoven we will get some idea of the intensity with which they attempted and succeeded in communicating with us. The emotions that arise from creating a Primary Relationship are akin to those that result from producing great art.

If these artists found an intense joy in their work we know that they also suffered a great deal. We can experience joy in sharing their work without suffering but we can expect to suffer sometime while engaged in our own creative efforts to engage others in a Primary Relationship. Imagine two people trying to connect with each other with the same kind of intensity as Keats or Van Gogh in their creative modes. Getting this close can be a fearsome project even between parent and child. When two persons can overcome their fears and engage in the aesthetic enterprise I call a Primary Relationship they have begun the process of Communion which may also be called a Sacrament of Encounter, or Primary Experience, the three names I give for what happens in a Primary Relationship. The persons involved in such a relationship may know times of great pain when it seems that the relationship will founder on the inability to connect for whatever reason and great joy in those moments when the connection seems perfect. The joy cannot be permanent because it results from having reached a certain level of development which must be left behind as they grow and aspire to the next level. With some experience in this project the persons involved may begin to experience the joy of anticipating the next level simultaneously with the pain of the difficult ascent.

Such intimacy is the ultimate in moral refinement. If morality has to do with how we act with, for and toward other humans, the persons involved in a Primary Relationship can never knowingly cause the slightest harm to the other person; nor can either be satisfied that the occasion for complete freedom for the other person has been achieved, that the vulnerability offered has not in some way been violated. We come so burdened with wants and needs that we may find it difficult not to let some suggestion of those wants and needs creep into our relationships with other humans. John Carse reminds us how difficult it is being perfectly silent in just listening to another person, to not have a script we would like them to use in speaking or in responding to us (1985:74). Having such a script manifests a lack of freedom to just be in the others presence. This can approach desperation when a person cannot chance a free response from the other. With the sacrament of love the two persons in the relationship in a sense commit to allowing a partner to want and to express wants, and not just needs, thus mitigating the taint of self-centeredness. In a Primary Relationship there is no question of suppressing wants after discovering that the joy in the relationship derives precisely from the sense of allowing the other a freedom that is as close to perfect as it is possible for humans to achieve. The gift of self-disclosure must be entirely free or it becomes an item for trading. If gift giving were on a continuum, the gifts in a Primary Relationship would be at the opposite end from the trading that sometimes goes on in relationships.

The pursuit of this higher morality I am describing is possible for everyone, in or out of religion. There are many degrees of satisfaction in connecting with other humans from the pleasure that a rapist experiences to true Communion or Primary Experience in an ideal Primary Relationship. Such a relationship does not exclude sex but since sex is a primary physical relationship and provides its own primary experience it can be limiting by creating the illusion that a Primary Relationship already exists and that sex is *the* Primary Experience. To believe that sex is the ultimate experience makes it impossible to have the Primary Relationship I am attempting to describe.

Primary Relationships with children develop unselfconsciously when their need continues to be met beyond infancy. But a higher degree of consciousness is required of the adult because meeting the need occurs in the context of socialization which seems to require some distance. There can be no doubt about a higher degree of consciousness being necessary for adults who wish to connect in this way, especially when we consider that adults generally do not come together with the natural openness of a child. The disposition to learn from others, and a readiness to self-disclose are the most important elements in such relationships. The relationship that exists between an author and a reader may help to explain. The author generally expends a great deal of conscious effort analyzing, synthesizing or just explaining something, e.g. Plato's *Republic*, from some perspective which can be made so clear that we are positioned to agree or disagree with either the author or Plato. The reader connects with the author by being consciously and critically involved in trying to understand what has been written. Authors and readers seldom have an interpersonal relationship but the learning patterns and disposition involved in writing a book or understanding one resembles what happens when these characteristics are mutual in an interpersonal relationship.

In the previous chapter we looked at relationships in which people are emotionally involved. In a Primary Relationship one experiences emotions, but that is not where they begin nor where they end. In the words of James Carse

> what is needed is that others relate to me in ways that call from me resources and responses that I need to be human, but did not otherwise experience as needs at all (1985:59).

This helps to the distinguish a Primary Relationship from a sexual relationship because for many men (I cannot speak for women) sex appears to be the dominant felt need. Whenever a need has been filled we experience satisfaction. I am saying that our greatest and least recognized need is to connect with other humans on the level I call Communion, Primary Experience, or the Sacrament of Encounter. Fulfilling that greatest need results in our greatest possible satisfaction. Imagine parents whose child is lost. Then imagine their feelings at the moment of recovery. Their joy results from the bond that they had perhaps taken for granted but the importance of which they now recognize. When relationships fail it may be that people understand on some level that this unknown need is not going to be satisfied. To the extent that a relationship is Primary there will be no disappointments proceeding from the relationship because it does not begin with expectations as in ordinary relationships wherein we often meet others in roles. When the two person involved have a certain degree of trust, each can begin to think that what the other does is somehow necessary for the other's growth and development and discover what it means to be perfectly non-judgmental.

In looking at the Decalogue we saw that the commandment that proscribes killing is central because life is central. Nothing is as important as life, followed closely in importance by freedom, the means for surviving and for gaining more life, at least when coupled with reflection. The child in the example above represents an expansion of the parents own life and survival in another dimension, viz., time. Freedom is expressed through choices and our choices result in either a greater or a lesser freedom. Choosing to learn, for example, generally gives us options we would not otherwise have. Learning Greek will give us access to Homer's *Iliad* as he wrote it. What we fail to learn or choose not to learn provides no choices at all. The ultimate limiting choice is suicide.

One of the functions then of a Primary Relationship is to extend or expand through a special kind of learning the possibility of choosing in such a way that life remains open and dynamic through mutual self-discovery, hence the most satisfying freedom possible in the total acceptance of each other. For many of us achieving Communion calls for us to eliminate obstacles to its attainment acquired since childhood. Fortunately, the attempt to engage someone in a Primary Relationship is at the same time a means of healing. All "substantial personal changes are mediated by intimate personal relationships" (Hudson p. 180). The thesis of this essay is that there can be nothing more liberating than allowing others to be free in their interactions with us. We may have learned unselfconsciously from an adult who fostered this liberty. If not we have to consciously learn it. Such knowledge can come in several ways. We may see others acting in certain ways that we identify as telling us something about ourselves. We are constantly being tested by one experience or another that teaches us about our talents and our limits. But nothing provides this self-knowledge to the degree that occurs in attempts to self-disclose who and what we are and what we think and feel to someone who is also committed to making the self explicit. Our self-knowledge is mostly tacit, hidden from ourselves until we engage someone this way. When self-disclosure is mutual both persons experience freedom offered to each other at the same time they acquire more. Two people free enough to be naked in each others presence, and experiencing the same kind of unselfconscious freedom they both have with their own bodies, even though they do not have a sexual relationship, provides a good analogy for the self-disclosures that take place in a Primary Relationship. It should be clear that concentration on what is being said is required of the person listening in much the same way that a person must attend to the words of someone who has written an explanation of Plato's *Republic*. To be listened to in this way will "calls from me resources and responses that I *need* to be human," [emphasis added] (Carse p. 59).

As noted above, whatever either person in a Primary Relationship does or says is viewed by the other as somehow necessary to that person's growth and development and is accepted as such. The ideal is to be totally non-judgmental, to listen in total silence as we learn from Prof. Carse, first with each other then ultimately with everyone else because that is one way Primary Relationships shape the persons within it. We think of friendship as a relationship between equals. This limitation does not apply to Primary Relationships which may exist in any combination of two humans, child-parent, teacher-student, two lovers, two friends, reader and author and so on. Primary Relationships resemble friendships somewhat, but two persons usually can be friends only to the extent that they are equal. We generally cannot be friends with a subordinate or a superior as such. Whereas Primary Relationships are unlimited in this respect. Generally they can exist between all classes, all ages, and all genders. In the Old South some white persons and black persons were able to have a deeply satisfy Primary Relationship while friendship between the two was impossible. They could not attend the same restaurants or play golf together. They could not marry or even sit together in church. Nevertheless their relationship showed that people can transcend class differences forced upon them.

A radical disposition of openness is required to have such relationship, i.e., an invitation to connect through learning about each other. In our competitive, adversarial society of winners and losers people tend to be guarded. An open disposition, like the infant's will remind many person on some level of their hidden need to connect in such a way, thus allowing relationships to blossom if only for a little while. Many of us have had the experience of connecting with someone on a journey. The lack of antecedent connections and the fact that after the journey we may never see our seat mate again allows us to open up in unaccustomed ways and leaves us with the feeling that the trip was all too short. This is a foretaste of what is possible in a long-term relationship when we work at erasing all boundaries in the mind.

The best place to learn what we need to know about relating to others in the way I have described should be among the intimate relationships available to us early in life. If we do not learn it there we may experience great difficulty learning it anywhere else. Parents or other caregivers should teach children how to learn from experience within a relationship as described by Maguire in the quotation opening this chapter. This cannot happen unless parents recognize that in the matter of interpersonal relationships persons are not generic so the rules cannot be generic. If, for example, a parent can admit having made a mistake the lesson does not have to be spelled out. The admission itself says, "I respect you and I have learned something significant from our relationship." The parent has also taught something significant, a multidimensional lesson in how to act toward intimates that might take hours to explain in words and not be nearly as effective. Parents who defend their damaged egos instead of admitting errors also teach effectively without direct statements. The lesson is the importance of *front* in a society of winners and losers.

Primary Relationships should first occur between parents and children. Parent-child relationships are the best place for them to develop because the relationship begins in necessity and lasts for several years. Also, they are a prototype of deeply satisfying non-sexual relationships, which is where all relationships should begin even if they become sexual later. And finally, they have always occurred in families without having been labeled, and by naming the relationship we can consciously use and hone those same skills in all of our relationships. Talking about Primary Relationships is, in addition, not subject to the problems we might encounter in talking about Christian love in a secular world. To simultaneously create an intelligent morality and its offshoot, a global community, everyone should be involved in the conversation.

We lack historical perspective for judging our own time, but except for style we probably act in general the way humans have always acted. We love, we lie, we work and play and generally seek advantages, only now we trade cars instead of horses, but above all we are generally better educated. We all know the importance of becoming a winner in our culture, and we do have to survive, but we are not required to let this aspect of our culture's grand myth dominate our thinking because it makes us adversaries and this adversarial disposition can find its way into interpersonal relationships where we become traders, hoping to get as much or more than we give. The destructive effects of the sociopathology in an adversarial society do not occur immediately. Like the Mississippi, a large, rich society can absorb a great deal of effluent before we notice the pollution. Unfortunately, even when parents are not trading the love and affirmation that children need for acceptable behavior, those parents may have bought into the grand myth of our culture which holds that one is either a winner or a loser and thus prepare their children to be winners, hence adversaries to all, thus creating further obstacles to the possibility of Communion.

If our grand myth prescribes competitiveness and limits cooperation, where do we draw the line, since in a competitive world our gains are necessarily someone else's losses? The question of how we relate to one another is unavoidable. I have frequently described morality as what people do with, for, or to someone else sometimes without distinguishing between good and bad moralities. Obviously there are people with divisive personal codes with whom we must deal. We have to act jointly to solve the problems they pose, but how to act wisely in regard to anti-social behavior is a complex problem that demands more thought than we have so far devoted to the problem, and we will not have begun until we admit that we all share responsibility for such social disorganization as we have (Cahn 1961:45-72). Disorganization implies a failure in communication. When communication breaks down between the DNA and the embryo the result is pathology and usually death. The DNA and the embryo are naturally organized so they can become dis-organized. People must choose to be organized, i.e. have intimate relationships. Infants and the mentally handicapped depend on others to make the connection. On a macro level our current mode of organization is tribal with the various tribes being adversarial to some degree, and to that degree pathological. It all goes back to not knowing what kind of creatures we are and the needs we have.

Every relationship has rules, but we do not ask potential friends or lovers to specify the rules by which we shall relate. Such rules are unselfconsciously developed over a period of time and for a situation not covered we negotiate or end the relationship. For larger social organizations sanctions may be necessary for maintaining the rules, but sanctions in interpersonal relationships signal failure. Sanctions are based on power differences, and power in an interpersonal relationship can only be used to get what we want, not to make or refine a connection. Getting what we want may provide some satisfaction but not nearly on the level of satisfying our most fundamental need. If someone gives under duress or perhaps gives to keep a relationship going and does not give freely and joyfully, further growth and development will probably be blocked. It is a trade that may come back to haunt the persons in the relationship.

In family relationships some rules are deliberately made for the physical safety of children, but many of the rules that concern interpersonal matters are developed over time, rules concerning touching, talking, and the sharing of things and space. Only the most basic rules can be taught in advance because they change as children grow. Rules for relating to others must grow out of the experiences of each person in the context of a relationship. When they are not learned this way, as when relationships are based on role performance or power, the subtle connections that are possible will be missed. Also, the dynamics of interpersonal relationships are limited when they depend on just the broad moral guidelines as, for example, those taught by the churches. Avoiding premarital sex, because it offends God tells us nothing about why it might be wrong. Still less does the rule inform us of the nuances of personal responsibility in our behavior with one another. When the churches talk of reflection they refer to a code which is outside of us, not the needs (what is "fitting") for the person with whom we are dealing. Our abysmal ignorance of what is behind the surface personality of others, the individual strengths and weaknesses of the persons with whom we attempt to relate should give us pause while we consider whether we have defined ourselves according to our grand myth, i.e., as adversaries to everyone, including friend and mates, and so responsible to no one and for no one.

The first rule for learning about persons is that our ignorance is standard, i.e., our normal condition. Beyond that most of us are afflicted with Ignorance II, faulty knowledge as explained earlier, meaning that we not only do not know, we know falsely. In any case such knowledge as we have of persons, whether intimate or not, is more often than not inadequate. Children come naturally equipped with this rule for learning. Whether they maintain it into adulthood depends mostly upon their early socialization. If parents present themselves as having certain knowledge in every respect or cannot admit mistakes, they demonstrate for their children how the children are supposed to act when they become adults. If winning is important a person had better not admit weaknesses or someone will take advantage of it. We are all aware of how children imitate their parents, so unless parents demonstrate an uncertainty and tentativeness about their own moral expertise neither will their children, hence they will not be open to learning, the basic requirement for a Primary Relationship, hence of the greatest source of satisfaction humans can have. We do not want children who will spend time imagining how life would have been better or less problematic if this or that had not happened. "If-only" thinking leads to an uninhabitable fantasy land.

Children who have not been raised with the idea that the responsibility for their behavior and its consequences belong to them may always be looking for some excuse, or for someone to blame when life does not provide the kind of satisfaction that everyone needs even when it is unknown and unexpected. Acts have natural consequences. Lack of food results in hunger; not enough sleep results in tiredness; not doing schoolwork results in failure. Life is full of opportunities for children to discover good and bad outcomes of their behavior. But these opportunities are lost to children who never get to discover natural consequences if their parents prefer to prevent mistakes being made. This teaches children to conceal problems and mistakes through fear of consequences, or to maintain a front. If a child fails a course or a grade in school we should help the child find the lesson in that failure. Such small setbacks are not a major tragedy in a culture where people must be learning all their lives. Parental example has always been important, but never so important as when our efforts fall short and we must cut our losses and go on. We are called upon to be helpful and supportive of children's needs, especially standing by them when they are in trouble.

I am suggesting that children who do not grow up with the experience of being free do not come naturally equipped to engage someone in a Primary Relationship, and may never learn, hence fail to achieve the kind of satisfaction I believe we are all born for. To that end children's behavior should not be controlled to the point of parents assuming full responsibility. Instead of operating decisively through conviction, whether right or wrong, children raised in this way have to defer to a parent's thinking, present or absent, which can never be an adequate resource for moral decisions in every possible circumstance. If parents have set an example of the kind of persons that children should be, and the channels of communication are open, life for the children may still turn out unsatisfactorily at times, but with such a background it is easier to cut losses and move on instead of looking backward and wishing that the past could be changed. Most importantly children will know they are responsible for their own satisfaction or dissatisfaction resulting from their behavior.

There is a widespread misconception about the meaning of discipline in regard to children as in, "I'm sending my kids to Catholic school because they have discipline." Unless discipline becomes self-discipline children will grow up behaving according to a force or lack of it outside of themselves. One of my young students, when asked why he did not do what he was told, said, "You didn't hit me." We have to walk a fine line, controlling where necessary and allowing children responsibility for their own behavior wherever possible, all the while explaining why it is that we do what we do . It is better to err on the side of less control despite the risks. If freedom is next to life in importance children must learn about freedom by exercising it in the context of the family where risks can be taken with parental support, as for example in reading books meant for adults. When parents are open to discussing the contents of those books not much harm will come to their children from such reading.

The major criterion of intelligent behavior for anyone requires that moral decisions be based on what is best in the long run. When we have been taught that our best interest is saving our "immortal souls" such a belief neatly complements the idolatrous belief that prosperity is God's or the gods' way of showing approval for our behavior, and so getting an education becomes primarily important for getting a good job and making money. This is a closed-end choice and one that ultimately diminishes our opportunities to choose instead of broadening them. Saving our souls is an abstract enterprise, and accumulating wealth to show that we are on track is a very concrete form of idolatry. Because much of what Jesus taught is paradoxical, such flat contradictions of the gospel as this attitude toward wealth have been able to survive in our myths. In the chapter on Genesis we saw that pleasing or appeasing the gods to get or retain favors may have been one of the earliest human responses to the idea of gods. Such thinking almost seems to be part of human nature because of its prevalence, but of course it is not. What is part of human nature is the need for knowledge to attain closure when confronted by the ignorance that generates anxiety. When we do not have answers we create them, and when we create them they may be empirical in the grossest sense. This accounts in part for prosperity being an acceptable marker for God's favor.

Martin Marty compared two preachers, father and son, Lyman Beecher and Henry Ward Beecher. The elder Beecher preached that, "The poor should be content with their assigned status [and not] attempt to transcend their class or fate. To the son's generation, poverty was always a vice. . . One must aspire, not to prove one's salvation but to become rich" (1969:105). There is the added advantage that wealth rewards those a who have it with the freedom of more choices, (including sometimes the choice of mates) and our intuition tells us that freedom is a superior kind of good. But choosing to accumulate wealth tends to be divisive because winning frequently results from someone's losing. Besides, the choices we make with money are not inherently liberating; we can think, for example, of someone being able to afford an expensive drug habit, and people with lots of money sometimes commit suicide.

In addition to furnishing examples of how to act, and being encouraging and supportive, parents can demonstrate an awareness of everyone's uniqueness by showing respect for their children's own perspective of the world. If we were capable of perceiving the world as it really is we would all perceive it in the same way. The fact that we do not is strong evidence that our perceptions are somehow created out of our individual experiences (Bateson 1980:38-40). Thus instead of trying to impose our world view on children (this never works anyway in a world of mass media) we should use a dialectical approach, expanding our own world view by examining theirs while sharing ours with them, thus generating a larger world view that comprises both. In order to do this children must be regarded with respect and honesty, and with the expectation that we will learn from them as we hope that they will learn from us. Applied to adults as well this is what Maguire, in the opening quotation, means by "fitting." This is the ultimate in moral behavior, and the prototype of what I call the search for moral refinement. One of the ways that parents can learn is by making explicit for themselves as well as their children the principles by which they relate to other humans, that is, to turn myth into philosophy so that they can discern the real basis for determining their choices, i.e., by reflecting on the consequences of their choices.

All our values have to do with relationships, directly or indirectly and some values blatantly contradict those of persons engaged in a Primary Relationship. With the possible exception of hermits, we are all engaged in supplying each other's needs and wants. How we manage this, i.e., the rules we follow in this enterprise is most of, if not all of our morality. Some social scientists (chiefly Homans 1964) see in this activity only one pattern, that of commerce. He calls it "exchange theory" (Gouldner 1970:395-396). According to this theory, we give only to receive. Like Lorenz's aggression and Ardrey's territoriality, when extrapolated to humans, this one is questionable because it does not fit everyone. A volunteer working among AIDS patients derives satisfaction from that activity, but it does not fit into the trading model as in giving a prostitute money for sex. The AIDS worker can derive satisfaction independently of whether the recipients are grateful or even know what the AIDS worker has done. Another closely related theory is "game theory," and a subset of game theory, related to the formation of coalitions (Lawler 1975). These sociological theories do not explain human behavior. They just describe the way humans act under the conditions of the experiment, or perhaps the subjects act as they do because most of them subscribe to the dominant myth of the United States in which the point is to become a winner instead of a loser, or at least to break even in order to deal another day. I have little doubt that marriages would fare much better if couples understood the concept of Primary Relationship and tried to create one before committing to a long-term sexual relationship.

Communication among other creatures seems less subject to misinterpretation than human communication. The sounds and signals other animals use to communicate have a very limited range of possible meanings. Those that live in groups tend to act as though the group were a single organism, existing by virtue of all of its parts consistently communicating with one another in what amounts to the one message: keep the entity alive. A troop of baboons resembles such an entity by mimicking this survival technique of all the parts working to maintain the whole, the way that the DNA and the developing embryo communicate. Their organization is analogous to the way healthy bodies are organized with all the parts working together. For contemporary humans, however, this is not possible. Perhaps people acted that way when they lived in relatively isolated tribes where each day they were faced with the problem of just staying alive but not in our culture. In large, complex societies communication does not occur naturally among the various parts; it is what humans achieve through effort. We still depend on others for survival, but this dependence is mostly anonymous once we have outgrown our dependence upon family. Anonymous suppliers of our needs, e.g., supermarket managers, do not have a stake in applying sanctions to force our conformity. Also the dependence is not absolute. Most of us can find another supermarket. And because contemporary life offers so much diversity in our culture we have to form voluntary communities for there to be any (Cox 1965:40-48).

In addition to promoting a global community, healthy interpersonal relationships are still worth pursuing for the high degree of satisfaction they produce and none is more satisfying than one that results in Communion. A person's past weighs heavily upon the dynamics of interpersonal relationships. So much has been and still is taken for granted in the way that people relate to one another. The need to connect is natural. The skill required must learned, or for those with talent, developed, so that we can satisfy the need we have to be social, without the fear, anxiety, and frequent disappointment of our

current system. This new system should work for all people in or out
of religion, whether they are mates, friends, family, or whatever, and
it should work across the boundaries of religious denominations.

Successful communication starts with the recognition that communication becomes increasingly problematic as it grows increasingly
significant. Language with value associations exhibits wide variations
in meanings, as was shown in chapter five. What we must do when
we wish to communicate ideas with strong value associations is be
open to what others are saying and doing in the way that our senses
become sharpened when we find ourselves in a hostile physical environment where the information gathering mode is only the first stage.
We must then process the information so that we know how to act or
how to find some meaning in it. This stage is the most difficult. If
we are not children, we already have in place a meaning system (our
personal grand myth) to which we refer all incoming data. Unless we
assume that the results of the information-processing stage is tentative
while we try to put it in the context of the other person's meaning
system we may simply disagree and regard the other person's thinking
or communication skills faulty or that they are just wrong. If we tend
to be judgmental, it may be in part because of the great variety of
cultural backgrounds from which our thinking arises while believing
that we speak the same language. The situation calls for patience and
a creative effort on our part for which most of us are not prepared,
precisely as in the case of the moral education of children. Heidegger
wrote that "creation is necessarily violent, and unless we understand
this violence we will not be able to understand any other." In the
language of psychobiology, such a person has established neuro-
chemical pathways that make behavior and thinking less flexible (Rose
1976 271-72).

Judging from the kinds of problems we have and the need we have
to solve them, we can legitimately extend Dr. Beck's thesis beyond
couples to the whole world. Love, especially the way it is currently
thought of, is definitely not enough. We can accomplish wonders
when we find love. On that rising tide of emotion there may be a
sudden release of thinking and activity that is nothing short of inspira-
tional. In this state people write poems, paint pictures, build houses,
go long hours without sleep. Love prompts us to demonstrate the
depth and degree of our sensibilities and our awareness of another.
We want to say and show how much we are committed to the person
we love. None of this comes about through habit. It is all the result
of conscious choices among a set of possibilities, greatly expanded
under the stimulus of love. Anything which arouses us to conscious
activity is good, even a reversal of fortune, or some great adversity,

but nothing does it so pleasantly as love. Love enables us to put aside fear, increases our tolerance for pain. It keeps us going when we would otherwise quit. It makes us feel great, and makes us more productive, because it quickens our imagination. We begin to see what we would not otherwise have attended to, and we are full of confidence that we can overcome all obstacles. Unfortunately, based as it is on the rising tide of emotion, we may be in store for a lot of pain when the initial tide goes out. Therefore, love as ordinarily thought of is not in itself a suitable basis for doing the hard work of building a community, whether of two or more. A lasting intimacy requires communication skills not generally taught, very likely because the teachers do not possess those skills.

We can have negative feelings about a person, and still learn from that person. The dissonance is telling us something about ourselves. Such learning may not be easy or pleasant, but it is still learning, hence still intelligent behavior. Also, the negativity that puts us off may simultaneously give a greater edge to our consciousness, and whatever does that is a plus. Thus the disposition we should always have toward every person is a disposition to learn that is independent of our feelings toward that person. With such a disposition we are more likely to be aware that understanding is an active process, a kind of reaching out for meaning from what we should perhaps think of as the mysterious, locked-in world of other persons. When I encounter a person with a problem who seems bent on inflicting the problem on me (someone acts nasty toward me) it is that person's problem; the idea is to not make it mine which is best achieved by responding compassionately by not taking the other persons's expressions personally. Compassion is a skill best honed in Primary Relationships.

When we have a disposition of radical openness toward the possibility of learning from others regardless of our feelings, we have what I call a Primary Disposition. A Primary Disposition is an openness or receptiveness toward others that is the basis for the Sacrament of Encounter. It starts with acceptance of the idea that we can learn from anyone, anywhere, anytime. This is also the disposition that is required if we wish to achieve the most satisfying kind of interpersonal relationships, relationships that are not based on fragile emotions nor standard cultural expectations of what another person will do for us or give to us. The commitment we enter into under these circumstances is not just to a person, but also to a relationship, and our satisfaction and growth as persons will depend on the creative effort that we put into the process, not on what others are willing to give. As with all creative efforts a high degree of self-discipline is required. Painters, musicians and dancers practice long and hard to master their craft, even when gifted with a great talent. Creating Primary Relationships similarly requires learning a skill or developing such talent as we have, and as with painting, music and dance part of the satisfaction in Primary Relationship comes from a task well done. The enjoyment is internal and satisfies a need, as noted, we may not know we have.

One of the more important lessons in my life occurred incidentally through an interaction with one of my sons. In the midst of a four-year-old temper tantrum he beat on my legs with both fists while crying. I thought of my father who would have spanked the child for such behavior. This did not strike me as an appropriate response. Instead I picked up my son and stroked his back as he continued to pound on me with his fists. Eventually he put his head on my shoulder and began sucking his thumb. I realized then that he had been demonstrating that he felt bad about something but lacked the communication skills for saying it. He had been using his fists to say that he felt bad and his actions were not a personal attack on me. Then it occurred to me that even adults do what my son did. Because anyone, child or adult may lack the skill to communicate bad feelings with words, or because the adult grew up in a culture that where such behavior was demonstrated rather than verbalized. Whatever the reason, the adult may communicate bad feelings by apparently trying to hurt me. The appropriate response is compassion not retaliation. By absorbing the hurt I create a moment in which the Sacrament of Encounter can take place. By acting this way the effect may not be immediately noticeable but by not returning hurt for hurt I will have correctly understood the message sent, and the other person will on some level know that. At the very least I will not have made another person's problem my own.

This kind of response to another person may be made easier for Christians by the thought that God is immanent in everyone, including those that seem to be trying to hurt us. Human hurts occur on many levels for reasons that most people are unable to make explicit. The hurt directed at us is more than likely a cry for compassion. Children find it easier than adults to understand that they are acting out bad feelings when the response to their acting out is compassionate. While adults may simply rationalize their acting out as an expression of justice in an abusive world. Thus, teaching children to verbalize their feelings may be one of the better ways of directing them toward an adulthood in which they will know the freedom that comes from peace within and without because they do not have to act out those feelings. Children cannot give much, but if parents have a Primary Disposition, i.e, have a radical openness to learning, they will recognize the radical openness of their children. Small children lack the obstacles to bonding that adults may have learned. They naturally begin with a Primary Disposition. Thus by responding creatively to their children's needs parents can learn to make concrete and explicit many vaguely understood determinants of their own behaviors. Consciousness of what we do positions us to make better use of our own skills and talents as every teacher knows.

Some animals, perhaps most, are born with some precoded knowledge of how to relate to others of their species. Scientists refer to this as species-specific behavior. Human babies become bonded to the persons who first provide their needs--food, touching, comfort and so on. The chief responsibility of parents, or primary caregivers is to provide models for children to learn how to act in their own best interest, mainly how to relate to other humans as a matter of survival. We need not create arbitrary frustrations. Enough real ones will occur naturally. As children grow and learn which things are dangerous they will also learn when they are treated arbitrarily, consequently that power may be used capriciously in relationships. We all act on feelings. Children usually have no other basis for acting. A team of psychotherapists (Efran et al 1990:157) describe emotions as bodily predispositions "that underlie, support, and create readiness for actions." Frustration breeds insecurity in children and early on they generally have only one predisposition--to connect with someone. Their most urgent need is to bond. Its absence causes them to focus on this need and diminishes their capacity to learn anything else, making them unable to transcend destructive feelings and act intelligently. In the meantime their models may be teaching them that manipulation is appropriate for getting what those with power want, generally conformity. If the adults of the world accept cultural values uncritically they will continue to present models of unintelligent behavior that children will imitate and pass on to their children. Instead of making truly intelligent decisions, children will, like their parents, simply rationalize what they want, and be unable to distinguish wants from needs.

The perceptions of each person are different. A Primary Relationship helps us to understand these differences by allowing us to see the world in unaccustomed ways. Something similar happens in foreign travel where the contrast is sharper due to the larger number of people who are obviously different. In our culture we are more likely to appreciate another person's perspectives if we value that person. This has a bearing on the growth and development of intelligence. Everyone presents us with possibilities for learning, which for Christians should be seen as revelation, i.e., contact with the God immanent in others, but we are most likely to discover this through repeated experiences within the context of positive relationships, particularly Primary Relationships. Thus the importance of always maintaining a Primary Disposition. Bateson uses the analogy of binocular vision to explain how we learn from those who think differently. It "gives the possibility of a new order of information (about depth) so the understanding (conscious and unconscious) of behavior through relationship gives a new *logical type* of learning (1980:148). This is Bateson's Learning II, described earlier, by which we are able to transcend our current state of knowing and become freer.

From a positive relationship we may extrapolate to the possibility of learning from other relationships, but the process must be consciously developed which is precisely the advantage we acquire in attempting to form Primary Relationships. However, when parents or other caregivers do not present children with models of learning persons they will have to find those models in others such as peers or teachers. Unfortunately the experience of peers may be no better than theirs, and they may not find teachers for whom they have positive feelings, or because they are confused they may simply be no longer open to that possibility. When parents do not present models of openness for children to imitate, they may experience great difficulty in achieving such openness. Their next best chance occurs with children of their own which is why it is important to explicate in detail Primary Relationships between parents and children.

Within the context of a positive relationship we may think: *If this person whom I value highly perceives some aspect of life this way, then that perspective must in some way be valid. This may mean that my perspective is in error, or that it is valid but in some different context.* I do not necessarily give up my own perceptions under these circumstances. It is within the realm of possibility that we may discover a perspective that comprises both, analogous to the way that Ptolemaic and Newtonian cosmologies may be viewed as special cases within Einsteinian cosmology for practical uses such as navigation and engineering. Once we have developed this pattern of learning from the way others view the world, we can apply it intellectually to relationships that are not Primary, or do not have the advantage of a prior emotional commitment. Thinking and learning in this way is not automatic, however. If we have been raised in a social environment where openness to learning was not practiced, we may be inclined toward zero-sum thinking, i.e., if my idea is different from another person's, one of us is wrong. We will not think that we can both be right within the context of our own thoughts but some larger context may comprise both. We assume the validity of our own view because of its relatedness to the rest of what we know, our personal myth, and relating to what others know takes time and effort and can only occur if we are aware that it is necessary and that it is possible.

In most of the literature of sociology, social psychology and anthropology we will not often find the expression *Primary Relationship*. When it is found it generally implies that such relationships occur naturally within "primary groups" (Vander Zander 1984:245, 551) George Horton Cooley developed the primary group concept (Coser 1971:307). Primary groups are understood to be those that have intimate face to face relationships--friends, family, kinship groups, and other relationships within communal living (Brinkerhoff & White 1989:70-72). This use is legitimate if it represents the social scientist's ideal type rather than reality. (See also Tonnies' Gemeinshaft and Gesellshaft in Heberle 1968:100, and Cox 1965:46-49, on personal and anonymous relationships). Primary groups contrast with secondary type associations that we form in the workplace, in clubs, and in general, everywhere outside of kinship and other such groups. Unfortunately the concept "primary group" does not permit us to distinguish among its members, those with positive relationships and those without. Nor are we able to distinguish various kinds and various degrees of either negative or positive relationships, e.g., parents and children who are hostile to each other.

Primary Relationships do not occur automatically when falling in love, getting married, being born, or having a child. In these instances the relationships are potentially Primary as described in this study. To make them actually Primary requires that we either have an talent for such relationships or deliberately choose to develop the skills required to create them. There has to be a more complete openness and sensitivity than is ordinarily found in families which too often are thought of as the place to prepare for adversarial relationships. In Primary Relationships we try to communicate at face value, without roles or masks. This is not easy, but it might be helpful to realize that roles and masks are probably perceived as necessary within the larger society where social reality requires us to be on guard, an attitude neither necessary nor appropriate within a family or other intimate relationships. If parents relate to each other through roles, father/husband to mother/wife, or parent to child, there is little chance of modeling behavior to aid our children in retaining the openness to learning, that is, the Primary Disposition with which they are born. But if social reality is constructed it is subject to revision and re-creation. Unlike the tablets of Moses, conventional social reality is not written on stone.

Except for our children we can never know in advance whether a

Primary Relationship is possible with any particular person, and so if Primary Relationships have a positive value for us we must be prepared when the opportunity arises. Thus we should maintain a constant Primary Disposition, another way of saying that we "must become as little children" (Mat. 18:3). A Primary Disposition presents the most complete kind of openness to the possibility of communicating with another person, but with the understanding that for adults, in a matter of such importance this may be a long and difficult process, partly because, as noted in chapter five, words may look and sound the same yet mean differently, also because growing up without some mental barriers in our adversarial society is difficult.

There can be no formula for establishing Primary Relationships. Each one is a unique event, the result of experimentation. Before we can even begin the process we must recognize that even maintaining a Primary Disposition is generally fraught with difficulty. The grand myth of our culture is built upon a competitive economic model, geared to creating winners and losers. Hence, we must either qualify the person with whom we anticipate having a relationship, to determine if he or she subscribes to the trading model before revealing our openness, or else be free enough and secure enough in our sense of self-worth to survive frequent failure, because an encounter between someone in the trading mode with someone in an open mode will lead inevitably to a failure in communication. If a person with a Primary Disposition self-discloses, the person with a trading disposition may simply be embarrassed or will wonder what that person wants in return. The person with the Primary Disposition may say or suggest that nothing is expected. This can only lead to conclusion by the other party that this is an attempt to confuse or deceive. Such behavior simply does not exist for those who live by a trading model.

Indoctrinating children in the idea of trading for emotional fulfillment is not the only obstacle that parents can place in the way of having Primary Relationships with their children, and of ultimately preventing them from having Primary Relationships with others. In fact if we examine most of the ways children can acquire obstacles to developing a Primary Relationship from parents, teachers, and other adults, we should be able to infer an initial set of rules for establishing and maintaining Primary Relationships by simply avoiding those obstacles. Afterwards, we may still need to remind ourselves that social reality is a created product, and that we will not plunge our world into chaos, nor be acting self-destructively if we recreate it. It is more likely that if we do not attempt to recreate social reality, we will not be acting in our own best, long-term interest.

All values are in some way related to survival. For most of the time that humans have been on earth surviving physically has been the chief concern. For such survival people have to be alert to what is going on around them. Experience and the information provided by our senses is the best way to survive in a hostile environment. One of the first rules we learn upon escaping the confines of our homes as children is--"Look both ways when crossing the street." And although certain urban areas have become extremely hostile environments, for most of us the kind of awareness those places require is not necessary. Having solved to a great degree the problems of physical survival, we are now confronted with a new set of problems for which we are not naturally equipped--psychological survival. When people struggled to survive physically, their psychic survival occurred naturally from the bonds formed and maintained by the communal struggle. In other words psychic survival came about unselfconsciously. In the absence of a lifelong common struggle, the situation for most of our contemporaries in developed nations, bonding must be done consciously and continuously, a fact that has not yet become part of our collective wisdom.

Most of us can distinguish between hallucination and the information we receive from the empirical world, and while the empirical world is itself always in the process of changing, it is constant enough on the level at which humans experience it so that it is not generally a concern. But in the psychological world there are no constants from one individual to the next, each mind is a unique creation, and each mind has its own constants. That is why we can trace one of the fundamental problems of humanity to the tendency we have to equate social and psychological reality with empirical reality and to believe that psychological reality is the same for everyone, thus fostering the illusion that we can have certain knowledge concerning the causes of someone's behavior and that we can make true judgments about another person. This is the position of Catholic theologian William E. May who claims that moral revisionists "fail to show how [their] basic claims] can be harmonized with such basic truths of Catholic faith as, for instance, that `all human beings. . .have the same nature and the same origin, a 'common nature,'and the same calling and destiny" (1991:117). Alasdair McIntyre seems to define human nature similarly. He writes, "Human beings, like the members of all other species, have a specific nature; and that nature is such that they have certain aims and goals, such that they move by nature towards a specific telos" (1984:148). The telos of other species is to survive as a species. Humans do not just survive; they become. The only common nature we have is biological and even that requires some qualification. Beyond that everything is unique, or as Prof. Max Otto taught, human nature must include what it can become. The belief that we can make true judgments about other humans maintains human stupidities such as the tradition of trying to solve interpersonal, intertribal and international problems by killing people.

If priests, ministers, therapists, and others committed to the solving of human problems had the answers, the problems listed above would be diminishing instead of growing, as they seem to be. The same may be said of astrologists, Tarot cards readers, teachers of transcendental meditation, and all the other means by which people search for answers or try to find a solution to the constant dissatisfaction they experience. Being necessarily social, yet finding ourselves necessarily disconnected we have to search for answers, because the current mess will not resolve itself. Even when parents produce children who are secure within themselves the children sometimes cannot tell why because they act intuitively and the knowledge upon which their security rests has not been made explicit as is frequently the case with adults. Still our best hope for change at this time is in the creative possibilities that such children bring with them into adulthood to pass on to their children, until such time as the principles for raising secure persons can be made explicit.

Some persons have difficulty trusting children, and although the feeling has become largely secularized, and traditional in many families, it has its roots in an overly literal interpretation of the doctrine of Original Sin, whereby children are thought to be born morally defective or even corrupt. However, the obvious weakness, neediness, and ignorance of children should be enough to convince any intelligent adult that children can be controlled and manipulated as much as anyone desires. The question we must reflect upon is: What kind of relationship should we have with children so that they will grow up emotionally and intellectually secure adults, accepting responsibility for their own behavior? The answer seems obvious. We have to present children with models of intellectually and emotionally secure adults who accept responsibility for our own behavior, and since our behavior is modeled on parents and other adults of our own childhood experiences, we need to be skeptical of our ability as models.

I agree with Gloria Steinem that the most secure children seem to come from "child-loving cultures, and those childrearing practices that . . . share a belief: that it is not possible to 'spoil' a child before the age of two or three" (1992:66). Adults who deliberately frustrate children in the belief that the children must learn that they cannot have everything they want are attributing to children the skill of making logical inferences from the way they are treated to the lesson, "I can't have everything I want." This logic is not possible, not even for older children. All they know is that they have felt needs that are not being met. Assuming the opposite would in fact be more appropriate. The search for an intelligent morality begins and ends with a high degree of skepticism regarding the value of our own training and education. Thus, a relationship with a child in our care requires a correspondingly high degree of uncertainty and tentativeness, behavior that manifests the wisdom we all need. This mode of acting with children is intelligent, because it will be in our long-term interest as well as theirs. There is no satisfaction in seeing our children come to grief. This may happen despite our best efforts, but we certainly increase the chances of it happening if we do not give our best effort. When we engage children in a grand experiment, actively involving them, and attending carefully to their attempts at communicating, instead of just telling them the way things are and the way they should be, we have engaged them in the dialectics of a Primary Relationship, the ultimate in interpersonal morality. Because it is intimacy without sex, such parent-child relationships can provide the best model for all Primary Relationships.

What holds for a parent-child relationship is also the case for adult-adult relationships, with the added advantage that with both adults consciously engaged in the mutual, intellectual adventure of a Primary Relationship it may be more intense and more fruitful. There are currently adult-adult relationships like this. However, they are fewer than they should be, because until a kind of relationship is named and described it may be difficult to deliberately choose to enter into one, especially in cases where so many of the obstacles cited exist. Everyone has some idea of what kind of relationship is meant by being friends or lovers, and even what it means to be friends and lovers simultaneously, and the possibilities thus engendered, but few are aware of the benefits flowing from Primary Relationships. While these relationships already exist and probably have always existed, making them explicit produces a genuine conceptual innovation that can enter the domain of conscious choices (Polanyi 1962:186).

The failure of the social sciences to recognize and deal with Primary Relationships is understandable. The canon of social science requires that social scientists view human behavior as fully determined by social forces (Durkheim 1973; Friedrichs 1972) or according to Homans by human nature (1967:15, 36). And Primary Relationships are of necessity freely created. Many social scientists seek uniformities in human behavior, and treat irregularities as elements of a complex order not yet comprehended, or as idiosyncrasies to be dismissed altogether. And while in primary groups, which scientists do study, Primary Relationships may occur, and even have a higher probability of occurring, they do not happen necessarily. In fact if we accept the assumptions of traditional sociology out of Durkheim, or Homans' behaviorist explanation, a Primary Relationship could not come into existence at all. To create a Primary Relationship we must be conscious of the tentativeness of all knowledge, particularly knowledge of persons, and have a sense of the constraints upon thinking and acting that any knowledge places upon its possessors on account of our tendency toward closure. With such a disposition we will be free enough to share our unique perspectives of the world, and resolve such differences as any two of us may have in order to achieve a more subtle sense of the way the world should be, particularly our own world, in short, a super-refined morality.

A Primary Relationship in its ideal form is an open intimacy between two persons, one in which intellectual vulnerability is total, so that neither is afraid of hurting or being hurt by the other. In an ideal Primary Relationship we will have found someone who not only understands what we say but also gives evidence of being able to understand beyond our present ability to express ourselves. *We might then find that our ability to self-disclose would expand for as long as the capacity to understand and accept in this other person challenged our ability to express ourselves.* The ideal further implies a commitment to the growth and development of the relationship, as well as each person in the relationship as a free and responsible individual. Fortunately, even a less than ideal relationship can be extremely rewarding, and just attempting to create Primary Relationships can play an important role in the development of an intelligent morality and can provide the best foundation for the development of an intelligent society, and may conceivably be the only way such a society can begin. If we can develop a Primary Relationship with one other person, we are more likely to contribute to the development of a larger, intelligent society, especially through our modeling of restraint and reflection. What enhances the possibility of becoming more intelligent in a Primary Relationship is the fact that because it is personal, we generally begin it with a positive intellectual commitment without the roller-coaster effect found in love relationships based primarily on feelings.

Ordinarily our feelings will be a more important spur to behavior than our thinking. A commitment to maintain good health, for example, must have feel-good connections otherwise we will not persevere. These connections might be the self-esteem we derive from achieving a goal, from the knowledge that we feel good after exercising, from the belief that someone whose opinion is important to us appreciates our efforts to stay healthy, and so on. The more of these kinds of connections we have the easier it is to decide to exercise, or stay away from fatty foods, or whatever, when we feel bad or feel the need to comfort ourselves. Anyone who has ever tried controlling an impulse to eat or smoke knows that the inevitable question arises--Why bother? Smoking, drinking, eating, dope, and sex provide comfort when we are feeling disconnected. If someone does not stroke us we will stroke ourselves or feel that life has no point.

Our emotional commitment to organizing a society of two in a Primary way can stretch our thinking by introducing us to a different view of reality, thus leading us to find broader contexts within which important differences among humans can make sense. Even when differences cannot be resolved in this way, we can respect the differences because we understand because of the advantages to ourselves and the global community of a pluralistic attitude, one of the basic characteristics of an intelligent morality, hence of a potentially intelligent society. The use of power by one person is destructive to the possibility of creating any interpersonal relationship, especially a Primary Relationship. Using power means domination by one person's ideas. It establishes a context in which the person using the power does not learn, while the one toward whom the power is directed may learn but the learning is likely to be unrelated to the intended lesson.

From the description of an ideal Primary Relationship we can see that only a limited number of relationships even approaching the ideal are possible for any individual due to the amount of time and effort required, and also because of the difficulty of finding those who are willing to make an equally serious commitment. Writing a book to share what one believes, because it involves a great deal of time and effort is the prototypical attitude of a person wishing to establish a Primary Relationship. A writer's chief reward may come from learning what she or he already knows by attempting to make it explicit for the readers. There is no way of knowing in advance how readers will respond, but by focussing on the possibilities of learning from the experience the writer will find satisfaction regardless of the outcome.

More than any other relationship, Primary Relationships are models of intelligent morality. They exemplify the pursuit of moral refinement in an ultimate sense. For this reason there is a value in understanding the dynamics of Primary Relationships--what they are, how to develop them, what the pitfalls are, why they are rare, why they fail to develop, and so on. Even when someone's belief is so contradictory to our own that no hope seems to exist for having a relationship, a Primary Disposition (such as a writer's) will lead us to sharpen our own world view through a critical assessment and a better articulation of our position.

Sex and other forms of biological bonding are possibilities in Primary Relationships not requirements, otherwise Primary Relationship between adults and children, or between friends of whatever sex would be problematic. In our culture, mates or marriage partners are frequently chosen under the influence of intense positive feelings, but they cannot for that reason be thought of as intending to create a Primary Relationship. There are two main reasons for this: 1) the concept of "Primary Relationship" is apt to be undefined for the participants; 2) the commitment is generally made to a person rather than to the relationship, so that if feelings turn negative, as they frequently do, the relationship falters or fails, a fact that apparently supports the idea that what we feel is, in our society, probably more important determinant of behavior than what we know. The distinction of commitment to the relationship in contrast with commitment to a person is not trivial. If after having attained a level of competence as adults we plan to live alone and not engage other humans, except on a most superficial level, such as talk about the weather, or whether the Phillies will make the playoffs, we can then say, "I know enough." But the requirements of close, interpersonal relationships, at least initially, will make demands upon us that will require us to extend our knowledge of self and others if we wish the relationships to satisfy and endure. We can only acquire this through open discussions where meanings are negotiated, i.e, through mutual self-disclosure. Since much of our behavior is a consequence of feeling rather than intelligent decision making, what drives us tends to be opaque, even to ourselves. If we try to make someone else understand, the probable result is often some plausible rationalization rather than what really drives us. A person may, for example, behave in a certain way on account of having been sexually molested as a child without even remembering having been molested. We must, as a consequence, be skeptical of the reasons we give ourselves and others for what we do. This is also an excellent reason for maintaining an openness to the Sacrament of Encounter by listening compassionately to others whether they are trying to make their bad feelings explicit with words or simply acting out.

If we assume our own knowledge to be certain and correct rather than tentative as has been proposed here as necessary for a Primary Disposition, then the other person's knowledge is in error when it differs from ours in matters affecting a relationship, actual or potential, and we must somehow get them to accept what we know in order for the relationship to work. One of three outcomes is possible under such circumstances: 1) One of the parties will submit; 2) the relationship will become an open conflict; 3) the relationship will terminate.

None of these possibilities can be called satisfying if what we want and need are close, personal relations with others. Submission on the part of one party to a relationship, so that there is no apparent conflict can only satisfy those who see their relationships as fulfilling the requirements of some preconceived structure, as exemplified by rules such as, "A woman's place is in the home," or "spare the rod and spoil the child," and a host of similar maxims. Every relationship between two people contains the possibility of a power differential, but use of such power to affect the outcome of the relationship is counterproductive with respect to learning what we need to know, and it makes trying to establish or maintain Primary Relationships virtually impossible. Another person's vulnerability is a grant of power to us that should arouse respect and humility. It is a power which must not be used. We should note at this point that parents rightly use power to prevent children from acting self-destructively in physical matters, crossing the street, playing with dangerous objects, and so on. The use of power is only likely to be destructive to a parent-child relationship when parents use the various needs of the child as a means of controlling what parent considers the moral behavior of their children when such behavior endangers no one or nothing. By withholding affection to obtain conforming behavior, for example, a parent is demonstrating to the child that it is all right to use the power that a personal relationship gives us in order to get what we want. Children will copy our behavior without force (Craig 1973). If we want honest and polite children the best way of achieving that goal is to act consistently, honestly and with respect. They will eventually get the message, just as they do in learning language without being penalized for mispronunciations.

The possibility of Primary Relationships between adults is subject to all kinds of difficulties, either because of prior learning or other contingencies. There is no way to create an exhaustive list of these kinds of difficulties. Fortunately for us, while knowing in advance the kinds of difficulties we might encounter would be helpful, it is not necessary. The rule to remember first, last, and always is that, despite appearances, we do not speak the same language in matters of importance, even if we have learned from the very best of parents, meaning ones who created no obstacles in us to the development of interpersonal relationships.

Each Primary Relationship is the result of a dialectic between two unique beings under a unique set of circumstances. Children are good imitators, but they must first witness what they will imitate or themselves be the subject of such a dialectic. Much of what makes for a good Primary Relationship exists in the heads of those who have one and may not be manifested in a way that can be understood, like a pitcher's ability to throw a slider. Creating a Primary Relationship is an aesthetic enterprise. The result is Communion, or in Bateson words, "ultimate unity is aesthetic" (1980:19), like painting a picture, or writing a poem. We can see the result of the artistic process in a painting by Rembrandt, or a poem by Keats, but we cannot simply imitate them. If we wish to be artists or poets in the field of relationships, we must develop our own unique style. Skills and strategies must be mastered to make our way in that world, but ultimately each relationship must be its own masterpiece.

We must expect to live the orderly life we have invented continuously conscious of the imminence of change....Brewster Ghiselin

EPILOGUE....Responding to student challenges has been one of the great delights of classroom teaching. In those exchanges the delight was nearly always immediate because I felt I was learning, i.e., overcoming my personal daemons whose names are ignorance, the one I arrived with and the false knowledge I latterly acquired. However, trying to teach by writing a book forces me to painfully await a response, if there be any. Some readers, perhaps many, will agree with me but I can't expect to learn much from them. I do anticipate help in my battle from those who challenge what I have to say, particularly those compassionate readers who can perceive my sincere stumbling about in strange fields of knowledge as I attempt to start a conversation on some very important, neglected topics. The worst fate of all would be to receive no challenges, for then I would remain locked in lone combat with my double ignorance. Certainly the ground for challenges, hence enlightenment, are many because I have done so much groping for ways to express what I think, and not always successfully if as T.S. Eliot reminds us, "Between the idea/ And the reality. . .Falls the Shadow.

Central to everything written here is the idea of making functional interpersonal relationships the foundation of the kind of world we want. Functional is hardly the ideal word to describe what I am hoping to achieve. Recall the claim of Charles Davis that truth is found in community; the community of two I have labored long and hard to describe is the place to begin the search. An ideal interpersonal relationship is the basic school for such truth wherein each person grants the other the freedom to be so that there can be no obstacle to learning between them.

Starting with Heidegger's premise that being is becoming I have difficulty imagining worse a condition for becoming than a relationship in which one or both persons meet with expectations (a script, as Prof. James P. Carse calls it) of what the other must be to sustain the relationship. I feel certain that my own freedom depends to a very

268

high degree on my simultaneously wanting the other person to be free in any encounter with me.

This grant of freedom to others requires a sense of security that not everyone has because it generally comes from a secure parent who fostered it by granting the same kind of freedom. For the rest it may be acquired in a loving relationship, especially in marriage where the fires of passion can remove the dross of ignorance from the gold of knowing if the couple persists and they have at least a tentative idea of what the outcome should be.

Unfortunately that is not how it usually works. If a couple in a passionate relationship does not know, or does not learn, what the goal should be, their chances of reaching it are poor. We do not have a teaching tradition that spells out that people should be aiming for, viz. Communion. So much has been taken for granted in interpersonal morality. Not being taught the need for Communion men and women come into a world of choice without the wisdom to make the choices that optimizes their becoming and they are not acquiring that wisdom. It has not become common sense, as in looking both ways before crossing the street. I have attributed this failure primarily to the church but that's an obvious exaggeration since there are so many other factors affecting modern couples. However, if there are other sources to the problem, the hierarchy bears the main responsibility for making it right on account of their claim to teach in the name of God. I am merely calling them to task.

APPENDIX A....LOVING AND BEING FREE

When other speaks the disclosing word, he draws the first person into a new relationship, out of the role of dispassionate spectator and into that of personal Communion....Reinhold Niebuhr

Being with you is simultaneously an opportunity to exercise my freedom and to learn ways in which I am not free. If the cues and signals I get from you are like the ones I get from others, then I am not in tune to your unique self. I am, rather, tuned into some typification, reflecting a flaw that obscures how different you are from everyone else.

While failure to perceive your uniqueness is not always an obvious event on account of my blindness, the discovery of who you are is clearly distinct, being unlike any experience I have ever known. This event can only occur when I see you without any preconception of what you might be, especially when I see you *without preconception of what I want you to be*. Wanting you to be a certain way is the most obvious indicator of some deficiency within myself, hence of my lack of freedom. This is so because the closest I can come to experiencing you as you are is to experience you as you occur. I shall never come to the end of learning who you are.

If I try to shape the way you occur, or if I simply want you to occur a certain way, I am in effect permitting only a narrow channel of communication instead of giving you the broadest possible option of presenting yourself as you happen to be at a given moment. Since even the most ideal circumstances are limiting when you are trying to disclose yourself, anything less and I will miss you altogether.

270

APPENDIX B....A REFLECTION ON PRAYER

Little boys shouldn't pray for pocket knives. . . . Gregory Bateson

I had never thought of prayer as problematic prior to teaching at a certain Catholic high school. The teachers at this school had been accustomed to begin each class with the prayer, "Let us remember that we are in the presence of God." Despite admonitions by the administration to always lead the students in saying this traditional prayer before each class, I never did. For reason that were at the time inexplicable I experienced an extreme discomfort at just the thought of saying those words. After agonizing over this for some time I thought of a formula that I felt comfortable with that I could use with my classes and that I could get away with: "Let us remember the presence of God within us." "The presence of God" in the prescribed prayer suggested someone being in the room with us, like the department head doing an evaluation. It was also a reminder of the guilt-inducing image of God from my childhood when I was taught that nothing escaped God's notice--the big eye in the sky which by this time I knew to be idolatrous since no one knows *how* or *what* God knows.

Why should I feel comfortable with one prayer and not the other when both expressions are said to reflect truths accepted by Christians who believe in God? The best explanation I can offer is that I felt more comfortable thinking about God as immanent rather than transcendent, the God "up there" or "out there." When Bonhoeffer wrote that we must learn to live as if there were no God I believe he must have meant God as transcendent.

Even after this experience I still did not give much thought to understanding prayer. Like most people I know, I had always thought of prayers primarily as words I addressed to God, an essentially silent God. Then another experience started me thinking again. I was with a group of Covenant House volunteers in formation prior to being sent to work at one of the organization's youth homes. When the director of formation began a discussion on prayer I listened for fifteen minutes before I realized that no one was going to offer a definition of prayer and apparently no one thought this strange, unless like me they were keeping their mouth shut in amazement. Is it possible to pray while not having a clear idea of what prayer is? I did not find the Catechism's definition of prayer very helpful in trying to resolve this. "Lifting of the mind and heart to God" reminded me of the problem I had with prayer as a teacher, but it was the unenlightened definition I had lived with up to that time. It offered no answer to the question of how God communicates with us. When, how and where do we get messages from God? I understand communication to be a two-way process, that it is *with* not *to*. Ideally it is a dialectical exchange.

Then recalling my school experience and how the thought of God as immanent resonated with me I realized that singing and praying together as in common worship can be understood as communicating with the God immanent in each other. We connect through the words we say or sing. In my ignorance I had been prompted by the Holy Spirit to express solidarity with my sisters and brothers as they did with me while simultaneously affirming our faith in the God within each of us. So it seems that sometimes I actually managed to pray without completely understanding why what I did was true prayer. I began to see that the connection with each other makes what we do the kind of prayer that made sense to me. Unconscious behavior is apparently the norm among humans both in our relationship with God and other humans as it had been for me till these two experiences made unconsciousness a problem for me. It also seems that I could only recognize my ignorance in retrospect, previously defined as Ignorance II, or false knowledge in the early chapters.

If we are communicating with God in worship services even when unconscious of how it takes place, there would seem to be an obvious advantage in being conscious of what we are doing. My understanding of what it means to be human is that it is a progressive evolution of consciousness. I am happy to have a carpenter build my house who is so familiar with tools and wood that he can sing or even talk with a coworker about Monday Night Football while working. But I have to believe that communicating with God ought to occupy my full attention while I am doing it, the way that crafting a love letter or a poem might.

Distraction while praying alone seems to be a common problem. The church teaches that it is probably a venial sin. Distraction seems to be much less of problem during various liturgies. While singing the praises of God or reciting words with others in thanksgiving for life and God's many lesser gifts I am more likely to be fully engaged. But without a clear idea of what prayer is no one should be surprised that distractions come easily when praying alone if we think that praying is talking *to* God or forming words mentally for the same purpose. Unless we are mystics God is not responding as when we talk with a person. Talking *to* God is certainly not wrong but I cannot be satisfied with what is just "not being wrong" when what I do concerns my relationship with God.

What about communicating with God as transcendent? We may legitimately think of God as both transcendent and immanent. I am unable to speak for anyone else, but God as transcendent leaves me in a state of stunned silence when I even dare to turn my thoughts in that direction. What can I say? What is there to say? I not only cannot say words, I cannot even think them. The silence is absolute and there can be no distraction in that moment. I am totally preoccupied by such terrifying circumstances. Once I am in that situation, what follows is inevitable. The message is an intense awareness of God's wholly, unimaginable otherness. I confront a black, terrifying abyss. Such feelings explain in part the reluctance I felt in school to say, "Let us remember that we are in the presence of God." I cannot deliberately court such moments.

Since my high school and Covenant House experiences I have become aware of another kind of prayer that is closer to the prayer in common worship but which requires a higher degree of consciousness. It is also communication with God as immanent, but it takes place in one-on-one relationships with other humans. Such prayer can also happen in a semi-conscious state as in common worship when the two persons involved happen to be saying some explicit prayer together because people may be semi-conscious of the God-out-there, but the prayer I am trying to describe does not require pious words or any kind of God talk. Communication with God as immanent sometimes depends on the human voice of the person with whom I am trying to connect, but as in the case of my communication with God as transcendent it may occur without words but also without the awesomeness. Ideally when I am with someone we should both be conscious of trying to connect with each other and thus with God in each other although it is enough for own my purposes that I am conscious of the indwelling of the Holy Spirit in the other person. Another person has to be present in some form in order to communicate with God this way. I can even do it, or at least initiate it without the conscious participation of the other person. When I give a poor person food, clothing or shelter my behavior counts as a statement to God, and a remembrance of Jesus' own words on what such behavior means is God's rejoinder. With an attitude of openness to learning if I am really listening to the other I may hear a cry of distress, another way that the God within others communicates.

Distractions may prevent this kind of prayer. Instead of seeing a person I may see a mask behind which, God in the other person is concealed. There is a bond of intimacy between ourselves and the immanent God that our masks may conceal from each other and even from ourselves and there can be no communication without contact and confrontation. For example, I may ignore the plea of a beggar I meet because I am distracted by dirt and unpleasant odor. Obviously God is not just immanent in clean, sweet smelling beggars, another reason why consciousness is important in prayer. This will not happen if I stay conscious all the time and thus pray always as Paul advises (1Thes. 5:17). With respect to prayer and the kind of consciousness I ought to have, perhaps the most startling realization of all is that God is not just immanent in beggars, clean or dirty. God is immanent in everyone. Jesus told us to be concerned for the poor and dispossessed, but those who are not in obvious distress have needs that should elicit our compassion even if their problems are not so obvious. Virtually everyone hurts in some way.

And what does it say of my consciousness when I fail to see God in those with whom I have a commitment to love and cherish forever? Sometimes I can be guilty of a negative idolatry. The image of God I carry around with me does not match what I see in the people who are supposed to be near and dear to me--wife, children, friends, parents. The opportunities for prayer abound. Everyone, especially the people I am close to, gives God a voice with which to communicate making it less likely that I will lose myself in that awesome, black void I mentioned above. Under ideal circumstances when everything is working and I am totally respectful of God within the other person, I listen. In those moments I cease to be what I ordinarily am, Homo Stultus, and become what I ought to be, a fully conscious human, a Homo Sapiens.

In prayer with God as immanent there are times when I am also silent and adopt a respectful listening mode in which the silence is total, within and without; I am not thinking of what I will say when the other person finishes. I listen with my whole attention. When I do speak it is in such way as to offer self-disclosure as well as to elicit the same. I believe that such self-disclosures reveal an infinitesimal aspect of God's that is in each of us. In this kind of prayer I am engaging others in the deepest recesses of their being no matter the subject we are exploring, or even if we are quietly sharing each others presence. I strongly suspect that given the opportunity, God would communicate with me continuously through others if I were always disposed in this manner. I would thus be praying always as St Paul says I should. However I am the one who must provide those opportunities by simply being conscious that I can learn what God has to say through the person with whom I am engaged, who may sometimes appears to be like me, a poor piece of equipment for the job.

The advantage of being conscious of what prayer is or should be becomes even more apparent in a one-on-one relationship than in common worship. I might be more compassionate toward someone if instead of reacting in kind when a person addresses me in anger, I heard the message, "I'm hurting." When Jesus quoted Hosea saying, "I desire compassion, not sacrifice," he described how I should react under these circumstances. Thus the other person's ability to speak in God's voice can only be recognized if I have what I call a Primary Disposition. The closer I pay attention to what another human is saying to me, the better God is able to communicate with me. Everyone who has had the experience of being really listened to in the way I am describing here will recognize the change in feeling that comes over one in this process. Even though God and prayer may not be mentioned, the person being really listened to intuitively recognizes that an important event is taking place. This can happen even if the other person is an atheist. There occurs in that moment of reverential listening an affirmation of everything that is true and good about the other and myself. An aura of love envelopes both of us even though love may not be mentioned either. There is a recognition that a bit of self has died for the other, than which there is no greater love.

If such events are so good, why haven't they occurred more often? In the past I have operated with the idea of prayer taught by the church, that I am talking to a silent God. Also I had not been aware that God has anything to say to me through the self-disclosures of other humans. Even when I was conscious of prayer as communal in worship services I did not understand how I could relate to others in prayer when there was only two of us and we were not engaged in formal prayer. The church teaches that the Holy Spirit dwells within each of us, but it has not always been clear how we connect with God in each other the way I have described it.

It takes some effort to learn what others mean when what they say

is colored by emotion, especially anger. It helps me to think the way
mothers do when they try to understand children who are just learning
to express themselves. When mother-child communication works, the
attitude, the Primary Disposition, of the mother overcomes the deficiencies in the child's expression by careful attention to all the cues,
audible, visual, contextual, and so on. The mother has an open mind
with regard to her child. She does not have preconceptions about
what the child means. She simply considers possible meanings until
she succeeds in understanding. The positive feelings the mother has
for the child makes the problem of communication worth the effort as
it does in the case of two lovers. The description I have given of
mother-child communication is analogous to the way God communicates with me through other humans. I need to listen to others the
way mothers listen to a child if I want to hear what God is saying to
me with a person's voice.

The consciousness-raising experience of mother-child communication and the communication between lovers is what I need to carry
over into my relationships with anyone, no matter my feelings for the
person. I need to foster a disposition that will arouse in another
person the kind of openness that comes naturally to a small child.
When I do this I have begun to understand what Jesus meant in bidding me to become like a child. There is in fact no other way for me
to communicate with God, or as Jesus put it, "to enter the kingdom of
heaven" (Mt. 18:3).

If "lifting our minds and hearts to God" no longer helps us to
understand the meaning of prayer we must reconceptualize it. To the
extent that we cling to *this* truth, *this* way or *this* thing that makes us
feel secure, we become Homo Stultus. Homo Sapiens is a highly
evolved state and its development comes about with great difficulty
unless perhaps as children we were recipients of a special grace such
as being raised by enlightened adults who were not themselves para-
lyzed by fear due to their ignorance and consciousness of their contingency. The significance of our relationships with children is that God
says in effect, "Become disposed like a child and prompt others by
your disposition to do likewise."

If I pray aloud or silently by myself, to whom am I talking, and
from whom do I expect a response? Any image I have of God is
inevitably idolatrous, e,g., the little boy who asks for a pocket knife
may imagine a kindly grandfather type. A consciousness of God that
we do not think of as residing in another human must be imageless
and might result in the state I described in an earlier paragraph where
there is not only nothing to say, one becomes conscious of words
possibly being blasphemous because they can spoil a moment of pure

intimacy.

From the foregoing analysis we should be able to see that whereas we may worship together once a week, prayer with individuals should occur more frequently, in fact in every single encounter with another human without exception. Furthermore, those of us who have intimate relationships such as committed couples and married persons, should recognize that the possibilities for such prayer obviously occur more frequently for us by reason of being together more often. I dare say that prayer should come close to being continuous when with significant others. The positive feelings with which we began such relationships should promote the progressive evolution of consciousness that is a significant part of our destiny. The failure to take advantage of the opportunity to pray always is more tragic for such persons than for those who are uncommitted. It is an avoidable tragedy, but a failure rate of fifty-percent for marriages and other commitments is evidence that couples are not clear about what commitment can mean for personal development and development of one's relationship with God. After nearly twenty centuries of church teaching that marriage is primarily for procreation it is time for a revolution in the theology of interpersonal relationships by reclaiming from the church the true meaning of prayer as all attempts at Communion with other humans that respect the integrity of the other.

We must be constantly open to learning because we will never completely understand what prayer means, or what Communion with others means. The wisdom Xenophanes gave us twenty-five hundred years ago should be posted where we can constantly refer to it. "Quite evidently the gods have not revealed everything to mortals at the outset; for mortals are obliged, in the slow course of time, to discover for themselves what is best."

RECLAIMING RELIGION FROM THE CHURCH

BIBLIOGRAPHY

Abbott, Walter M., S.J., (Gen. eddy.) (1966)
DOCUMENTS OF VATICAN II, New York, Guild Press.

Ardrey, Robert (1966)
THE TERRITORIAL IMPERATIVE, New York, Delta.

Avis, Paul (1989)
EROS AND THE SACRED, Harrisburg, PA, Morehouse,
Publishing.

Bateson, Gregory (1980)
MIND & NATURE, New York, Bantam Books.

Bateson, Gregory & Mary Catherine (1988)
ANGELS FEAR, New York, Macmillan.

Baum, Gregory (1971)
MAN BECOMING: God in Secular Experience, New York, Herder
and Herder.

Beck, Aaron (1988)
LOVE IS NEVER ENOUGH, New York, Harper & Row.

Becker, Ernest (1971)
THE BIRTH AND DEATH OF MEANING, New York, Free Press.

Berger, Peter (1963)
INVITATION TO SOCIOLOGY, New York, Anchor Books.

Berger, Peter, and Thomas Luckmann (1967)
THE SOCIAL CONSTRUCTION OF REALITY, Garden City, N.Y.,
Doubleday Anchor.

Boff, Leonardo (1988)
WHEN THEOLOGY LISTENS TO THE POOR, San Francisco,
Harper & Row, Publishers.

Bok, Sissela (1979)
LYING, New York, Vintage Books.

Bokenkotter, Thomas (1986)
ESSENTIAL CATHOLICISM, Garden City, N.Y., Image Books.

Bonhoeffer, Dietrich (1976)
LETTERS & PAPERS FROM PRISON, New York, Macmillan
Publishing Co, Inc.

Bourke, Vernon J. (ed.) (1960)
THE POCKET AQUINAS, New York, Pocket Books.

Brinkerhoff, David B. & Lynn K. White, (1989)
ESSENTIALS OF SOCIOLOGY, St. Paul. West Publishing Co.

Brown, Peter (1988)
THE BODY AND SOCIETY, New York, Columbia University
Press.

Bruner, Jerome (1968)
TOWARD A THEORY OF INSTRUCTION, New York, W.W.
Norton & Co.

Budziszewski, J (1998)
"The Revenge of Conscience," *FIRST THINGS,*, No. 84, June/July
1998.

Cahn, Edmond (1961)
THE PREDICAMENT OF DEMOCRATIC MAN, New York, The
Macmillan Co.

Carney, James (1987)
TO BE A REVOLUTIONARY, San Francisco, Harper and Row.

Carse, James P. (1985)
THE SILENCE OF GOD, New York, Macmillan Publishing Co.

Catholic Encyclopedia (1967)
"Revelation," Vol. 12, pp. 441c, 444b.

Churchland, Patricia Smith (1997)
"The First Neurophilosopher," in *IMAGINE THERE'S NO HEAVEN*, The Council for Secular Humanism.

Cogley, John (1968)
RELIGION IN A SECULAR AGE, New York, Frederick A. Praeger, Publishers.

Collingwood,R.G. (1956)
THE IDEA OF HISTORY, New York, Oxford University Press.

Corbishley, Thomas (1964)
THE CONTEMPORARY CHRISTIAN, New York, Hawthorne Books.

Coser, Lewis (1964)
THE FUNCTIONS OF SOCIAL CONFLICT, Glencoe, Free Press.

Cox, Harvey (1965)
THE SECULAR CITY, New York, Macmillan.

Craig, Sidney D. (1973)
RAISING YOUR CHILD NOT BY FORCE BUT BY LOVE, Philadelphia, Westminster Press.

Crossan, John Dominic (1998)
THE BIRTH OF CHRISTIANITY, New York, Harper Collins.

Curran, Charles E. (1970)
A NEW LOOK AT CHRISTIAN MORALITY, Notre Dame, IN, Fides Publishers, Inc.

D'Amico, Robert (1989)
HISTORICISM AND KNOWLEDGE, New York, Routledge,

Chapman & Hall, Inc.

Davis, Charles (1967)
A QUESTION OF CONSCIENCE, New York, Harper & Row, Publishers.

Dewart, Leslie (1966)
THE FUTURE OF BELIEF, New York, Herder and Herder.

Dulles, Avery (1978)
MODELS OF THE CHURCH, New York, Image Books.

Dulles, Avery (1985)
THE SURVIVAL OF DOGMA, New York, Crossroads.

Dulles, Avery (1992)
MODELS OF REVELATION, Maryknoll, NY, Orbis Books.

Dulles, Avery (1990)
REVELATION THEOLOGY, New York, The Seabury Press.

Durkheim, Emile (1966)
SUICIDE, New York, The Free Press.

Edokimov, Paul (1995)
THE SACRAMENT OF LOVE, Crestwood, NY, St. Vladmir's Seminary Press.

Efran, Jay S., Michael D. & Robert J. Lukens (1990)
LANGUAGE, STRUCTURE AND CHANGE, New York, W.W. Norton & Co.

Ewing, A. C. (1962)
THE FUNDAMENTAL QUESTIONS OF PHILOSOPHY, New York, Collier Books.

Fagan, Sean (1979)
HAS SIN CHANGED?, Garden City, NY, Image Books.

Fletcher, Joseph (1967)
MORAL RESPONSIBILITY, Philadelphia, The Westminster Press.

Freidrichs, Robert W. (1972)

THE SOCIOLOGY OF SOCIOLOGY, New York, The Free Press.

Gatto, John (1991)
"Why Schools Don't Educate," *THE FAMILY NETWORKER*, Sept./
October 1991, pp.55-59.

Gerard, R.W. (1968)
"The Biological Basis of the Imagination," in *THE CREATIVE
PROCESS*, (Brewster Ghiselin, ed.), New York, Mentor Books.

Getzel, J.W. and Jackson, P.W. (1963)
"The Highly Intelligent and the Highly Creative Adolescent," in
CREATIVITY, P.E. Vernon, (ed.), Middlesex, Eng., Penguin
Books, Ltd.

Ghiselin, Brewster (1952)
"Introduction" to *The Creative Process*, New York, Mentor Books.

Gouldner, Alvin (1970)
THE COMING CRISIS OF WESTERN SOCIOLOGY, New York,
Avon Books.

Graham, Dom Aelred (1971)
THE END OF RELIGION, New York, Harcourt, Brace, Jovanvich,
Inc.

Greeley, Andrew M. (1983)
A PIECE OF MY MIND, Garden City, N.Y., Doubleday & Co.,
Inc.

Greeley, Andrew M. (1998)
"Prospects for 'Evangelization'," *AMERICA*, Jan., 17., p. 9

Hall, Edward T. (1969)
THE HIDDEN DIMENSION, Garden City, New York, Anchor
Books.

Hall, Edward T. (1963)
THE SILENT LANGUAGE, Greenwich, CT, Fawcett Publications.

Hassenhuttl, Gotthold (1974)
"Church and Institution," in *THE CHURCH AS INSTITUTION*,
New York, Herder and Herder.

Hays, Charlotte (2001)
"Solving the Puzzle of Natural Family Planning," in *CRISIS*,
Vol. 29, No. 11, (Dec.).

Hays, Richard B. (1996)
THE MORAL VISION OF THE NEW TESTAMENT, Harper, San
Francisco.

Heberle, Rudolf (1968)
"Ferdinand Tonnies" in *THE INTERNATIONAL ENCYCLOPEDIA
OF SOCIAL SCIENCES*, New York, The Free Press.

Hefner, Philip (1976)
CHANGING MAN, Garden City, NY, Doubleday.

Heidegger, Martin (1961)
INTRODUCTION TO METAPHYSICS, Ralph Mannheim, (trans.)
Garden City, NY, Anchor Books.

Holt, John (1972)
FREEDOM AND BEYOND, New York, E.P. Dutton & Co., Inc.

Homans, George Casper (1964)
"Contemporary Theory in Sociology," in *SOCIOLOGICAL
METHODS*, Norman K. Denzin (ed.), Chicago, Aldine Publishing,
(1970).

Homans, George Casper (1967)
THE NATURE OF SOCIAL SCIENCE, New York, Harcourt, Brace
& World, Inc.

Hudson, Liam, (1975)
HUMAN BEINGS, Garden City, N.Y., Anchor Books.

Huxley, Julian (1958)
RELIGION WITHOUT REVELATION, New York, A Mentor Book.

John Paul II (1993)
THE SPLENDOR OF TRUTH, Washington, DC, US Catholic
Conference.

John Paul II (1997)
CATECHISM OF THE CATHOLIC CHURCH, (2nd ed.),

Washington, DC, U.S. Catholic Conference.

Johnson, Paul (1976)
A HISTORY OF CHRISTIANITY, New York, Atheneum.

Johnson, Roger (1987)
RUDOLPH BULTMANN, London, Collins Liturgical Publications.

Kaufman, Philip S. (1995)
WHY YOU CAN DISAGREE AND REMAIN A FAITHFUL CATHOLIC, New York, Crossroads.

Kennedy, Eugene (1976)
A SENSE OF LIFE, A SENSE OF SIN, Garden City, NY, Image Books.

Kuhn, Thomas (1970)
THE STRUCTURE OF SCIENTIFIC REVOLUTIONS, Chicago, Phoenix Books.

Kung, Hans (1976)
THE CHURCH, Garden City, NY, Image Books.

Kurtz, Paul (1988)
FORBIDDEN FRUIT, Buffalo, Prometheus Books.

Lakoff, George (1987)
WOMEN, FIRE, AND DANGEROUS THINGS, Chicago, The University of Chicago Press.

Lawler, Edward (1975)
"The Impact of Status Differences on Coalition Agreements," *JOURNAL OF CONFLICT RESOLUTION*, Vol. 19 No. 2, (June).

Letkemann, Peter (1973)
CRIME AS WORK, Englewood Cliffs, NJ, Prentice-Hall, Inc.

Lippmann, Walter (1964)
A PREFACE TO MORALS, New York, Time, Inc.

Lorenz, Konrad (1971)
ON AGGRESSION, New York, Bantam Books.

MacIntyre, Alisdair (1984)
AFTER VIRTUE,, (2nd. ed.), Notre Dame, IN, Notre Dame
University Press.

McCormick, Richard A. (1989)
THE CRITICAL CALLING, Washington, D.C., Georgetown
University.

McSweeny, William (1980)
ROMAN CATHOLICISM: The Search for Relevance, New York,
St. Martin's Press.

Maguire, Daniel C. (1979)
THE MORAL CHOICE, Minneapolis, Winston Press.

Maguire, Daniel C. (1968)
"Moral Absolutes and the Magisterium," in *ABSOLUTES IN
MORAL THEOLOGY?*, (Chas. Curran, ed.), Washington, D.C.,
Corpus Books.

Martos, Dr. Joseph (1981)
DOORS TO THE SACRED, Garden City, NY, Doubleday.

Marty, Martin (1969)
THE MODERN SCHISM, New York, Harper & Row, Publishers.

Maslow, A.H. (1971)
THE FARTHER REACHES OF HUMAN NATURE, New York, The
Viking Press.

May, William E. (1991)
AN INTRODUCTION TO MORAL THEOLOGY, Huntington, IN,
Our Sunday Visitor, Inc.

Mazur Allan and Leon Robertson (1972)
BIOLOGY AND SOCIAL BEHAVIOR, New York, The Free Press.

Midgley, Mary (1985)
EVOLUTION AS RELIGION, New York, Methuen.

Milhaven, John Giles (1970)
TOWARD A NEW CATHOLIC MORALITY, Garden City, NY,
Doubleday.

Mills, C. Wright (1967)
THE SOCIOLOGICAL IMAGINATION, New York, Oxford
University Press.

Moran, Gabriel (1966)
THEOLOGY OF REVELATION, New York, Herder and Herder.

Moustakous, Carl (1967)
CREATIVITY AND CONFORMITY, New York, Van Nostrand
Reinhold Co.

Murphy, Robert F. (1971)
THE DIALECTICS OF SOCIAL LIFE, New York, Basic Books.

THE NEW AMERICAN STANDARD BIBLE, (1977)
New York, Thomas Nelson, Publishers, for the Lockman Foundation.

Nhat Hanh, Thich (1987)
BEING PEACE, Berkeley, CA, Parallax Press.

Niebuhr, Rheinhold (1952)
THE IRONY OF AMERICAN HISTORY, New York, Charles
Scribner's Sons.

Niebuhr, Rheinhold (1962)
"Christian Love & Natural Law," in *NINE MODERN MORALISTS*,
Englewood Clifs, NJ, Prentice Hall, Inc.

O'Connor, D.J. (1968)
AQUINAS AND NATURAL LAW, St. Martin's Press.

Otto, Max (1949)
SCIENCE AND THE MORAL LIFE, New York, A Mentor Book.

Ouspensky, P.D. (1974)
THE PSYCHOLOGY OF MAN'S POSSIBLE EVOLUTION, New
York, Vintage Books.

Paul VI (1969)
Humanae Vitae, Boston, Pauline Books & Media.

Pearce, Joseph Chilton (1980)

MAGICAL CHILD, New York, Bantam Books.

Piaget, Jean (1971)
THE CONSTRUCTION OF REALITY IN THE CHILD, New York,
Ballantine Books.

Pius XII (1950)
HUMANI GENERIS, Boston, Pauline Books & Media.

Polanyi, Michael (1962)
PERSONAL KNOWLEDGE, Chicago, University of Chicago Press.

Popper, Karl (1966)
THE OPEN SOCIETY AND ITS ENEMIES, Vol. I, Princeton, NJ,
Princeton University Press.

Popper, Karl (1968)
THE LOGIC OF SCIENTIFIC DISCOVERY, New York, Harper
Torchbooks.

Potter, David M. (1965)
PEOPLE OF PLENTY, Chicago, The University of Chicago Press.

Ramsey, Paul (1962)
"Religious Aspects of Marxism, in *NINE MODERN MORALISTS*,
Englewood Cliffs, NJ, Prentice-Hall, Inc.

Robinson, John A.T. (1963)
HONEST TO GOD, Philadelphia, Westminster Press.

Rondet, Rev. Henri (1961)
DO DOGMAS CHANGE?, New York, Hawthorne Press.

Rondet, Rev. Henri (1972)
ORIGINAL SIN, Shannon, Ireland, Ecclesia Press.

Rorty, Richard (1979)
PHILOSOPHY AND THE MIRROR OF NATURE, Princeton,
Princeton University Press.

Rose, Steven (1976)
THE CONSCIOUS BRAIN, New York, Vintage Books.

Russell, Bertrand (1961)
RELIGION AND SCIENCE, London, Oxford University Press.

Ryle, Gilbert (1978)
THE CONCEPT OF MIND, Middlesex, England, Penguin Books.

Sanders, Scott Russell (1998)
"The Faith Factor: Hope in the Here and Now," *THE SALT JOURNAL*, Vol. 1, Issue 3, April/May 1998.

Sartre, John Paul (1965)
THE PHILOSOPHY OF JEAN PAUL SARTRE, Robert Denoon Cumming, (ed.), New York, Vintage Books.

Schneiders, Sandra M. (1991)
BEYOND PATCHING, New York, Paulist Press.

Sobrino, Jon (1978)
CHRISTOLOGY AT THE CROSSROADS, Maryknoll, NY, Orbis Books.

Sorri, Mari and Jerry Gill (1989)
A POSTMODERN EPISTEMOLOGY, Lewiston, NY, The Edwin Mellen Press.

Steinem, Gloria (1992)
THE REVOLUTION WITHIN, Boston, Little, Brown & Co.

Stinchcombe, Arthur L. (1968)
CONSTRUCTING SOCIAL THEORIES, New York, Harcourt, Brace & World.

Thavis, John (1996)
"The new danger, Ratzinger says, is relativism," *NATIONAL CATHOLIC REPORTER*, Vol.32, No. 44, Oct.18.

Thomasma, David C. (1990)
HUMAN LIFE IN THE BALANCE, Louisville, KY, Westminster/John Knox Press.

Von Hildebrand, Dietrich and Alice (1966)
MORALITY AND SITUATION ETHICS, Chicago, Franciscan Herald Press.

Vander Zander, James W. (1984)
SOCIAL PSYCHOLOGY (3rd ed.), New York, Random House.

Watts, Alan (1972)
THE SUPREME IDENTITY, New York, Vintage Books.

Wickler, Wolfgang (1973)
THE SEXUAL CODE, Francisca Garvie (trans.), Garden City, NY, Anchor Books.

Wills, Gary (2000)
PAPAL SINS, Structures of Deceit, New York, Doubleday.

Wilson, Edward O. (1999)
CONSILIENCE, New York, Vintage Books.

Winch, Peter (1963)
THE IDEA OF SOCIAL SCIENCE AND ITS RELATIONSHIP TO PHILOSOPHY. London, Routledge & Kegan Paul.

ISBN 1-553954430-0

9 781553 954309